Brothers of War

THE STORY OF
WILLIAM HARRISON HOLT, S/C 1
UNITED STATES NAVY
And others

Lew Holt

To my friends in Dallas

Lew Holt

Brothers of War

THE STORY OF
WILLIAM HARRISON HOLT, S/C 1
UNITED STATES NAVY
And others

Beginning at Pearl Harbor
December 7, 1941

USS PHOENIX
Light Cruiser (CL-46)
1941 - 1943

Lew Holt

What others say about *Brothers of War*

Frode from Norway writes after reading Coco's account of the sinking of the Belgrano "... a speech about what I would anticipate was the most emotional moments of his life. A speech with undertones of sorrow, comradeship, pride and love for a weapon as a national symbol of national heroism."

:: :: ::

From Arlie Holt – "Well, I found myself crying it was so moving. One could not dredge this out of one's creative imagination if one tried. Great stuff."

:: :: ::

Coco writes – You have to forgive me not to answer quickly, but I need enough time to read carefully this wonderful book. I read completely and, let me tell you that it thrilled me, and I need to congratulate you to write this book. It's fascinating

:: :: ::

Dear Narendra Sethia: Your letter made me tremble. I am very pleased to meet you. I have to thank Mr. Lewis Holt, a very good friend, to make it possible that you and I can be in touch. Coco

:: :: ::

Hello Lew

Now that I have finished your vast tome – of which I read every single word – I wanted to write to you to say a few things. What a document.

You know, Lew, in a way you have brought Bill back to life. Here I am, thousands of miles away from you and we have not even met, and yet, in spite of the differences in our age, background and life story, having corresponded with you and read your work, I feel I know something profound of you and your family, and am honoured that you have shared such an important part of your life with me. Through your efforts, Bill will not be a faceless, forgotten victim of a long-ago war in a far-flung land. He is now as real to me as he is to your family, and as I write I can even see his face and imagine who and what he was.

Your hard work and research were worth every minute. I am not exaggerating when I say that it is probably the most touching biographical work that I have ever read. It reminded me that, regardless of our geographical origins or our place in time, we laugh for the same reasons, we cry for the same reasons, we are happy for the same reasons and we endure the same struggles in life.

There was Bill, more than half a century away, and here I am, reading his letters all these years later and looking at his photograph. Yet, there is no void, no gulf, just that singularity of human spirit which transcends time and makes us human. (N) Narendra Sethia

:: :: ::

I cannot add anything to the Pearl Harbor attack except a passage from the movie that was shown the night before the attack. One of the stars in the movie, THE LITTLE FOXES, said, "Take us the Foxes, the little foxes that spoil the vines, for our vines have tender grapes." Not until much later did I learn this passage, though it may not be exact, came out of the Bible. Approximately 2,128 young men lost their lives there.

I wish you well, and I am sorry to learn of William's death.
Sincerely, Tom (Tom F. Shook)

:: :: ::

You are absolutely right that a work of fiction could never have produced a story so extraordinary and so human. That, I feel, is its strength – had you written it to be a best-seller, I think it would have lost much of its human quality. It's REAL, and it's about real people, real events, real hardships, real joys, real tragedy – and it therefore appeals to the innate sensitivities of real people. What a wonderful legacy for your family, children, grandchildren and their grandchildren. (N) Narendra Sethia

Contents

Bill Holt
Graduation picture, June 1941
Dallas, Oregon High School

Bill Holt, U. S. Navy
December 2, 1941
Honolulu, Hawaii

PREFACE

Lewis (Lew) Holt, born April 11, 1929 in Vernonia, Oregon. I was 12 years old when Pearl Harbor was attacked. I have had to go back many years to tell the early part of this story. I have taken the liberty to just "visit with you informally " to tell the story of my brother, Bill, and the others who have become a part of his story. The story about Bill opened many doors that I could not have imagined.

In the summer of 1939 we lived in White Salmon, Washington where my father worked in a gypo logging camp. That fall he moved his wife and three sons across the Columbia River to Colton, Oregon. The fourth son, Charles, stayed with him at White Salmon to help finish a logging job. Just a couple of weeks before they were to join us in Oregon, my father, 48-year-old Charles Valentine Holt, was killed in a logging accident on November 1, 1939. My brother, Charles, was there and held his father's hand as his father died under a log. Charles returned home to Colton where we were living. In the spring of 1940 my Uncle Lewis found a little farm near Dallas, Oregon that he thought we would like. We bought the 5.5 acres for $1000 with payments of $15 a month. That fall, Charles started attending Oregon College of Education in Monmouth, 9 miles from where we lived. My younger brother Arlie and I went to the one room Bridgeport School just across the Little Luckiamute River from the house. I was in the sixth grade and Arlie in the fifth. Bill rode the school bus to the high school in Dallas for his senior year. It was his fourth high school, a different one each year.

In the spring of 1941, Bill joined the navy and left home on June 16th – just a few weeks before his 18th birthday. He died of tuberculosis in 1945. In the mid eighties I became curious about Bill's short life. The many years since his death made it difficult to find answers. Many of the veterans of the attack on Pearl Harbor were getting older. Many had died. Some had forgotten the specifics of the attack. Some did not wish to remember the attack. But some shared their memories of the attack with me. I will be forever grateful to them for sharing their letters and stories with me. Now I can share them with you.

My own memory of Bill has dimmed over the years. I was 12 years old when he left home and the years that followed were busy ones for me – high school, college, marriage, family, work, hobbies, and now retirement. For many years Bill was a sad memory and a picture on the shelf. It wasn't until I started collecting and putting all of his letters together in a book that I again thought of Bill and the part that he played in the lives of our family many years ago. And the life he lived after he left home.

I think of Bill as having "come from behind." When he was a toddler, a burning piece of paper fell from the wood burning stove. He attempted to stomp out the fire. His clothes caught on fire and he was burned badly which left scars on his side. He was not as tall as most of his cousins. The Navy offered him independence, the opportunity to get away to "see the world" and to get off the farm. When he became ill with tuberculosis, he no longer had that independence and no matter how hard he fought, he could not conquer the disease that eventually led to his death. Bill's letters to us at home were always very positive. They showed his pride and most of all, his desire to not cause his mother to worry. He did not want his mother to know how seriously ill he was.

Now I would like to share with you letters and information about Bill, his friends and "his ship." It was difficult leaving out many letters to shorten this book. This project involved literally hundreds of hours of interviewing people, collecting material, reading, writing hundreds of letters, editing twice as many letters and untold hours at the computer. Many excellent letters from Bill, friends and others had been "tucked away" over the years by my mother. If she had not saved Bill's letters, I would not have been able to write this book. They were the key to creating my curiosity about Bill, the time he was in service and until he died. My desire to find out about these few short years between high school and his death, I never realized that my curiosity would take me so far. It was a thought that eventually became more than a dream.

When I started I never realize that it would become a book. I was just collecting a few stories.

I sent out more than 350 letters to Phoenix veterans, made phone calls, acquired the 1938-1945 microfilm of the crew of the Phoenix, visited with many people and read many books to get information and a background for this book. My only regret is that I did not start my research 10 or 20 years earlier – before time took its toll – either by death or memory of those who served on the Phoenix. I was lucky to be able to have received many letters from veterans who were on the Phoenix at Pearl Harbor on December 7, 1941. These veterans of the attack on Pearl Harbor had ringside seats to this historical event. I was touched and moved by their concern and their willingness to share.

Originally this was to have been "Bill's story;" just his letters that he had written to us and letters that he had saved that were written to him. I could not have imagined that when I started that it would lead me to people in Australia, Argentina, England, Japan and many places in the United States. "Bill's story" became the story of people from five nations and five continents that were involved with Bill, or the Phoenix. Or they were involved with the story's beginning at Pearl Harbor on that December day in 1941.

My research has brought many interesting and exciting moments. Locating four men on the Phoenix who remembered Bill, finding Bill's girlfriend in Australia after 54 years, locating a sailor from Argentina who was on the Belgrano/Phoenix when it was sunk during the Falkland Island War in 1982 by a British submarine, locating a sailor from England who was on the submarine that sank the Belgrano/Phoenix and then the experience of bringing these two former enemies together as "brothers of war." Also, being able to visit Pearl Harbor when Alice and I were celebrating our 50th wedding anniversary, and later a dream coming true when I received letters from two Japanese airmen who participated in the attack on Pearl Harbor. I could never have imagined that later I would go to Japan to shake hands with two Japanese aviators who participated in the attack on Pearl Harbor – young men who tried to kill my brother. Mr. Harada flew escort in a Zero over the Japanese fleet while others attacked Pearl Harbor. I sat in his home in Japan visiting and having lunch. Mr. Maruyama released a torpedo that struck the USS Oklahoma during the attack. We had lunch together, sharing pictures and stories.

As with Coco and N in Argentina, Mr. Harada, Mr. Maruyama and I were no longer enemies but rather "brothers of war." The trip to Japan would not have possible if it were not for Chris in Japan. We are "brothers of fiddling." I owe him as much as any one person.

Finally at the end is the story of two young Argentine sailors who died during the sinking of the Belgrano/Phoenix. They represent the 323 young men who died that day when their ship was struck and sunk by torpedoes from a British submarine, HMS Conqueror.

A British veteran who was on the HMS Conqueror that sank the Belgrano/Phoenix on May 2, 1982 wrote the following. Later you will meet N and come to know the part he played in this book about Bill.

N writes:

March 8, 2000. Lew Your hard work and research were worth every minute. I am not exaggerating when I say that it is probably the most touching biographical work that I have ever read. It reminded me that, regardless of our geographical origins or our place in time, we laugh for the same reasons, we cry for the same reasons, we are happy for the same reasons and we endure the same struggles in life. There was Bill, more than half a century away, and here I am, reading his letters all these years later and looking at his photograph. Yet, there is no void, no gulf, just that singularity of human spirit, which transcends time and makes us human. Thanks for sharing Bill's story with me. N

The story is not complete, even yet, but it has reached the point where it is time to share it. I have enjoyed this project. I hope you will enjoy reading what I have written.

Lew Holt

*Bill Holt (arrow) freshman at Kalama High School
Kalama, Washington. Possibly 1937.*

*Bill Holt on the farm a short time
prior to leaving for the Navy.*

*Bill Holt graduated from Dallas
High School, taken June 11, 1941.*

CHAPTER ONE

BILL JOINS THE NAVY

June 16, 1941. On that morning, many years ago, Vintie Holt and three of her four sons were up early. They quickly did the morning farm chores, ate breakfast, packed lunches and walked the gravel road a half-mile to ride with Mrs. Harvey to work in the berry fields. They got into the Model A Ford with Mrs. Harvey and her daughter, Jeanette. Mrs. Harvey drove four miles towards Dallas (Oregon), slowed up, turned on to the side road at the Guthrie School and stopped. Seventeen-year-old Bill got out of the car and closed the door.

We told Bill goodbye. No hugs, no tears. We left him standing there waving goodbye as we drove off down the graveled road a few more miles to pick berries in the hot sun. It was the last time that eleven-year-old Arlie and I, twelve years old, saw Bill alive. Our mother saw him briefly four years later just a few weeks before he died.

Mom (Vintie) Holt taken in 1941.

Looking back almost 70 years, I wonder what we might have been thinking as we walked across the bridge by our house, by the one room school and down the graveled road. We had our lunch buckets. Bill had a little bag of things he would need. Arlie and I never wondered that day as we picked berries what our mother might be thinking. She had told her second son good-bye. Nor do we know what Bill thought as the Model A Ford drove away leaving him standing there on the edge of the highway. Bill hitchhiked into Salem to begin his new adventure. He could not have anticipated the historical experience he would have in just a few months at Pearl Harbor or the events that were to follow which eventually lead to his death four years later.

U.S. Naval Training Station
June 22, 1941
Dear Mom,

I have just got back from chow, breakfast to you, and have to wait till time to go to church so I thought I might write a few lines. Here is a summary of the days since I left home.

Mon. 16.   went to Salem visited Charles.

Tues. 17.   took exam in Portland, left 10:10 P.M.

Wed. 18   spent day on train

Thurs. 19   arrived at training station at 1:30 P. M. Took final exam and was vaccinated for smallpox, took one typhoid shot & went to a show.

Fri. 20   was issued clothes, assigned company and assigned bunk.

Sat. 21   rolled clothes, drilled, and washed clothes.

I received 4 white jumpers (shirts) 12 handkerchiefs, 4 pants, 6 white socks, 21 work blue jumpers, 4 blue socks, 2 work blue pants, 2 neckerchiefs, 1 dress blue jumpers, 4 pairs of shoes, 1 dress blue pants, 1 pair rubbers, 1 swimming suit, 1 heavy coat, 2 outfits of underwear, 3 towels, 1 pair of gloves, 1 sea bag, 1 stocking cap, 4 white sailor caps. 1 shoe blackening outfit, 1 comb, 1 hair brush, 1 mattress, 1 hammock, 3 mattress covers, 1 pillow, 3 pillow cases. Boy you ought to see me now, my head looks like a peeled onion because they cut off practically all my hair.

We have to shave, take a shower, and wash our clothes every day, brush our teeth twice a day. Starting tomorrow our hard work will begin. Starting tomorrow we begin to walk the grindstone (parade grounds). It is now just about time for chow (supper). After that we will go to a program and after that shave, brush my teeth, take a shower, and roll some clothes. I will close now so I can mail it while at chow.

What is Mr. Ressler's address?
Remember my address is
William H. Holt Company 41-75
U. S. Training Station San Diego, Calif.
Bill

Bill Holt
U. S. N. T. S.
San Diego
June 1941

:: :: ::

Bill (arrow) noted on the back of this photo, "Barracks pennant held two weeks. 5 mistakes first week, 0 mistakes second week."

June 24, 1941

Dear Bill,

We have 5 cards from you since you left home. Was sure glad to hear from you as many ask about you. We are still picking berries. My fingers are full of stickers and we just finished in the rain and it is still raining. Arlie and I came home. I built a fire and laid down on the davenport and taken a nap. Old kitty Tom is on it asleep now and sounds like he might be some person snoring. Charles came home Sunday after noon stayed till Monday morning. He milked the cow for Lewis. Uncle Lewis came over from the ball game. They are having club over at the hall this afternoon but it felt so good to set by the fire so I stayed home. Lewis picked cherries for Mrs. Lee yesterday on shares. I canned 15 qts and he went back today but hasn't got home. Mrs. Sleighter takes her mother up there then goes home goes back late in the afternoon after her so Lewis and cherries come too. We picked for Mrs. Hedeen on shares canned 5 qts so we will have several qts of cherries after all.

Bill, Mae Campbell, Mr. Campbell's daughter died with double pneumonia and was buried last Sat. I got to go with Conmiches. Conmiches is going to cut the grass in the schoolyard for me. There is lots of clover in the grass. Well, Bill we have made $18.00 and worked Thur and Fri this wk. Arlie and I made $1.90 but the berries haven't ripened good are so small and knotted. Our last row was good and they was finishing up so they doubled up on us. You got a nice graduation card from Mr. Deetz of Colton and at last Uncle Chester and Sue wrote a letter thanking us for the gift and thanks for your picture and so on. We got a letter from grandma and she said they got a letter from Aunt Eliza in Calif but that Uncle Ralph had died and one of Uncle Nelson's boys had died but I haven't heard from them myself.

Do you have to pay for your clothes or how is it? Let me know so I know what to do this summer about my hay and roofing. The roofing is my worst worry. Uncle Lewis is going to see the man that put his roof on and he paid his by monthly payments just buy from him and let him do the work too so I wouldn't have to worry about getting it done. What all do you have to do and how do you like it? And what have you made up your mind to do?

David Baker is going to work on the electric line right away and so is Frances Harvey. I was just talking to Frank he said he would see Mr. Esaw about some hay for us. I subscribed for the Oregon Farmer paid $1.00 and sold him $1.00 worth of those beer bottles and got it for 7 yrs. I always like to read the Oregon Farmer magazine. Well Bill it was sweet of you to write and let us know how you are. What did you have to say over the air? And how many boys was there that was in your group? I wish I could of heard you on the radio. (Bill talked on a radio station in Portland – probably something to do with his enlistment. He had written about it in a letter.)

Well I will send an order off for Charles a slack suit, shorts, socks and a pair of tennis slippers. He gave me the money to get them with. Say Bill that pup is the cutest thing and growing so fast fat as a pig. Stays out side busy playing under the house or out in the yd somewhere. I guess Thomas cat has been catching rabbits he came home yesterday just covered with fleas. I got a100 lbs of sugar, a sack of flour, a sack of potatoes and some other groceries. Got my check cashed at Irish and Warners store. Gave Uncle Lewis some money to make a payment on the place and get my barn shovel and a stone jar with cover on it to put my butter in and I taken that roll of film in Sat. Uncle Lewis is going to get them for me for I may not go to town till after the fourth. What will you do on the 4th? Phil at the berry yard the short fellow his niece that worked up in his berry yard was coming down the hill from his house on her brother's bike and taken a spill down hill and broke a leg. Phil was the only man that was there. He said he put boards on her leg so he could handle her better to put her in the car to take her to the hospital. She is a big tall girl with dark brown eyes. Of course Mrs. Harvey went to several for tickets to get her a present I haven't gave her any yet. We worked so darn hard to get what we did get. They have turned down several carloads of pickers as he has all he wants. He told Arlie and me that we did fine and had a job as long as there was a berry to pick so that don't sound bad at all. Lewis has got home done the milking and I have more cherries to can now. I am getting Lewis some supper. It is cold and we have had a warm fire in the heater all afternoon. Well Bill the sun is trying to shine between big black and white clouds this morning. I hope it can shine to ripen those berries as I want to make about $23.00 all told this wk. I would like to have about $35.00 or so. We will be picking after the fourth too. Let me know how you are and tell me how you are getting along and hope you do your best so you can do good. And what are you doing? Well I must close and get busy canning cherries and do a washing and train those beans as they are all vines. Write.

As ever Mom.

:: :: ::

June 25, 1941
Dear Bill,
I don't expect you to answer this letter but I am writing anyhow. I would like for you to get me some matchbooks from Calif. or anywhere else you go. Next time you write tell about the radio program. I want your album because you won't need it. I want to see if I can have both of them full by the time you come home at the end of the three years. I only picked berries one day after you left. And that was last Sat.

Lewis

:: :: ::

Dallas, Ore
June 25, 1941
Dear Bill,
Hope you like the Navy. What kind of work do you do?
What did you broadcast at Portland? Did you see anything very interesting out of the train window or was it too dark at night? Did you manage the group of boys very well? How do you like your haircut? Is the weather very good in San Diego?

In the berries we do about half the field at a time. At the end of the week we should have more than 20 dollars.

The puppy is growing fast I think.

I've only been in swimming once since you left. We are having winter weather because it rains quite a bit of the time.

Arlie

P.S. Be sure to answer my questions in your next letter. May I have your stamp? Send me things like you said.

:: :: ::

June 30, 1941

Dear Bill,

We sure was glad to get your interesting letter. We have enjoyed reading it over and over. I took it into Uncle Lewis. He had lots of fun reading it. We are all well and hope your poor old arm isn't so very sore. We picked berries and made $3.40. Sure is warming up now. Today was hot but last Sat. was cool. We worked till 1 o'clock and to about 2:30 today. I went into Dallas Sat. with Mrs. Harvey and gave Charley Gregory $20.30 berry check that I drew Friday. We have to pay Charlie G. (Gregory) $35.00 interest on the $500.00 so you see where part of our berry money went to. Was we disgusted. All our plans was shot to the dickens. So I still have $14.60 to pay him to pay as soon as I can. Charles came home Sat. nite from that barn dance you heard them talking about in the berry field with Charlie Joslin. And we filled your suitcase full of socks, shorts, lettuce, butter, and bread and it was full and he started out a foot. He says he is looking for a letter from you. His address is 340 W. Jackson St. Monmouth, Ore. Aunt Leona she is spending a wk on the coast with a friend this wk. Uncle Lewis will join her the fourth. I guess we just go over here to the hall to a picnic and go back to the berry field Sat. to make all the dollars we can. Uncle Lewis said a big down payment we make on our roofing the smaller the monthly payments is. So send as much as you can and I will put in as much as I can spare for I will have to buy hay. Mr. Conmick didn't charge me anything for cutting and racking the grass in the schoolyard. We have to get that off the ground before the fourth. And the berries are ripening more all time that means we have to stay busy. We picked everyday this week but the fourth. Uncle Lewis got us or I had him to get us a barn shovel that I saw in the store so it won't be so bad of job to clean out the barn.

Flo Etta and Ralph were here last wk. I don't remember if I told you or not. We got your letter the same day we sent you one. Aunt Pearl said Little George got married and left his wife for a 7-month trip to Alaska. Say Bill Bossy Cow got into our garden ate our kale and cabbage, beans and corn off. Sure made a good mess of it so the boys and I cut brush and piled along the fence and with the barbwire that you put on the lot fence. She sure ate those big beans down close. My garden sure is growing nice.

Tuesday morning. The boys are milking and feeding the calf. I am already to go pick berries. Oh that cow sure ate up about all our garden down below. We fixed more fence or cut down trees and piled along the fence and shocked hay too last nite. The boys are so tired. I have just been on the run ever since 4:30. The boys are coming so I have to strain the milk and go. So write. Bye. As ever be good. Mom.

:: :: ::

Dallas, Ore.
July 12, 1941
Dear Bill,
Received your letter and both the pictures. I found you O. K. in the big picture of all the boys. I opened the one with no name on it so I opened the others just to see the face of the boys that went down there with you. But I put them back in the wrapper. Today is Sat. and sure is warm. I haven't done much this afternoon only set around and visited with Dora Mae Hart and Beth. Mr. Esaw and the boys went and got a load of hay Sat. nite after it cooled off and put part of it in the barn and dumped the rest out on the ground so we put the rest in this morning while it was cool and he said he might go get the other load tonite as next wk he will combine and will be busy. I am paying $14.00 for two loads.

Oh say well I just happen to think about it. Mr. E. J. Roesler, Claflin, Ks. That is his address you asked for it and I have forgotten to send it to you ever time I write. We got a card from Mr. Mrs. Oscar Kellar that they have a new son born July the 9th and we got a letter from Grandma and it was so hot there and she was sick. I sure did get a mess of wet hay out of the barn last evening. Will be nice to put on the garden this fall. Jessie was telling me she got a letter from you yesterday and she had answered it. Mrs. Baker, Chas., David, Dorothy, Jimmy, and Teddy, Mrs. Breedon, Jessie, Ela Mae, Leota, and myself set out in the park and rested by a camp fire and also Marvin.

After supper. I have been down to the garden on the river everything is growing nice all but the potatoes we planted the first time. I guess the trees and bushes takes the moles out of the ground. We sure have lots of hoeing to do and I sure will be glad when we get done picking berries as bad as I need the money for I hate to see things grow up in to weeds. We sure have lots of poles to cut and saw since they cleared the electric lines right away. Some of these trees are large and some of them are in the river back of the barn and we can see up to Harvey's now. There is going to be dance tonite. I can hear some cars driving but I don't think I will go as I am so tired. I worked two afternoons in the hot cleaning out the barn and besides picking berries and I sure was wore out today. I felt like I couldn't hardly move my arms and so sleepy.

Uncle Lewis and Aunt Leona spent Sunday with us and was it hot. Charles came home with a friend that was going to Falls City. Ate dinner with us. Loaded up his bag you gave him and started back to meet this guy out on the highway. We picked berries yesterday. Will today.

Tuesday 15. Have one more picking after today. Am in a hurry as we are getting ready to go. James (Holt) is in Alaska now.

As ever Mom. Write.

:: :: ::

Company 41-75 ... U.S. Naval Training Station, San Diego, Calif. 26 June 1941
I.O. Black, CTC, Company Commander ... L.S. McDaniel, C.B.M., 2nd Platoon Commander

Bill (arrow and inset)

The following names were written on the back of the picture:

Charles Lloyd Parker Independence, OR	William Ruffin Baker, OR	Gordon Hansen Spokane, WN	Kenneth A Spangler Veneta, OR	Lewis A Trow Trent, OR
Raymond Webb Lebanon, OR	Emery L Neil Portland, OR	Ernest W. Smith Pondosa, OR	Thompson, Robert Spokane, WN	Fred O Rask

23

:: :: ::

Dallas, Ore.
July 22, 1941
Dear Bill,

Will answer your letter that we received yesterday with the pictures and money. The 5 spot as you called it thanks a lot. I just gave Charles a 5 spot to pay his rent as he didn't want to draw any of his $20.00 he has in the bank at Monmouth. It is cool and cloudy so we are working out side. I have been pulling weeds out of the lawn and giving it a good soaking. As with the calf and the goat they keep the grass ate down short.

The boys bought them a nanny goat she is just a pet. Her and the calf bawls after each other when we put them each in their barns. We keep the goat at nite in one of the hen houses. I sure do have to water good now as it has been so hot and dry. And we are trying to get our garden down in the river hoed out. It looks better then I thought it would after the cow ate it down so close. Lewis and Arlie are getting forked sticks to put the hose in above my beans so I can get water over to my tall beans.

That woman that is such a card player that comes to Uncle Lewis's was here last Sunday. She thought I had pretty nice garden. Bill we made $53.00 picking berries but I am holding $14.00 to pay for hay. Gave Charles $5.00, $20.30 to Charles Gregory. Bought some groceries out of it. Bought a bunny house $1.50 from Harvey as we have two does of Mrs. Hedeen to keep this summer and raising two batches of baby rabbits. Your pictures are nice. I will have two of them enlarged and more made later and keep those for you if you want me to.

Where was your boils this time? I hope they can give you medicine to drive them out of your blood. Charles, Lewis, and Arlie sawed up some trees the linemen cut down into wood that was in the river. He is coming back Sunday and saw some more then we throw the blocks up on the bank to dry out for wood. All helps out. I got my check yesterday. I have to fill out a paper again to show them I am still a widow. I will go in with Mrs. Harvey tomorrow. I hope later you will have more money coming so you can send at least $10.00 so I can get a new roof on this house before it starts in raining. We are just living out of our garden. Don't buy much had to buy $5.00 worth of feed for cow, hog, chicks and rabbits. Charles said you wouldn't send any money this month but I told him I bet you would. If peaches aren't too high I would like to buy a few to can so we just have a few. We may pick prunes for Bakers in a day or so. There aren't many to pick.

Bill –I got the rest of that Australian set of stamps. It is some firing guns. I got a Cuba stamp so has Arlie.

Lewis

Yes anything you want me to keep for you send it home and not try to have very much there with you. I will put everything away and keep it for you. I want to get a moth proof bag and put your suit away and take good care of it for you.

Well I hope you won't have no more boils. Oh, yes, I don't remember if I told you Oscar and Bunny has a boy born July 9. I will have to have some of those pictures made and send them one. Charles got him a nice slack suit tan color. He is getting a few clothes along and he works hard too falling away in weight.

Say have you gained any yet?

Well it seems nice to be at home and get my outside work done. I already have orders for beans. So I want to try and raise a lot to make money to help out. We never got to get any clothes or nothing much out of our berry money but I tell you it sure came in mighty darn handy I tell you. Well I must close and get busy again.

Write, we are all well. Old Lewis is looking good and filling out a little isn't so poor as he was. Write. Mom. The Baker girl is engaged to a Bill in the Army if she hasn't wrote you.

(Information from micro film records) "CORRECTED COPY"
REPORT OF CHANGES of USS <u>PHOENIX</u>
for the month ending <u>31st</u> day of <u>August</u>, date of sailing　　　(1941)
from _____to _____

Names	Service Number	Rate	day month
1. Hodges, Lawrence A.	510 02 73	V-6 USNR	7 Jan. 41 Tacoma, WA
2. Holt, William H.	**393 56 14**	**A. S.**	**17 June 41 Portland, Or**
3. Hopper, Drexel L.	272 07 42	S. C. 1c	11 Sept. 40 Mare Island, Calif.
1. USN.　SCM. 8/4/41	Tried 7/28/41 sent to be conf period 1 mo lose $18 per mo for 4 mos tlp $72, App ISIC 6/1/41		
2. USN.　REC.	**8/14/41　R/S, San Diego, Calif., for duty**		
3. USN.　Tran. 8/26/41	NTS, San Diego, Calif., for a course of instruction in Cooks and Bakers School		

:: :: ::

Aug. 25, 1941

Dear Bill,

We was more then glad to get your long thoughtful letter. Was not worried about you but just couldn't but think of you. I am glad you got to go over there as it is all new to you and I hope you will enjoy yourself. I have been so busy till I haven't had time to worry since I got done making mattresses I been picking beans. Made $17.18 in 6 days. Would leave home at 6 and get back at 6 or after drove 42 miles there and back. We went through Airlie about 10 or 12 miles beyond there. Mrs. Harvey, Mrs. Joslin, Ruth, Clara, and myself. Went in the old Ford. Gee I am sure tired tonite. I think will forget everything as soon as I get the bread baked and go to bed. It was last wk I picked beans. This wk will can pears, peaches and beans and also make pickles and do a washing get ready to pick prunes and hops. But some of the prune picking will be on hop picking days.

Mr. Hart came and asked me if I wanted the job washing the schoolhouse windows. So we are going to do that for a little money. We will soon have a new roof. Will cost $78.00. I had to pay $4.55 for insurance. Paid out $8.50 for wood from Fern sawmill at Fall City. Got me two new kettles and a small dish pan. The kettles are blue and the dish pan is white trimmed in red. I just got home a little while ago from town. I have been to Dallas and Independence with Mrs.

Harvey. Got myself a pr of brown colored slacks and a pink slip out of my bean check. All I got out of my berry check was 2 prs of panties for 25 cents. My overalls are about gone so I had to have something else to wear out to work in. Yes dear I am sure proud of the pretty pillow top you sent me. I showed it to everyone as I think it is so pretty and also the pictures. I gave Uncle Lewis his a wk ago last Sunday and Charles and his school mom came over too. He has a sweet girl. Her father is dead and she knows how it is to get along with out a father like we are.

I have back interest paid up and owe $15.00 on the books and owe $8.00 to Joslin. Have you paid your dentist bill if not send me the money and I will pay him. I got your pictures I had enlarged today. I had Uncle Lewis to get them for me. I had the two of you holding your gun and the ones in your suit just one. I will have some of you made soon as I can get time to take care of them but I am so busy now trying to get my canning done. And am so tired out we went to the county fair at Monmouth last Sat. nite. Never got home till about one and I haven't got rested up yet. I hope we can get on our feet this winter. I will have to get my wood sawed.

Well next morning got a good nites rest feel lots better and ready for a busy day's work. Had a good rain last nite that means lots more beans to sell glad as it all helps a lot. I bought a no 3 burner for our big lamp and I wished I had done it years ago as it makes so much more light and when I work away from home

I have to do a lot of my work by lamp light. Oh, yes the evergreen berries are getting ripe so I want to get lots of them canned. Mrs. Kingsberry gave the boys a arm full of coats, two sweaters, two polo shirts, a suit coat, pants, and vest all pretty good and right about the right size for them to wear. All helps. And at the fair a man gave me a big loaf of home made bread and a big angel food cake boy was it good and it sure helped out a big lot for I didn't have any bread at all. Seems like luck has been with me and I guess it was for a good cause for I am not in debt only $4.00 for hay and I owe that to Mr. Esaw. I got a ton of clover hay from Mr. Campbell for $8.00. Cost $2.00 to get it hauled that was my berry money. I paid $10.00 mo. on the roofing.

Say why didn't you take up cooking or baking instead of gunnery? Charles he said you should of as he thought that would be the best. He sure is working hard saving his money. Had $20.00 in the bank. There will be about a month that there is no school and he will keep on working there and do his other jobs in the evening such as mowing lawn and watering. He gave me $2.00 for a permanent as my hair is getting so long and it's hard to do anything with. I got a card from Uncle Bud asking about work out here. There is a big cry for help in hops, beans, and prunes. Mrs. Foster is having a time to get any help. The hops are not quite as heavy as they were last year but we must try hard to make all we can. I bought us a kind of scales. We can set a box on to weigh our beans. Cost $1.49 only. They are white trimmed in red.

I put your picture you sent me last in my tablet I use at my work and show them to the folks. I am sure proud of them. Can I have the one where you have a smile on your face? I am going to have one enlarged off of that one sometime for I think it is good of you. I have the one in town you want some made off of it. Getting them enlarged. Can you have anything only just your clothes with you? I have asked you once. I will tell you how the mattresses are made later as I have so much to do right now. I am trying to keep my beans nice and green for I can sell lots of them. The boys are good to help but sometimes they get out all the papers and toys all over the house and forget to pick them up.

The Dixon's children have come over and Anne Palmer's too but they need a little time to play for I don't have much time to do much... This is an old letter but I will send it to you. I was about ready to send it and I got your letter that you soon move so I waited. I have lots of beans to sell now. Have sold to Detta Gage, Ora Shutt for canning and to Aunt Leona 50 lbs. Taken in 25 lbs yesterday for her to sell. Her daughter and 4 other ladies want beans so I didn't think it would be hard for her to get rid of them. And will be a lady out Friday evening for beans. I already have $2.75 saved up of bean money so all helps. Are you going to send me money to help pay for the roofing I hope so. Well Bill I haven't done much yet today. I feel so tired. I will tell you how we made those mattresses. First make the tick then the cotton was in 500 hundred lbs bales. Weighed out 50 lbs of cotton. Put it out on blankets out in the air and sun. Pull it all a part then we had muslin cloth. We weighed out 3 lbs and pinned the insides and beat 3 minutes on each side. Make 3 of them and put inside the tick. We put in 5 layers of 3 each and then one extra one in the center. Put extra bunch of cotton in the corners but at each layer we pined the tick together and beat 5 minutes after it was all done sewed the tick together by hand. Beat 30 minutes then make the roll with a needle 5 inches long with heavy waxed twine and that is hard on hands. The ticking was the blue and white striped. There was 6 yds left over and it was given to me.

This was in with the letter –
a part of the old letter she mentioned above.

Dallas, Ore.
Aug. 6, 1941
Dear Bill,

Gee son I am sure proud of my pillowcase and am sure glad you think of your old mom here at home working hard and on a run. I had a little rest today. I only cut out two ticks and helped Myrtle Stouffer on her mattress some. Anne Palmer helped her too. There is a bunch from Falls City coming tomorrow. Friday is my dead line to work. I get 25 cents for my work and I won't have to pay for my mattress. I have two big fat ones so soft and nice hard work to get them but they are nice. I go over to the hall at 7 to 7:30 to open up. I am the head of the committee. I guess have wrote you once about it. Charles came home Sat. nite and he and Willis Hart finished the roll on my first one. Then Mrs. Hart put him and Dora Mae to work on the other one. He stayed with it till he had it ready to be sewed then I went over Tuesday morning at 6:30 and sewed on it. The folks came. We finished one for them and made another one and Mr. Falk finished mine and hauled it home for me. Charles and Willis carried the other one over. So now I have two dandy ones. Have to take a broom stick and beat them 15 minutes on one side then turn over and beat 15 minutes more for

14 days before using them. I have had 3 sties since doing this work. Charles got us a lawn mower so we can keep the yard looking nice. Oh Bill that popcorn is so high and those beans. Oh are the vines thick and it will be some job to pick them. We sold Frank beans. Mrs. Crowley, Anne Palmer beans. So we will make a little bit off of our garden. We have nice cabbage. My tomatoes are nice now. I had a time of getting them to grow. I sent Oscar's (Keller) son a baby book and they wrote right back thanking me for it.

Unsigned

:: :: ::

USS Phoenix
Pearl harbor, T. H.
Oct. 16, 1941
Dear Mom,
Just a few lines to let you know I am O. K. I hope you feel better now. The reason I haven't written is, that I have been to the Philippines. A package will follow. Give Charles the billfold. Lewis and Arlie the stamps and eversharps. Uncle Lewis the deck of cards. Aunt Leona the fan with the ship on it. For you the broach and the light colored rose fan. Keep the rest for me. I am enclosing $10. Tell Charles I thought of him on his birthday. Tell him to write. I am now in Honolulu so I will sign off.
Bill
William H. Holt
USS Phoenix Div. 4
Pearl Harbor, T. H.

:: :: ::

Bill
Honolulu, Hawaii

Bill & Friend
August 31, 1941
Honolulu, Hawaii

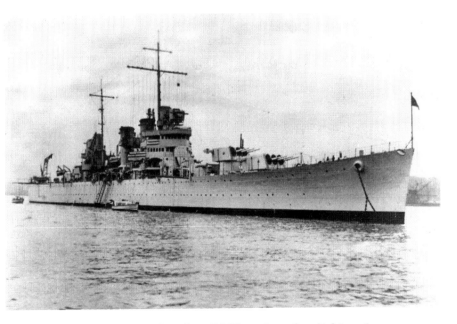

Bill was assigned to the USS Phoenix, a fast light cruiser
(CL-46) with a crew of around 1000.

USS Phoenix   (Post card)
Oct. 21, 1941
Dear Detta,
Mama mentioned something about you wanting
some post cards. I hope you are feeling fine. Give the
rest of the family my regards. I am having a swell
time have been to the Philippines. On the way over hit
a storm. Since I have joined the Navy I have gained
10 pounds and 1 inch in height. I hope you are
making out O.K. We are now in Pearl Harbor.
    Bill

:: :: ::

USS Phoenix
Nov. 11, 1941
Dear Mom,
I imagine it is cold in Oregon now but here all I
wear is a pair of shorts and an under shirt. I was very
much surprised when I received your letter because we
were at sea at the time. I have received your pictures.
I have started a picture album and I have over 100
pictures of the Philippines and Hawaii in it. I am
now a qualified helmsman. If you don't know what
that is, ask Charles. A helmsman is the person who
steers the ship. A ship and a car are very different
when it comes to steering. The trip to the Philippines
was very interesting. We stopped at Manila, Ilails,
Tanaboauga, and Cebu. Have Lewis and Arlie find
these places on a map. Today is Armistice Day and we
are having holiday routine. In your next letter give
the addresses of Aunt Pearl, Aunt Cassie, Aunt Gladys,
Grandma, Uncle Arlie, Uncle Bud, Uncle Chet, and
Glenn. I hope you received the package O. K. Be sure to
tell Charles to write. I have written him and he hasn't
answered. Also tell Uncle Lewis to write. Give every body

my regards. Tell Lewis and Arlie not to work to hard.
(I don't.) I have gained 10 pounds and my muscles
are getting hard as rocks. Oh, yes, tell Charles I said
if he would have been good he wouldn't have gotten
in trouble and after this for him to take it easy. I hope
you are in the best of health.

Bill

P.S. The 2 pictures marked X give to Charles. I have
more I will send later. I am having an allotment
made out where you will be sent $10 a month and
I won't have to worry about it. I will send $10 this
month. The allotment will start next month I think.

:: :: ::

USS Phoenix
Pearl Harbor, T. H.
Nov. 11, 1941
Dear Lewis,
You like to fly and to see the world but you would
rather fly than see the world but here is a way you
can do both. Join the <u>Navy Air Corp</u>. As for the types
of airplanes you can't fool me for I know the different
types better than you do because I have to know for I
am lookout.

If you want some big shells come around sometime
after we fire. Be sure and find the following places
on a map. Manila, Iloilo, Zamboanga, and Cebu. I
have been to those places. And in the dictionary look
up carametta. I have ridden in them. Did you swim
much this year? How are you and your chipmunks
getting along? Don't <u>study</u> too <u>hard</u>.

Bill

P. S. Please write. Ask questions because I can't
think of much to say

S.P.S. How did you like your stamps – can you work

your eversharps? The eversharps cost 30 centavos or 15 cents.

:: :: ::

USS Phoenix
Pearl Harbor, T. H.
Nov. 11, 1941
Dear Arlie,
  I am sending you and Lewis a picture apiece, more will follow. How do you like your stamp and eversharp? The mountains around Pearl Harbor are nice and green and very rugged. The Philippines Islands were very nice. As for the water you get used to that. I go swimming but not in the ocean. For Christmas draw me a picture of a Hawaiian girl and send it to me. (Better make it good) The mountains around here are covered with sugar cane. Remember if you ever join the Navy, you can't be a baby. Say don't get too thick with your teacher. Don't work or study too hard. Keep asking questions it gives me something to write about.
  Bill
  P. S. Remember to write.

:: :: ::

USS Phoenix
Pearl Harbor, T. H.
Nov. 20, 1941
Dear Mom,
  Being today is Thanksgiving and I have nothing to do I thought I would write you a few lines to pass away time. I feel pretty low today. I went ashore yesterday and went swimming and bought something to eat. I only spent 50¢. I imagine you are having a big feed today. I know we are. Don't send anything

for Christmas except maybe a shaving kit, which I don't need but I tell you what I would like that is a piece of fruit cake or some peanut butter cookies.

What is Francis Harvey doing? Tell him to write. What school are Wanda and David going to? Is Vic still staying at Palmers? Yesterday was payday and I now have $25 saved up. I will send $10 home the next time I write. How is Charles feeling? Tell him to be sure and write. I got a letter from Uncle Lewis and Aunt Leona.

I am sleepy but will write more after chow. Well I had a good sleep and for chow we had asparagus, fruit cake, butter, pumpkin pie, candy, nuts, celery, and olives and boy am I full and I am still eating candy.

Be sure and send pictures to put in my album. Tell some of the young people around Bridgeport to write. I will answer all letters. How is Oscar, Bunny and the baby getting along? Did you send them those pictures? Tell them to write. I will sign off now. Write soon.

Bill

William H. Holt

USS Phoenix Division 4

% Fleet Post office Pearl Harbor, T.H.

P.S. Tell Charles to write.

:: :: ::

Bill writes above, "I feel pretty low today." No place in any of his letters do I detect him being homesick – except in this letter. He wanted "Mom's cookies and fruit cake." He has been gone from home for six months. Typically a sailor will have a leave after boot camp but Bill wanted to be on the Phoenix so he had to forgo the leave and go to Pearl Harbor to be assigned to the Phoenix. We were excited and pleased for him so we didn't think much about it. As he stated in an earlier letter – he had joined the Navy for three years so he would be home then. But that was not to be.

CHAPTER TWO

PEARL HARBOR, DEC. 7, 1941

My own personal recollection of December 7, 1941 is clear even after 60 years. We did not have electricity so we didn't have a radio to hear the news of the attack. Glenn and Detta Gage lived 3/4 of a mile west of our place towards Falls City. They had heard about the attack by the Japanese on Pearl Harbor on their radio and came down to tell us. They knew that Bill was at Pearl Harbor and knew that we should be told about the attack. They pulled up in front of our place and parked. We went out to see them. I remember we stood by their car as they told us about the attack. Now I wonder what my mother thought about that evening and the days that followed. You can imagine the thrill we felt when we received the following letter from Bill. It was a simple mimeographed form letter but it was valued more than any letter we were to receive. Until we received the letter we did not know where Bill was or if he was alive.

(Form letter – mimeographed)

Date   *December 10, 1941*

Dear   *Mom*

I am well and send love to (*you*) (all)

I received your *letter* dated *Nov. 24*
          telegram
          parcel

      Bill   Sign as desired

W. H. Holt

Name - Initials

:: :: ::

:: :: ::

I am O. K. Don't worry.

I am enclosing $10.00

W. H. Holt
Name - initials

:: :: ::

Date *December 15, 1941*
Dear *Mom*

I am well and send love to (*you*) (all)
I received your ***letter*** dated   *Nov. 25, 1941*
                    telegram
                    parcel
                    Bill   Sign as desired

W. H. Holt
Name - Initials

:: :: ::

I received your long letter and I appreciated it very much. I want you to write whether you hear from me or not. I hope you like your Christmas presents. The belt is Charles', the knives are Lewis' and Arlie's, and the rest is yours. The allotment I made out will start in January. Well I can't think of anymore to say so till next time. Well a Very Merry Christmas and a Happy New Year. Oh, yes, I hope you got my $10 O. K.

Holt, W. H.
Name - initials

:: :: ::

Date *December 15, 1941*
Dear   *Uncle Lewis & Aunt Leona*

I am well and send love to (you) (<u>all</u>)
I received your _letter_ dated   *November*
                    telegram
                    parcel

  <u>Holt, W. H.</u>
Name - Initials

Just a few lines to let you know I am O. K. I hope
you received your Christmas present alright. It isn't
much but something to show. I think of you and the
things you have done for me. Well I wish you a very
Merry Christmas and a Happy New Year. Give Glenn
my regards. Well don't worry and try to keep Mamma
from worrying.

                 Bill

  <u>Holt, W. H.</u>
Name - initials

I suppose you heard from Bill but incase you did not I am mailing
this to you. Also Cassie's card. I may have to go away to work any day
now. L. H. Holt

                :: :: ::

Date   *December 15, 1941*
Dear   *Charles*
    I am well and send love to (*you*) (all).
    I received your <u>letter</u> dated *November*
                    telegram
                    parcel

  <u>Holt, W. H.</u>
Name - Initials

Just a few lines to let you know I am still O.K.
and still on top. I am sorry I couldn't answer your
questions and send you the things you wanted. I had
a long letter written but didn't send it. I imagine you
will have a good time Christmas. Well I wish you a

Merry Christmas and a Happy New Year. Don't worry
and try to keep Mamma from worrying.

Bill

Holt, W. H.
Name - Initials

:: :: ::

USS Phoenix
Dec. 26, 1941
Dear Mom,

Just a few lines to let you know I am O. K. I am in
the best of health. I am enclosing $15.00. I want you
to pay my dentist bill. I think it is $3. Tell him I am
sorry I didn't pay it sooner. The rest of the money is
yours.

I had a swell time Christmas. We had a big feed
with all we wanted to eat. I received letters from
Bunny & Oscar, Grandma, Aunt Gladys, Rose, and
Claude. Christmas cards from Uncle Lewis and
Grandma. I am sorry I didn't write sooner.

Well I hope you had a nice Christmas and received
my package O. K. I can't think of anything to say so I
will sign off.

Bill

William H. Holt
USS Phoenix

P. S. I received pictures from Aunt Gladys and Rose.
There was one of Rose, one of Claude, and one of Rose
and Aunt Elsie (Uncle Arlie's wife) and one of Aunt
Gladys and her husband. I got the picture you sent.
Thanks a lot.

Well don't worry.

:: :: ::

These letters were valuable. We did not know where Bill was but receiving these letters let us know that he was OK. The first one was especially valuable. For all we knew, he might have been dead. Even after receiving the letters, we had no idea where he was, nor could we begin to guess where he might be. In gathering material for this book, I found out many years later that the Phoenix went to San Francisco just a few days after the attack on Pearl Harbor. One of the guns had been damaged while firing at the attacking Japanese planes. The gun was replaced in San Francisco. Leaving San Francisco the Phoenix escorted a troop ship to Australia.

Bill wrote this account of the attack on Pearl Harbor for an extension class while he was in a naval hospital in California. After his death it was printed in the *Dallas (Oregon) Itemizer Observer* 12-6-45.

Pearl Harbor Attack Described In Paper Left By Late Sailor

William Holt, son of Mrs. Vintie Holt of the Bridgeport community was on duty on the Cruiser Phoenix in Pearl Harbor on the morning of December 7, 1941. Later he contracted tuberculosis in the service and died February 6, 1945, at the Veterans' hospital, Walla Walla, Wn. Among his papers was found an account of his experiences on that "day of infamy" which he had written during his stay in various hospitals.

_____

On the morning of December 7, 1941, I was on the boat deck waiting for "turn to" when about 0855 someone said "Come here and look. They are making a practice air attack on Ford Island." About that time colors were sounded. Right after colors I crossed from the port side to the starboard side and I saw planes coming in over the yards, airfields and the battlewagons. Two battlewagons were already hit and listing and burning. At that moment the general alarm was sounded and I proceeded as fast as I could to my battle station which was on the starboard side of the forward machine gun platform.

Everybody was so surprised at first they didn't know what to do but it didn't take long to get into action. Someone started unlashing the awnings. Then someone broke out a big knife out of the galley and the next thing I knew the awning and gun covers were over the side and the guns were clear for action, and did they go into action!

The planes came over in two waves, one just before 0800 and the other around 1000. When the attack started most of our officers were ashore but it didn't take most of them long to get back.

We got orders to get underway. We had just cast off from the buoys and the order came to pick up the buoy again. Again we started to pick up the buoy and the order was changed. Now we were going out for sure. We started out one way and we had to change because a battlewagon was beached and they weren't sure if we could get through or not. So we turned around and steamed out right past the yards and battlewagons (time 1200-1300). We could see most of the damage that was inflicted to Pearl Harbor. I was on lookout and I had a pair of 6 X 30 binoculars and I got a good look. It was not a pretty sight either. Ships were hit, some down, burning and some even turned turtle, but the sailors were still in good spirit and they cheered us when we went out.

As we made the turn and headed straight out we began to put on speed and by the time we cleared the outer harbor we were going full speed (33.5 knots). Boy, was I glad when we got out far enough that we could zig-zag, because there were submarines lying out there waiting for us. We sailed out in company with two light cruisers and six destroyers. The rumors were we were steaming at full speed and the enemy was 50 miles away and were we scared. The rumor was false.

We soon met a few heavy cruisers and some more cans. Felt somewhat better. And still later out of the mist loomed a carrier, more cruisers and cans. Boy, did that make me feel better.

For the next three days, (Dec. 7 - Dec. 11) we sailed along standing watch and going to G Q at the slightest irregularity. For the first two days I was sick but I didn't miss a watch. On December 11 four cruisers and an escort of destroyers headed into port. We just squared off and headed in when the second cruiser began to flash a light and the first two cruisers went one way and the other two another way and swish, swish, two "fish" went sailing by.

We took on supplies and fuel and stripped the ship and sailed out the following day for the States.

There are two things I won't forget. One – two planes made their run on a battlewagon and were pulling out and they were raked from stem to stern with machine gun fire and they both hit the water in one, two order. Two – A plane made his run over the battle wagons and pulled out right by us and a machine gunner began to pour lead into him on the quarter and continued till he was on the bow. Apparently the pilot was killed because the plane continued on in an even climb. He cracked into the side of the hill and burst into flame.

If anyone tells you he wasn't scared, don't believe him, because everyone I talked to who was there said he and all those he knew were scared.

Phoenix

The USS Phoenix is at the extreme left around 0800 Dec 7th in this view by a Japanese airman. Note Japanese planes at center and extreme right.

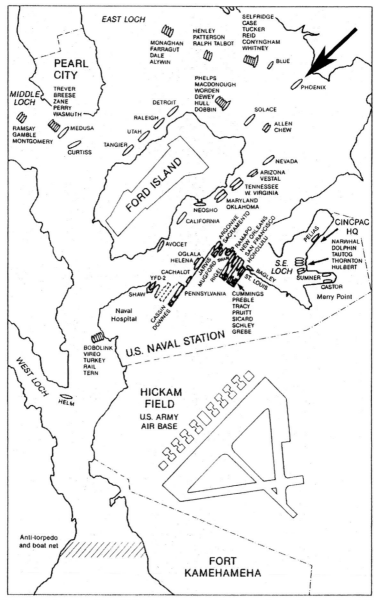

Ship locations at Pearl Harbor prior to the attack on December 7th.
Of the 96 ships positioned inside the harbor, 18 were sunk or
heavily damaged. Contrary to popular belief, only about
half the of the fleet was present.

*USS Phoenix leaves Pearl Harbor and the burning battleship
USS Arizona after the initial Japanese air attack of WWII.
This historic event on December 7, 1941 eventually
led to Bill's death four years later at the age of 21.*

DEPARTMENT OF THE NAVY -- NAVAL HISTORICAL CENTER
805 KIDDER BREESE SE -- WASHINGTON NAVY YARD
WASHINGTON DC 20374-5060

USS Phoenix, Report of Pearl Harbor Attack
CL46/A16
(0202)
 U.S.S. Phoenix
   December 11, 1941.

From: The Commanding Officer.
To: Commander-in-Chief, U.S. Pacific Fleet.

Subject: Report of attack on Pearl Harbor --
December 7, 1941.

Enclosure: (A) Brief Narrative of Events.

1. Enclosure (A) is forwarded as directed.
2. No direct damage to enemy planes by this
vessel can be definitely established. Three planes
which were under fire of several ships including
Phoenix were seen to crash.
3. No damage was inflicted on this vessel by
enemy fire. Number 3 - 6″ gun was placed out of
commission owing to swollen barrel.
4. There were no individuals who were
outstanding in the performance of duty.

[signed]
H.E. FISCHER.

Copies to:
  Combatfor
  Comcrubatfor

Times marked with an asterix are fairly definite.

TIME

EVENT

0755* First attacking planes sighted from signal bridge attacking from north of Ford Island. Plane had all guns firing, passed over stern of Raleigh and proceeded toward Ford Island Central Tower and dropped bomb.

0800 Bombing attack on battleships (Plane markings: varied "U.S.--", Swastika's and Rising Sun, painted on fuselage).

0806* Phoenix made radio signal to ships of sector four to "prepare to get underway".

0807* One plane burning in water at end of pipe line astern of berth F-8.

0810 Machine gun battery opened fire on attacking planes.

0815 AA Battery opened fire.

0845 Ship ready to get underway.

0900 Formation of 11 planes crossed over fleet on heading 070, high altitude. Approximately 10,000. Planes appeared to be painted silver. Expended approximately 50 rounds of 5". No apparent damage to planes.

0910 (Approx)

Second bombing attack on battleships. Expended approximately 60 rounds 5" ammunition.

After planes came out of dive and turned toward berth C-6 planes were brought under fire of machine gun battery.

0900-0915

Dive bombing attack on ships berthed northern side of Ford Island. Attack made at about 30° angle

opposed with AA battery and machine gun battery.
Expended about 20 rounds 5″.

One plane was entirely disintegrated by DD fire.
0900-0930 Effected periodic fire on planes
delivering low level bombing attack on Navy Yard
and ships berthed there.
1010 Got underway, but returned to berth C-6 on
receiving orders not to sortie.
1030 Got underway and started out of north
channel, but received message from Tennessee "From
Cincpac do not sortie". Turned around in channel
and started back to berth C-6. On receipt of orders
from Commander Cruisers, Battle Force proceeded
via south channel and completed sortie and joined
Commander Task Force One.

TOTAL AMMUNITION EXPENDED:
353 - 5″/50 Cal.
35 - 3″/25 Cal.
4500 - 50 Cal. Machine Gun.

Source: Enclosure (E) to CINCPAC action report
Serial 0479 of 15 February 1942, World War II
action reports, the Modern Military Branch,
National Archives and Records Administration, 8601
Adelphi Road, College Park, MD 20740.

CHAPTER THREE

1942 In Australia

There were no letters that Mom saved from Bill in the box from the December 26, 1941 — following the attack on Pearl Harbor — until we received the following letter in March of 1942. We did not know where Bill was or what he was doing.

Miss Rita Barron
40 King St.
Perth, West Australia
8th March 1942

Dear Mrs. Holt,

I suppose you will be surprised to open this letter & find it is from a strange girl you haven't heard of or seen.

Well I will explain how you got this letter, I have been going out with your son "Bill" and he asked me to write to you and tell you that he is quite safe and well and he is having a good time. Bill said not to worry, he'll soon be back.

Mrs. Holt, Bill said when you write to anybody don't say that you heard where he was and how he is getting on. You believe me, he is enjoying himself. I will see that he does, he wants me to send a photo of myself in my next letter and you are to keep it for him till he gets back. I think Bill is very nice, we've had a lot of fun together.

Well Mrs. Holt I hope that now you have heard news of Bill you will not worry too much. He is always telling me about you. I feel as if I have known you for years. I will write again & tell you how Bill is keeping & I hope you will write & let me know you received my letter. Hoping this finds you safe & well.

I remain yours truly,
Rita Barron

The above letter from Rita Barron was an exciting letter. It was news about Bill, which had been very rare. For over 60 years pictures of Bill and Rita have been on an end table at the family home at Bridgeport near Dallas, Oregon. Over the years we have wondered about Rita, who she really was, what might have been her life after Bill left – she was a letter and a girl in a picture on the beach with Bill. That was all we knew about her. But 54 years later our questions were answered. But wait, I'll tell you more about her later. My mother received one more letter from Rita but it has been misplaced or lost.

Rita and Bill in Freemantle, Australia in early 1942

:: :: ::

May 12, 1942 - Post marked) (Bill's birthday was on July 5th)
Monmouth, Oreg.

Happy Birthday SAILOR
Here's wishing you
smooth sailing
on Your Birthday,
blue skies overhead
straight to the
Port of Happiness!

Dear Bill,

Just a word to let you know that we will be thinking of you when your birthday anniversary comes around. Besides doing a little work I hope you are having a little fun. I am trying to have my share of it. I think that I will receive a letterman's sweater this term. It has not been decided definitely. You should be here to help me in my English courses. It has been recommended that I take Freshman English again. We had Sophomore examinations the other day. My scores were better than average or superior in every thing except English fundamentals.

Well write to Mom and me and let us know all that you can.

I am trying to enlist in the Aviation Cadets Reserves. If I can do that there will be another term of school left for me. If not I'll be in service soon. With my teeth fixed I may be in the navy Thurs. I am getting a cap on my front tooth. Love from all

Charles and rest

:: :: ::

There are no other letters during 1942. If there had been, he could not have told where he was or what he was doing. Either he didn't write or the letters were lost.

The United States of America Navy Department
Bureau of Navigation
Navy training course Certificate

William H. Holt

having completed the Navy training Course Seaman

First Class with a mark of 3.1 , is awarded this certificate this 29th day of October, 1942.
   Notation of this effort has been made in his service record.

John J. Slattery   D. L. Erwin,
Ensign, U. S. Navy Res   Commander, U.S. Navy
Division Officer   Commanding USS
              Phoenix

:: :: ::

CHRISTMAS GREETINGS to you, Son
A Christmas wish for happiness,
A greeting to convey
The loving pride that fills each thought
Of you, dear Son, today;
The torch of liberty shines bright
And freedom is our fate
Because fine men, fine Sons like you
Have made our nation great!

Nov. 13, 1942
Dear Bill,

Just a few lines on a Xmas card from home. We are O.K. And hope you are the same. We are busy getting in two cords of fir wood in the shed and it is nice wood. We sure have been having cold frosty nites but it is clouding up today so we may soon have rain. We want to get the rest of our potatoes dug soon as we can and get our work done for the winter. Write.

With love, Mom - Lewis - Arlie - Charles

:: :: ::

Bill received many Christmas cards from Aunts and Uncles and friends.

CHAPTER FOUR

DEAR MOM HAVE BEEN SICK

```
R17 VIAMACKAYRADIO=F SANSO. IGINE AMBOYO NDT NFT
(1943 JAN 29 AM 9 27)
     DKT VINTIE O HOLT
     RTE 2 BOX 134 (DALLAS ORE)
     =DEAR MOM HAVE BEEN SICK AM IMPROVING NOW
NEARLY WELL LOVE


     BILL HOLT
```

Bill must have sent this telegram from the Army Hospital in Townsville, Queensland, Australia. It was postmarked from Salem, Oregon on Jan. 29, 1943. We had no idea where he was when he sent the telegram. This telegram signifies the beginning of an illness that would eventually lead to his death three years later. Bill was transferred to US Naval Hospital in Oakland, California where he continued to struggle attempting to conqueror his illness. But eventually tuberculosis would cause his death at 21 in the veteran's hospital in Walla Walla, Washington.

REPORT OF CHANGES of USS _____ PHOENIX
for the month ending 27th day of _____ January ___, 19 43 date of sailing from _____
DANGEROUS WATERS _____ to _____

1. BOZICK, Wilfred Rudolph	300 27 12 S1c.	4 Dec. 40	Chicago, Ill
2. GATES, Arthur William	302 17 44 F1c	12 Mar 40	Los Angels, Calif
3. GEORGE, Maurice Murphy	273 64 12 OM1c12	Sept 40	Mare Island, Calif.
4. HOLT, William Harrison	**393 56 14 S1c**	**17 June 41**	**Portland, Ore.**
5. POLLAK, William Louis	250 47 31 RM2c	16 May 38	Pittsburg, PA.
6. RUSH, William Porter	272 32 01 RM3c	11 June 40	Birmingham, Ala.
7. SHINGLE, John Gilbert	375 9784 GM3c	8 Nov. 39	San Francisco, Calif.
8. STRANSKY, Castmer Edward	242 84 14 GM(PA)	9 May 42	Fremantle, Aus.
9. WYATT, Verlin Dale	372 10 66 SM3c 6	Oct. 39	Denver, Colo.
10. HENDRIX, Myron William	382 50 35 F3c 21	July 41	Los Angeles, Calif.
11. WILLIS, James Ray	249 92 95 SM1c	No Records	Auth Letter Bu Per 4-22-42

:: :: ::

1. USN   REC   1/23/43   COMSERFORSOWSPACFOR for duty.
2. USN   REC   1/23/43   COMSERFORSOWSPACFOR for duty.
3. USN   TRAN 1/26/43   R/ship or Sta on West Coast of US for assign new construction by COMSUBORDCOMSERF
4. USN   TRAN 1/26/43 US Army Hosp, Townsville, Aus, not misc. records & accounts US Nav. Observer Brisbane.
5. USN   TRAN 1/26/43 R/Ship or Sta on West Coast of US for assign new construction by COMSUBORDCOMSERFORPACFLT.
6. USN   TRAN 1/26/43 R/Ship or Sta on West Coast of US for assign new construction by COMSUBORDCOMSERFORPACFLT.
7 USN   TRAN 1/26/43 US Army Hosp, Townsville, Aus, not misc. records & accounts US Nav. Observer Brisbane.
8. USN   TRAN 1/26/43 R/Ship or Sta on West Coast of US for assign new construction by COMSUBORDCOMSERFORPACFLT.
9. USN   TRAN 1/26/43 R/Ship or Sta on West Coast of US for assign new construction by R/Ship or Sta on West Coast of US for assign new construction by COMSUBORDCOMSERF ORPACFLT.
10. USN   TRAN 1/11/43 USS Helm for duty treatment completed
11. USN   TRAN 1/8/43 USS Mugford FFT HMAS AUSTRALIA
Suth Letter Bu Per 4/22/42

Copy to: Bupers. COMSUBORDCOMSERFORPACFLT.

ComSerForSoWesPacFor. (signed) R. W. Clark

Commander, U. S. Navy

Executive Officer.

:: :: ::

The months that followed Bill's transfer from the Phoenix led to Bill's mail being sent to addresses where he had been. He had been transferred from the Phoenix to the hospital in Townsville, Australia. He was there only a short time so his mail didn't arrive until he was transferred to the Naval Hospital in California. But eventually his mail caught up with him.

(V-mail letter)
Mr. William H. Holt Sea 1/c   Vintie Holt
U. S. Navy USS Phoenix   Rt. 2. Box 134
% Post Master   Dallas, Ore.
San Francisco, Calif   Feb. 21, 1943

Dear Bill. A few lines on a pretty spring like day. We have had over a week's nice weather and I have been working outside too. I have gotten the garden spot all spaded between the house and bridge and started on the other side of the house. The ground is just right to work up good. I am over my cold now. Lewis has one. Arlie's wasn't so bad as Lewis's and mine but we keep going and eating so we weren't too bad off. Uncle Lewis was out all last week grubbing scotch bloom and he has a job. They are so tall and the high water just laid them down to the ground. He has a small grub hoe so he stays with it. I have sowed some clover seed. The cows look good. Daisy is a pretty thing. She will be fresh next month. Write when you can hope you are well by now. Love Mom

(Mom wrote this letter on February 21, 1943. She would have known that Bill was sick but didn't know that he wasn't on the Phoenix. The envelope was postmarked Mar 5, 1943, May 15, 1943, and June 13, 1943. The letter was forwarded from the USS Phoenix to the 12th U.S. Army Hospital A. P. O. 922. This was probably the Army Hospital at Townsville, Australia where Bill went when he left the Phoenix. By the time the letter got to the hospital he had been transferred. It was forwarded to A.P.O. 723. Part of the address is scribbled out. Another penciled note says, "N.I.F. 4/17/43." Final stamp says, "Forwarded Jun 28, 1943 Fleet Records Office San Francisco, California." Eventually it was sent to the US NH in Oakland, Calif. Bill had arrived there by this time.

:: :: ::

(V-mail)
Mr. William H. Holt Sea 1/c
U.S.N. SS. Phoenix
% Fleet Post Office
San Francisco, Calif.

Vintie Holt
Rt. 2 Box 134
Dallas, Ore.
Mar. 8, 1943

Dear Bill,

I haven't written to you for a long time so will write a few lines now. We've been having pretty weather here lately so we've been spading and planting some garden. Uncle Lewis has been out and is cutting all the scotch broom in the pasture. It's fun to burn it.

I worked all night last Friday helping George Riggs test chickens.

Then Saturday night I went to a dance. I danced with most everybody there except the ones I didn't know (that was in some Paul Jones two steps) I danced with some people I knew.

Your brother, Arlie

Arlie wrote this letter at school. We are all well.

Mom

(This letter followed the same route as the previous one.)

:: :: ::

(To avoid delay have correspondents use your full name, rate, service No. and latest address.) Post marked May 18, 1943, No Record-FRO Navy 128-S-9 JUN 27, 1943, and Forwarded Jul 14, 1943 Fleet Records' Office San Francisco, California. USN HOSP Oakland, Cal 63-A (63-A would probably be his room and bed number.)

(V-mail)

Mr. William H. Holt Sea 1/c   Vintie Holt

U.S.N. USS Phoenix   Rt. 2 Box 134

% Fleet Post Office   Dallas, Ore.

San Francisco, Calif.   Mar. 22, 1943

Dear Bill,

A few lines to let you know we are O.K. and we are having dry weather. We had a snow storm a week ago. Today is cloudy but warm so we may get some rain. I am as busy as a bee doing two big washings a week besides our own. Mrs. Kingsberry and a neighbor that moved up from Calif since you left. (The McGinities) They moved the building up on the hill by the old Gage place from down on the creek. They are both teachers. The Mrs. teaches at Falls City now. He is farming. Well I hope you are feeling better by now. Uncle Lewis is O.K. Write when you can. Love as ever Mom.

:: :: ::

May 14, 1943
My Rosary for Mother
May God's peace and richest blessings
be in your heart on Mother's Day
and always
To Mama
From Bill

:: :: ::

Happy Birthday
MOTHER

TO MAMA
With Love From Bill
I'm thinking today of the nice things you've done
To make others happy each year.
I'm thinking of all of your sweet, thoughtful ways
That bring so much gladness and cheer;
I'm thinking today of your love and your care.
And hoping with all my heart, too,
That the sweet things you've done will return one by one
To make each day happy for you

:: :: ::

May 31, 1943
Best Wishes to YOU in the Hospital
May your hospital stay
be so cheery,
May the cure be
so splendid indeed,
You will soon become
known as the patient
Who recovered with
very great speed!
Love Mom

May 31, 1943

Dear Bill,

Will start a few lines. I have so much to do I don't know what to do first. I did Mrs. Kingsberry's washing and my own, got dinner and made one sheet out of feed sacks have another one started, have my iron heating up as I think I had better get my other neighbor's washing ironed. They owe me $7.50. June 1 Well Bill 9 o'clock in the evening just came in from planting beans. Lewis and Arlie covered them. I went to town this morning with a neighbor. Came out with Uncle Lewis. He put the water pipes in wrong into the water tank and made the water much slower to heat so he came out and changed them. I gave him a pt of cream and a qt of buttermilk. June 2. A few more lines I have been hurrying to go out and work but now it is raining so I can do my ironing, clean house or sew. I have a slack suit cut out. I can find plenty to do. Oh Bill I sure hope Aunt Hetty could go see you and if she does tell her to write to me.

I know you will enjoy a visit with her. The boys worked till 9:15 last nite. They are so anxious to see our beans get to growing. I got me a pretty red slack suit yesterday and two prs of red anklets. I have 2 pr of red play shoes. One with no heal or toes and I paid down on me an overall work suit light blue. I need something like that as I am out side working so much of the time and I don't have much time to sew. Take time out to write to you, Charles and Caroline. I must write to Claude. Oh yes the boys finally got the fence up around the barnyard. Lewis has worked so hard and faithful at it and be so tired too while Arlie would be setting reading movie magazines. We made $30.05 last wk. We put wks before last on the place and I will save out some out our last wk to pay on it too. We owe now $75.00 and I want to have extra money for taxes as they will be high. That downie (downie mildew) is getting in the hops and it some times kills the vine and as soon as the weather is better, I can work because it means lots of money to us. I want to get wallpaper and paint to make our house look and feel more comfortable for in the winter as we don't have much time in the summer. It is getting lighter so maybe we will get something done outside.

I am trying to get the boys started out to clean the hen house. Lewis he is busy working on airplane models and Arlie reading about movie actors. Well I almost forgot to tell you about our trip to Buxton. The kids are out now and I can think. It rained all day couldn't take any pictures. Bunny, she wanted to take pictures so she could send them to you and Charles. We cleaned off the graves the best we could put flowers on them then went to Cassie's. We met them on our way over there . Aunt Cassie wasn't feeling so very good and it was getting late and raining so that's why we started over there. William's car was a head. He stopped after passed up and the cars all bumped into each other. Hurt Aunt Cassie some they all came back home so we had dinner at her house. Uncle Geo's was there. Uncle Gilbert is sick and isn't able to be out at all. Had the flu went out to work too soon and taken a back set and has been awful sick. Devera came on the bus. William and his wife have two baby boys and expecting another one. Magdalene has two girls and expecting another one. Mary E has one boy and expecting again. Aunt Pearl's was there. Beverly she sure thinks she is cute. Lazy and crazy about the boys. Virginia she isn't so fat any more and she has her a steady boy friend. Linnie is so big fat and awful homely. We had all we could eat and I just ate and go back and eat some more. We had two tables full of eats. Well I guess I had better close and get this letter out in the mail then I will have to take time out and write to Charles. It makes Lewis feel good to tell him he is so much like you for he is proud of you dear. Love, Mom

:: :: ::

Bill received many get well cards — too many to include here.

:: :: ::

November 3, 1943
Dear Mom,
Well I am in the letter writing business so I thought I would include you in my business for today. It has been nice the last few days. Sunny and not a cloud in the sky. But true to California tradition, it is cool

59

in the morning and nice in the afternoon. There has been fog a couple times since I have been here. I am going to send you some more pictures of the hospital here. I guess it is a nice place if I could see it. All I saw was just a glimpse when we came in. About fifty yards from the ward is a lake. The only way I can see it is get up and the nurse gives me the devil if she catches me up. She doesn't catch me up very much because I don't get up very much. Some ladies came to the ward today and passed out cookies, apples, and some relish. The relish is really good. You have made lots of it.

I have been studying most of the day. My shorthand is getting easier every day. The educational officer asked me if I had any questions. He said I hope not because he knew less than I did about it. So far there aren't any questions. I got my second book on Algebra today. I should finish the other one in a few days. I wrote to the Oregon System of Higher Education for information on correspondence courses. I want to take some that will count on college credit. As long as I haven't anything to do I might as well put my time to a good use. I'll bet I study more than Lewis and Arlie. Today I studied from 8:30 to 11:00 and from 12:30 to about 3:00. It is just a typical day. Sometimes I read a book but I keep busy. The doctors advise a patient to keep busy to keep your mind off your worries.

I got a letter from Charles and Norma today. Charles didn't have much to say. Norma was telling me about her troubles she was having going to school. From the way she writes I'll bet she is pretty smart. She is also very active. It is getting along towards evening and it is cooling off. I don't know what is wrong with me tonight I am making more errors than usual. Maybe it is because I am trying to make a little speed.

I guess I had better slow down.

I am getting tired so I will sign off. Before I quit maybe you saw pictures of the USS Savannah in the paper the last few days. The reason why I mentioned that is the ship I was on was of the same class. They are good ships, too.

W.H. Holt, Sea 1/c
U.S. Navy   *Bill*

:: :: ::

Dec. 6, 1943

An early winter view
of the Grand Lake in Labrador
when the trappers
still travel in canoes

Bringing you Holiday Greetings
and every good wish for
the New Year.

To Mama, Lewis, and Arlie
from Bill
Don't worry I'll be home someday.

:: :: ::

We found this poem in Bill's duffel bag when it was sent to us from Walla Walla after he died. The poem must have had a special meaning for him. Was it Rita in Australia? Was it the hope and anticipation of coming home? Or was it his dreams of a future that he never had?

WHEN YOU RETURN

BY Anderson M. Scruggs

When you return I shall not question you
On all your little deeds since that far day.
Time wedged our paths apart. I shall not say,
As others might, who missed your presence, too.
How do you like the town of so and so?
Or some such phrase friends utter, unconcerned;
What use are casual words to those who learned
One day, in silence, all they need to know?

I shall abide my time and when, at last,
The clamor and the greetings all are done,
Our eyes shall meet, and silently, as one,
We shall relive one moment in the past,
And you shall know, though lips let no word fall,
That in my heart you did not leave at all.

:: :: ::

OREGON STATE SYSTEM OF HIGHER EDUCATION
CORRESPONDENCE STUDY DEPARTMENT

December 8, 1943

William H. Holt, S1c 393 56 14
US Navy Hospital, Unit 2
Corona, California

Dear Mr. Holt:

The General Extension Division is in receipt of
your application for the course in Principles of
Good Writing, with your money order for $4.85 to
cover half the expense of the course. A receipt is
enclosed.

We are sending herewith the first assignments
of the course, also a list of suggestions we shall
ask you to follow carefully in preparing your

written reports. Your text will be mailed from the University of Oregon Cooperative Store and should reach you in a short time.

Your registration will have no definite date of termination, as men in the service are allowed an indefinite period for work on a course. While you are free to go ahead with the assignments, the final credit will not be recorded until the remaining half of the fee is received from the Armed Forces Institute.

We are very glad to have you working with us, and trust you will find the course entirely satisfactory. Let us know if we may be of assistance at any time.

Sincerely yours,
Miss) Mozelle Hair
Head of Correspondence Study
by Dorothy S. Jones

:: :: ::

U.S. Naval Hospital
Corona, California
December 25, 1943
Dear Mom,
Christmas 1940 home, Christmas 1941 Pearl Harbor, Christmas 1942 Sydney, Australia, Christmas 1943 U.S. Naval Hospital Corona, California, and Christmas 1944 home again (I hope).

Well Mama I am filled up to the gills. You can see by the menu that we had plenty to eat and I ate too. Besides that I have eaten lots of candy and nuts that weren't on the menu. The way I've eaten the last week I should gain a little weight this week.

It is sure quiet today but wait till Monday and

it will be as noisy as ever. It is cloudy today but the sun is trying to shine so it isn't such a bad day. I've seen lots worse days. I sure was busy last week. I wrote over 20 letters. Don't think I will have that many this week. I hope not because I want to work on my autobiography. I want to send it in the latter part of next week. I sent my application in for the Veterans of Foreign Wars yesterday. Boy I've enough combs now. I only have 8, 3 in my sea bag and 5 with me.

I imagine all is quiet up your way too. Are you having much rain up there? I have enough hand lotion to last me the next year. I just have two large and one small bottle of Jergen's Lotion.

Well I think I will close and take it easy being this is Christmas.

William H. Holt, Sea 1/c
United States Navy   *Bill*

(Looking back this is one of the saddest letters from Bill. At the time it was one of the most exciting letters. Bill would be home for Christmas 1944 – what a beautiful thought. Now I feel that he was giving himself hope but most of all he was protecting his mother and trying to present himself as getting better so she wouldn't worry. Also, it was written on Christmas day when millions of young men and women would liked to have been home with their families.)

:: :: ::

Eng C III William H. Holt, S 1/c 393 36 14
RECEIVED
U.S. Naval Hosp. Unit 2   JAN 13, 1944
Corona, California   GENERAL EXTENSION DIVISION

Assignment 1   Page 1

I am lying in a hospital bed looking across the lawn at the hills beyond thinking of my past.

The greater part of my childhood was spent on a farm in Oregon. When I was about eleven years of age my father went to work in the logging camps, and for six years we followed the job, moving from camp to camp. In spite of changing schools, I kept up in my subjects and managed to get average or above grades.

In my last two and one-half years of high school, I was prominent in school activities. Basketball was my favorite sport, and even though I did not excel in journalism, I worked on the school paper. In my junior year something happened that probably changed my journey through life -- my father was killed in a logging accident. Consequently we moved back to the farm. If he had lived I would have probably followed in his footsteps.

By the time I finished high school the war had begun in Europe, and the outlook for the United States was not very promising so I joined the Navy. It was another milestone in my life.

At the age of seventeen I joined the Navy. While I was in training and until I went aboard a cruiser for duty, I was among men of my own age. Aboard ship life was different since most of the men were old timers. Prior to my joining the navy my mother took care of my clothes and money and told me to do this or do that. Now Mama was thousands of miles away, and I couldn't run to her for every little thing.

I had to wash and press my own clothes, take care of my money, and do what the Navy said and not what I wanted to do.

What a thrill it was, going aboard a transport bound for Hawaii, the Pearl of the Pacific. I was in for a big disappointment because I still believed the pamphlets and posters I saw when I took the examination for the Navy. I looked everywhere for some true Hawaiians. What did I find? I found every nationality except Hawaiians.

Things were going along just fine until one morning hell broke loose. All around me ships were being attacked, some burning, and some sinking. In a few hours young kids became battle-tried veterans. A short time after that we put to sea and headed for parts unknown. There was quite a change in visiting the different foreign ports - new places, money, customs, and people. I was progressing all right until I became sick and turned into the "sick bay" with a high fever.

Seventeen days later the doctor said, "We are going to send you to the hospital because it will be better for you." Reading my mind and realizing that I didn't want to leave the ship, he said, "Don't worry, you will be back aboard ship in a couple of months." I felt better then, but the doctor didn't know I was destined to be in the hospital for along time.

I was sent to an army hospital in Northern Australia and eventually to a Navy hospital in the United States. It was in an army hospital that a doctor told me I would probably be in the hospital two or three years and that I would be unable to continue the work that I had been doing.

I have been in the hospital a year now and after being discharged I hope to further my education.

(A teacher writes) *You've had hard luck. Maybe studying will relieve your boredom (I should think you'd become very weary of inactivity), and certainly the more required courses you can dispose of through Extension the more quickly you will be able to finish school when you are discharged.*

:: :: ::

U.S. NAVAL HOSPITAL
Corona, California
February 9, 1944

SWORN STATEMENT in the case of William Harrison
HOLT, S1c, U. S. Navy

From January 1, 1943 to January 26, 1943
I was attached to U.S.S. Phoenix. On January 26,
1943, I was transferred to the U. S. Army Hospital,
Townsville, Queensland, Australia for treatment.

On March 23, 1943 and while still in a
patient status I was further transferred to 118th
General Hospital, U. S. Army, Sydney, Australia.

On April 10, 1943 and while still in a
patient status I again transferred to U.S.S. Mizar
for further transfer to the United States.

I arrived in the United States on April
28, 1943 and was transferred to the U. S. Naval
Hospital, Oakland, California.

On October 16, 1943 I was transferred to the
U. S. Naval Hospital, Corona, California.

_____

WILLIAM HARRISON HOLT

Signature witnessed.

T. J. Mikulis,
CHIEF PHARM., USN.

Sworn to this 9th day of February 1944

JOSEPH TAYMOR   Lieut.Comdr., (MC), USNR.

:: :: ::

I found the above letter very interesting. It shows a time line of where Bill was from Jan. 1, 1943 to February 1944. It would have been nice to have more detail.

:: :: ::

U. S. N. H.
Feb. 21, 1944

Dear Lewis,
Say, do you want a job? I want you to help me write some letters. I had only 7 to start with. This is my 5th. I don't know why it seemed like everyone waited so I would get them all the same time.

That is O. K. about the money. There is no hurry about paying it back. I won't need it for some time.

I read "Under Cover" also. And I too had the same impression.

Do you still write to that girl in Kansas? Say, how much do you get for working in the hops now?

I'm feeling fine. What is the idea of starting school at 8:00? It is trying to be good for a while. If you listened to Jack Benny or Bob Hope, you have heard about the weather we have been having. This is all for tonight.   Good night.

W. H. Holt, Sea 1/c   Bill
U. S. Navy

:: :: ::

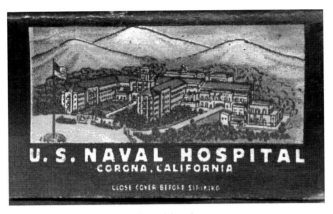

Matchbook

Bill Holt March 5, 1944 U. S. Naval Hospital
Buildings from back to front
Corpsmen's Quaters, S. O. Q., Ward A-2

*Cloen, George, Jack
Cheney, Me
U.S. Naval Hospital
Corona, California
March 5, 1944*

William H. Holt S 1/c, 393 56 14   Eng C III
Unit 2 Ward B-1   Assignment 6
U. S. Naval Hospital   RECEIVED MAR 31, 1944
Corona, California   GENERAL EXTENSION DIVISION

MY DEFINITION OF A SUCCESSFUL LIFE

Whether it is happy or sad, rich or poor, life is what one makes it. A successful life depends on personal achievements, home, profession and income.

Health, above all, is the most important. Wealth or position are of small value unless you have good health. Friends, social life, respect of the community, and strength of character are closely related. Usually if a person has one, he has the others. Personal achievements give one self-confidence and the feeling that he is of some value to the human race.

If one's surroundings or environment are not congenial, his health will soon deteriorate. Also, a person's social standing is affected by the location of his home. For example, people across the tracks are usually considered in the lower social bracket. A man's family probably influences his happiness more than any other thing. A person takes great pride in his family. He or she will sacrifice health and wealth for his wife (husband) and children to see that they have the proper care.

A person should choose a profession which he desires, for which he has had training, and one which will give him a periodical vacation. In many cases people will do work which doesn't appeal to them for some desire of their own or the desire of their family. A person is happier and more contented doing a job he likes.

If a person has good health and a good profession,

71

he shouldn't have to worry about his income or security for the future: that is, if he lives within the means of his earnings. Some people with a large income have less and are not as happy as people with a small income. It isn't so much the amount one earns, as it is how he uses what he earns. Freedom from financial worries aids happiness immensely.

My definition of a successful life is for one to have attained personal achievements, a good home, a well liked profession, and an income which is adequate to provide for his present needs and, also, for his future security.

Bill writes a note at the end of the assignment: I may be transferred soon and I was wondering if I could get the information concerning my term paper. The reason for this I don't know what kind of library I will have access to.

:: :: ::

ASSIGNMENT RECEIVED
APR 20, 1944
GENERAL EXTENSION DIVISION

HOW TO BE A SUCCESS IN THE NAVY

In the Navy, you do as you are told, not as you want. And it is on how you do it, and how you handle yourself that your success in the Navy depends.

When it comes to judging a sailor, the first thing a person notices is your appearance. It, therefore, pays to have your clothes clean, shoes shined, hair cut, face shaved, and your body clean. They aren't as strict now as they were in the peace time. Then they were very strict. I know. I had a hard time when I first went aboard a ship. I had to wash clothes and shine shoes every day, get a hair cut once every two weeks, and have my locker and bunk in order at all times. You couldn't tell just when they were going to have inspection. What would happen if you didn't do these things? Well, if it was just your division P. O. (Petty Officer) who noticed your appearance, you might get off with a verbal chastisement, a few extra watches, a little dirty work, or a few hours of extra-duty. (You usually got the extra-duty when you had something special planned.) If your division officer or one of the higher officers caught you, you might get extra-duty or restriction of your liberty. Another important thing is to be friendly, because you have to live and work with the same people day after day, and it can be miserable if you are not friendly. How you get along with your shipmates indicates how you will make out in your work.

The most important thing about your work is to be able to take orders. And I mean that is tough. Especially if you are in the deck force. Many men are giving you orders. Many times your orders will be mixed up and contradictory. The only thing you can do in that case is to do what you are told and let the man who gives you the orders be responsible. Also, when you are told to do something, do it cheerfully. Arguing and grumbling only lowers your P. O.'s opinion of you. Co-operation is very important, because you work in small groups. If one person shirks duty or does his job just half way, it makes it all the harder on the rest of the group. In war time, co-operation is more important. There are numerous watches. Maybe your P.O. in charge is on watch and some leading seaman will be left in charge. Many people resent taking orders from a seaman. I know that for a fact, because I have been put in charge of a cleaning detail when only a seaman and had other seamen under me.

How far you go in the Navy depends on how hard you work and study. To go up for a rate, you have to be recommended. Your first recommendation comes from your division P. O. and your division officer. If you are recommended by them and pass your preliminary examinations, you will be recommended by your Executive Officer. Here you have to study. That is what you did in peace because of fleet competition.* Then to make it harder, you had to have 4.0 (perfect) in conduct and proficiency. The qualifications weren't that high. But because of the numbers trying for the same rate, you had to have almost a 4.0 record.

Your living conditions and daily routine affect your personality. It isn't so bad at a base, but aboard a ship, especially small ships, the quarters are close. Your daily routine is the same day after day. Here is a typical day in port - 0600 (6:00), reveille, 0630 (6:30) turn to, 0900 (9:00) maybe quarters for muster and drill, 1130 (11:30) sweep down, 1200 (12:00) dinner, 1300 (1:00) turn to, 1530 (3:30) liberty, 1600 (4:00) (sweep down, 1700 (5:00) supper, 1900 (7:00) sweep down, 2055 (8:55) tattoo (?), and 2100 (9:00) taps. If you have any watches to stand, you have to stand them. The number of watches you stand depends on your rate and qualifications.

* Fleet Competition is all the men in the division (Referring to ships) compete for rates and in peace time there would be only 3 or 4 rates given out every quarter (3 months).

:: :: ::

(V-mail)

W. H. Holt S 1/c   Lt. D. R. Anzeline
Unit 2 Wrd B-1   2nd Field Hosp.
U. S. Naval Hosp.   APO 322, % P. H.
Corona, Calif.   S. F., Calif.

Hello –

We've done a bit more moving and now that we've settled temporarily I can get to our letter. The country up here is still the same – doesn't vary much – all mud, jungle & heat. Yes, it even rains more here than in Calif. – and I'm sure this isn't exceptional weather.

That milk sounds good – have an extra shot for me. 144 lbs sounds good. It doesn't seem as tho it were a whole year since you left Australia – sometimes tho it seems 20. Jeepers, if we don't get home some day soon they'll just carry us from the boat to the veteran's home – & I'm not kidding.

Miss Fryer is in Letterman General in S. F. We had a letter from her last week. She is feeling better & needless to say very glad to be back in civilization.

It is about that time so I'd better put on my boots & wade back to the ward tent–

Keep on improving – you'll reach the 200 lb mark eventually.

Good luck

Dorothy Anzeline

On the backside Bill writes: This is a typical letter I receive from the nurse I had in Townsville. Save it for me.

:: :: ::

Elsie Harber lived near Bridgeport where we lived and rode the same bus to school that Bill did in 1940-1941. She was several years younger than Bill. Mom knew Elsie's mother so she probably got Elsie started writing to Bill.

Elsie wrote many letters to Bill. I have chosen not to include all of Elsie's letters – numbering 40 – even though her letters were most

75

often humorous, I feel that she felt a genuine concern for Bill. There might have been a teasing "Dear" but never any words of affection. Her letters were not love letters. Bill wrote many letters to Elsie. He must have felt very close to her but realizing his health, he probably never expressed his feelings. On the surface she was a patriotic girl writing to a serviceman in the hospital.

:: :: ::

Peggy Harber	Wm H. Holt, S1/c
347 N. 12th St.	Unit 2, Ward B-1
Salem, Oregon	Corona, California

May 10, 1944 (Letter continued from yesterday)

Dear Bill,

How do you like the way I write to you on the installment plan? There's nothing like being different I always say. I'll bet you can't guess where I'm writing this – I'm sitting under a hair dryer. I had to wash my pretty little golden locks this morning. I just hate to do that too. Anyhow it's nice and warm under here and that's more than I can say for the weather out doors – Brrrr.

I get so amused at one of the doctors on the hospital staff. He is quite old and has the reputation of taking people home. Practically every night he seems to manage to finish his calls so he can take me home when I get off duty. Last night I was rather late so he asked me how much longer I would be and I told him ten or fifteen minutes and not to wait. He said, Wellllll – I'll go out in the kitchen & get a drink. (First time I knew it took ten minutes to get one drink of water!) Anyway, he came strolling back and proceeded to escort me home. He's just as apt to go down to the nurse's room and gab with the nurses as not. Honestly, he's a swell old guy but he tickles me half to death. That reminds me – the girl at the office who is such a good friend of Dr. Joseph's had a letter from his wife saying she had had a cable from him. He apparently has reached his destination overseas.

Well, I finally got off seven day duty at the hospital. It really wasn't so bad though. I guess I should be able to do that much – often what some of the boys "over there" are doing. That reminds me – the Navy is doing a grand job "out there," don't you think. (Personally, I'm not capable of it!)

It seems like most of the boys I graduated with that are in service chose the Navy. Everett Mott is overseas. You probably read that in the paper. I think he was the first to go across from our class. Oh, yes, tell me some more (tall) sea stories.

Boy, did I get the surprise of my life this payday. I got a $25 raise. I'd had 5 & 10 dollar once before but never a $25 one. That really made me happy.

Well, I'm almost out of paper so I'll write you a continuation tomorrow. Aren't I mean?

Be good and don't do anything I wouldn't!!!

As Ever, Elsie

:: :: ::

May 11, 1944
Dear Bill,
Well, here I sit writing on the third installment. Don't you like my stationery? I'll bet you're just beginning to love me for these silly letters. I just got a mean streak and it's sticking.

If you hear a loud explosion pretty soon, don't be surprised. My sis and her girl friend are experimenting – it's only a cake but I'm still waiting for the explosion.

Gee, did I ever have a streak of luck when I landed my job at the hospital – tonight I was informed that I got two weeks vacation with pay and only my first year of work. There are so many things I have planned to do though so I'm certainly not a bit sorry. I only hope the weather is nice so I can get a lovely sunburn.

Well, Bill, if you don't hear from me any more you'll know why – we are going to try the experiment. Well, it wasn't too bad even though it was Mayonnaise Cake.

Guess what? Tonight just as I was leaving the hospital one of the doctors called up & said he was sending in an emergency appendix. It's getting to be so common that no one thinks of them as "emergencies" anymore. We were so amused at one of the little fellows in the children's ward who had had an appendectomy. He was so proud of his operation. I prefer to keep mine thank you.

Did you hear about the excitement? Some one tried to escape from the penitentiary. One of the guards got shot in the hip, another in the arm and a visitor that happened to be there got shot in the excitement!

With that – I'll close before I get any cornier. I'll have to get busy & dig up some more stationery for tomorrow.

Peggy Letter will be discontinued until further notice. (Elsie Harber) May 13, 1944

:: :: ::

To Mama From Bill   Dear Mom,
Here is something else so as to show you I thought about you on your birthday. Love Bill

It isn't much I'm saying...
Just a brief I LOVE YOU, MOTHER,
But you know that I am thinking
What we mean to one another;
And I'm most sincerely hoping
That this Mother's Day will add
To the memories you cherish
And the happiness you've had

Whatever you consider
The best that life can bring
In making up my birthday wish
I'll ask that very thing –
And it doesn't matter what you want
Or what you want to do
I'll hope that in the year ahead
Your wishes will come true

(Mom's birthday was May 19.)

:: :: ::

Sunday, May 14, 1944

Dear Mom,

Guess what day this is. Do you mean you give up? Just a minute, I'll give you a little hint. For the last month all you have heard is "Remember _____ on _____'s Day." "Buy a so and so for _____ on _____'s Day," and "remember the sweetest person on _____'s Day. Take her to Flick's for a lovely evening." Have you got it yet? That's right. It is <u>Mother's Day</u> and since it is, I thought I would drop you a few lines to let you know I'm thinking about you on this very lovely day.

That is right this is a nice day. It was clear last night. I thought surely I'll have to pull on more covers tonight but I was badly mistaken.

I can't win for loosing. I get caught up on my correspondence, then I get a slew of letters. Then I'm way behind again. I received 3 letters today. I was lucky. Two of them were from the same person. Elsie H. is sure crazy. She has written 3 times in the last four days. She said she was, but I didn't know if she was serious or otherwise. She is going on a vacation soon.

I have some more letters to write so I will make this one short.

W. H. Holt, Sea 1/c

U. S. Navy   Bill

(On the back of the envelope) You have clumb another rung in Life's ladder. Keep up the good work and good luck.

:: :: ::

May 17, 1944 Pvt. Charles H. Holt 19102881   (Bill's older brother.)
Portland, Oregon   Co. K 397th Inf APO 447
                      Fort Bragg, N. C

Dear Bill,

Well, I'm on my way back to North Carolina. It wasn't so bad, but I noticed that I didn't mind the slowness of bus. It didn't bother me nearly as much as before.

I lay over here until 8:00 tonight then I have solid riding for the next two or three days. That will put me into Chicago and a short while later I'll leave for Washington. I have a darned big lay over in Wash, D. C. If it weren't for those lay overs in Wash., I would have had another day at home.

I came all of the way home just to lay around and sleep. I spent Friday and Saturday in Monmouth. I still like that place. Everyone there is doing O, K. But the trouble is there aren't very many there. Right now there are less girls than there were boys when I went to school.

I think that I'll close and go make some telephone calls. One of the WAVE girl friends from Wash, D.C. is now stationed at her home here in Portland. She should be home by now. So bye until tomorrow.

Your bud Charles

:: :: ::

June 30, 1944   (Bill's birthday was July 5th)

A happy birthday greeting
And best wishes sincere and true
From one whose heart will ever hold
The kindest thoughts of you.
Love, Mom 1944

Dear Bill,

Saturday morning all alone. Have lots to do. I won't get lonesome. How are you? I feel sore, sleepy, that's all. I went up to Phil Muller's Berry yard yesterday got 8 carriers at 20 cents per carrier but the next picking should be much better. The truck comes by at 10 minutes after 6 and picks myself and Ora Shutt up. The Breeden girls, two girls in Fall City in this end of town then about 5 more as they go through and then Dora Mae Hart, then Myrtle Wagner, Ora's sister. We sure had a good time laughing. I thought maybe it would be a change for me to get out away from home. The boys are shocking hay for Ernest Hoisington. He comes and gets them. I will go into Dallas this afternoon with Mrs. Jones – the folks that bought the Baker place. She is a nice woman. About my age. They have a nice car. They have a son about Arlie's age but Arlie don't like him they will have some time this year on the school bus I am afraid. Yes, Bill old Arlie is doing better. He always works but he had to fuss just so much now he goes ahead and says nothing. Oh, he is one of those kind that likes to talk and be cute but he is a little more sensible about it now. Well, Bill, I guess I will have to cut this letter short and get busy have dishes to wash, milk things and clothes to sprinkle down and clean up the house and myself to get ready to go to town.

Write long letters. They are all so sweet.

Love, Mom We enjoy every one of your letters.

:: :: ::

Bill received many birthday cards in 1944. His birthday was July 5. (His 21st birthday) The cards and writers all wished him well, a long life and all of those kinds of sentimental words that birthday cards express. In reality it was to be Bill's last birthday. All of the good wishes for the coming year expressed in the cards were what people are often told but they were not to be for Bill. Most of the birthday cards were from neighbors and relatives. There were too many to be by chance. Mom was a great letter writer so she must have written to relatives and, also, asked neighbors to send Bill birthday cards. I have chosen not to include the birthday cards because of space.

:: :: ::

August 10, 1944   (Another jig saw puzzle letter.)
I'M ALL BROKEN UP!
Dear Bill,

I just decided to take you up on the proposition. I'll write you two or three letters a day and your promise was to answer them all. All I have to say is that "you'll be sorry."

Thanks very much for explaining your shorthand. I couldn't figure out that one word "----." I guess it was just because I wasn't familiar with the term.

How do you like my radio program? I'm enjoying it very much between writing, fighting with the cat and fighting with the cat's fleas and swatting mosquitoes. They may raise mosquitoes in Missouri but they raise monsters in Oregon.

Bottom Button is on my lap taking a bath – in between chasing my pen around. She was playing in the kitchen a while ago and she backed into her bowl of milk. Consequently, Bottom Button has a wet bottom. I really wish you could see her – she's so affectionate (like her mistress – ha ha) and really a panic. She certainly has done a good job of keeping me entertained while I'm all alone. It looks as though I'm at the bottom so I'd better close.

Love, Elsie

PUZZLE LETTER 33 Pat Rights Pen. Fresno Art Novelty Co. Fresno, Calif.

:: :: ::

E. Harber   W. H. Holt, Sea 1/c
1844 Court St   Unit 2, Ward B-1
Salem, Oregon   U. S. Naval Hospital
                         Corona, California

Date 8/12/44   Episode No. 15

DON'T FORGET TO WRITE SOON! WEEKLY CHATTERSHEET Hi, Kid
A COMMUNIQUÉ OF NEWSY BITS FROM: Elsie to Bill

Sports Department

Yesterday I went to the dentist and had a couple of rounds with him. The only trouble is he won. If that knighthood still remains in you – now's your chance – boy, is that little guy tough!

Special Messages from:

Invitation

There's a beautiful moon tonight simply going to waste. Maybe I should take you up on that date you asked me for (you wolf) I'll bring the sandwiches and the bottle (of milk).

News About

VISITORS   Do you want to hear some more about my cat? I'll admit it's RELATIVES getting a bit monotonous but she's getting tougher everyday.

BOTTOM BUTTON It's going to take two of us to handle her yet.

People who want you to write:

Elsie Harber

"   "

"   "

Event of the week

Tonight I'm going to my girl friend's wedding. It's at 9:00 o'clock. The poor girl didn't have any better sense than to take the final step. We had a shower for her the other night – more about that later – it was really a panic.

Miscellaneous Chatter

I'm home in Dallas for my day off – and am I off – in more ways than one. It sure has been a nice day. I hate the thought of going back to work at 7:00 A.M. in the morning.

YES! WE'RE REMEMBERING PEARL HARBOR Bond Purchases to Date _____

Question Dept. (Send Answer If Possible)

? How do you like my new type of stationery? When you want two or three letters a day – I have to find a streamlined form.

Doodling Space

XXXX XXXX

0000

OLD GANG NEWS

Don't know any old gang news – in fact I don't know anything (period) all of which is nothing unusual.

They're in The Service Now

1. Bill Holt
2. " "
3. " "

:: :: ::

Elsie wrote many letters to Bill. I have chosen not to include all of them in this book.

:: :: ::

August 28, 1944

Dear Son,

Here comes a few lines before I start my work. I ate my breakfast and the boys are milking and Lewis he feels tired. He said as he had a long day of it almost 10 hrs. He help set up sacks while the dew was on but this morning he goes to work an hour later. I will have to make Arlie do more at home so Lewis can rest he is busy but it isn't as hard a work lifting on those big sacks. Well Billy my eye is about O.K. Now my sty turned out to be a boil in the corner of my right eye next to my nose and I couldn't wear my glasses so I was very upset and nervous. But I feel fine now. Well Sweet Heart your letters sound so cheerful and I am glad you looked at life the way you do. It will take time to get well and by taking and looking at life like you do you will get well all the sooner and I am glad Elsie takes such a great interest in writing to you like she does. I didn't think she was such a kick but you have lots of fun and I am glad. Well dear here is my story. Canned two sacks of corn, about bu. of peaches, a big washing for Campbells. The lines full of clothes I washed yesterday. I went up in the afternoon and helped Mortenson get corn ready to can. Arlie helped get it in from the field. Well dear the boys are coming in for their breakfast. Well I will just wait when you can come home. I saw Rex Kingsbury he sure has a tan. He has been over the waters where you have been taking supplies to the boys.

As ever love, Mom

:: :: ::

RECEIVED

AUG 31, 1944
GENERAL EXTENSION DIVISION

In my first assignment, you asked me if possible, to tell about some of the places I've been. I will now attempt to do it.

Picture yourself on a ship, a large luxury liner, for instance. The ship is lit up and the orders of the day are gaiety and happiness.

You, after much fan fare, sail proudly out of the Golden Gate. In a few days, you make a short stop at the wonderful Hawaiian Islands. Being thoroughly disgusted because you didn't find all the hula maids, you sail on to the Philippines.

After an uneventful voyage, you sail through the San Bernardino Straits into the quiet waters of the Philippine Islands. All is calm. If you would look around with a pair of binoculars, you would see the natives on the beach or in their small canoes going about as if they didn't have care or worry in the world. Here and there you would see a plantation.

Day passes and it is getting late, you go up on topside to witness a much heard about sunset. I guarantee you that once you see one that you won't forget it (I can't find words to describe one.) Gradually as the sun sets and it gets dark, you will see lights pop up here, there, and everywhere all along the beaches.

There is an abundance of activity. The crew is preparing to enter port and the passengers to disembark. The ship slows down, picks up a pilot and proceeds on. You enter Manila Bay - the scene of Admiral Dewey's great victory of 1898.

The average person would disregard the points of land. As far as you are concerned, it is just the Island of Luzon. But if you to ask or look at a map, you would see on your right Carabao Isle on your right, U.S. Naval Yard at Cavite, and Corregidor and on your left Bataan Peninsula. Say, what is this? A battleship? I thought we weren't supposed to have any out here. You look again and ask a few questions and your battleship turns out to be a fort, which from a distance resembles one.

You can now see Manila. Over there is the world famous Manila Hotel. Yeah and over there is Pier Seven - the dock to which you go along side. If you are lucky, you will see the president's yacht, a sleek trim little craft.

(The instructor writes, "I suppose the Japs are enjoying it now."

After docking, you go sight seeing. You go here and there and after you get back you can tell about the Walled City with its massive walls, old buildings and narrow streets. Oh, yes, you must not forget to tell about the curio shops, where you have been dickering with the manager.

After spending several days, weeks, or months, AND lots of money, you reverse the procedure and come back to the good old United States.

Again pictures yourself on a ship. It may be the same ship but what a change. It is blacked out, bristling with guns, stripped for action and painted war color. On a cold dreary Frisco morning, you slip out of the Golden Gate. Destination unknown. You sail a zig-zag course and your guns are manned and ready for immediate action. You keep your life jacket with you at all times. You have run to your abandon ship station so many times that you can run there blindfolded.

The rumors are flying fast and furious. You are going here. You are going there. Probably only the high officers know and they aren't sure because orders can be changed at a moment's notice.

You pull into some desolate island, which has been converted into a Naval Base, refuel, and get underway again, going west and your destination is still unknown, too.

Then from over the loud speaker, a voice pipes up, "Attention all hands. Attention all hands." All men stop what they are doing." Quietness prevails. The voice continues, "Our destination is Manila. Our destination is Manila." Some men cheer. Some men are silent. Those who guessed right say, "I told you so, See what did I tell you." etc. etc.

You sail amongst the islands. Only the beautiful sunset prevails. Even that is marred by memories, ships sunk and burnt, and the landscape ravaged by war.

Again, you prepare to enter port, except this time you go ashore to work and not to play. You pick up your pilot just as before. The pilot wears the uniform of the U. S. Navy. He is to pilot you through the mine fields.

You take interest in the places you pass because most of them will go down the annals of history. There is Carabao Island which has been thoroughly bombed and shelled. You see it commands the entrance to Manila Bay. Off to your right is the vaunted Rock (Corregidor). To your left is Bataan which is covered with hundreds of graves, some marked and some not, of brave Americans and courageous Filipinos. The Navy yard is hurriedly being put back into use after most of its facilities were destroyed when the Japs pulled out. As you get closer you can see what remains of the Manila Hotel and Pier Seven.

The Walled City, which you enjoyed as much in past time, has been all but destroyed. Just a skeleton stands. The highways, which in peacetime were crowded with taxis, bicycles and caramettas, have changed, too. They are lined with burnt vehicles and are crowded with military trucks. Say, why all this day dreaming? There is work to be done, so, let's get busy.

Bill adds – *There are two hospitals in Walla Walla. One Army and one Veterans'. Most of the Dallas boys have gone to the Army Hospital. I will go to the Veterans' Hospital because when I go, I will be out of the service. Glen Holt. He is stationed at the marine base at El Centro, California.*

How's the weather up there? It is a little warm here. Bill

The instructor adds the following note: I didn't know you could be discharged until you were completely well. Anyway, you'll be a little closer home.

I knew Glen was at El Centro – poor thing. I lived there for three years and can imagine no worse place – and I was never there during the summer. I saw Lucille when she was here and tried to persuade her not to go down there until October. I'm afraid she couldn't stand the heat or the living conditions. However, I expect she's there to be with Glen. Maybe someday he'll get out to see you. Corona's heat can't hold a candle to El Centro's. It was 100 in Eugene Tuesday, but today it's almost cold. Last night it rained. But I'll still take Oregon.

:: :: ::

The Racial Problem in the U. S.

(I don't know why Bill happened to write regarding this subject. Is it original thinking? Or is it from a book or magazine article? I'll share part of it with you.)

The racial problem in the U. S. is funny, to me. I guess I shouldn't say funny because it is more disgusting. Just as soon as some other country starts to prosecute a group of people because of their race or creed, we are the first to holler. Good present day examples are the Germans of their treatment of the Jews and the Japanese and their treatment of the rest of people. I say that the United States should, if they are looking for someone to prosecute for racial discrimination, look at home. They are just as guilty of it as any other county. The only difference is that we don't kill or intern them in concentration camps or do we make an issue of it. To get a clear picture of our racial problem, one should know a little about its history...

(Remember, this was written in 1944.)

:: :: ::

U.S. NAVAL HOSPITAL
CORONA, CALIFORNIA

A I R M A I L
23 September 1944
Mrs. Vintie Holt
Route #2 Box 134
Dallas, Oregon

Dear Mrs. Holt:

I regret to inform you that your son, William Harrison HOLT has been suffering from TUBERCULOSIS, Pulmonary, Chronic, Active, Far Advanced #1103, and his condition is now considered to be serious.
You will be informed of any new developments.

Sincerely yours,
M. T. BATES, Lt. Comdr. (MC) USNR
Officer-of-the-Day
By Direction

:: :: ::

We didn't fully realize the significance of this letter at the time. It was a bad omen of things to come.

Oct. 2, 1944
Dear Bill,
Just a few lines before I start my days work. Have beans and corn on cooking in jars. Canned 15 qts of shelled beans yesterday. The boys helped me get them ready and they hauled in some wood at the house. I hauled in some at the school house. I am beginning to get my jars filled up. Today looks like it will be a nice day and I have a big washing to do for Kingsburys. Oh Bill I sure laughed at the boys yesterday. Lewis was in his boat and if he don't stand just so it will turn over. Well he didn't. Well Arlie and Jeanette Harvey was on a raft and Arlie was throwing water on Lewis. Lewis he started to throw water on Arlie and he got wet clear up to his shoulders. That was how deep the water was where he jumped in. Did we all laugh. Well then that stopped the fun. Lewis made Arlie help him carry his boat to the house so he could change his clothes and it was chore time. Arlie is so big and ruff. It is all Lewis can do to handle him sometimes. They are sure some pr. But people will say isn't it an awful job to take care of two so close together but they have made up for all their work just watching them grow up. Oh I got a letter from James Holt. He is in Maryland. He sure has been on a move. He wrote a long letter gave me Grace and Johnnies address in case you get a leave from the hospital you can go see them. He don't know you are a sick boy like I do does he. Well you just rest and I will do your work for you someday you can do mine. Can't you. Love Mom.

Thinking of You
A warm, friendly greeting,
A hearty hello,
A "Hi there – how are you
And how do things go?"
Been thinking about you

And wanted to show
That you are one person
I'm lucky to know!
Mom

:: :: ::

Oct. 11, 1944
M C Dawson
1831 Phillips Way
Los Angeles 42, California

HELLO
Jes' got to thinkin' of you
As Ah so often does,
An' thought Ah'd
send a little card
To ask you –
HOW YOU WAS?
Mrs. Dawson

Tuesday P. M
My Dear Bill,

I found this little card the other day so am sending it on to you. I tho't maybe you would get a chuckle out of it as I did.

I found another one I am sending to Gordon. Scolding him because he hasn't written for such a long time only it is all funny about an old auto tire used for a spare. I love to look at and buy many, funny cards every time I go in an Art store. I went to Pasadena Tues. – and shopped some.

I done something today, I've never done before. Because I do not believe in going any place just to see things or people. Just thro curiosity but a neighbor invited me to go to Forest Lawn Cemetery to see the flowers on Amie McPherson's grave. Thousands of people done the same thing and I must say I never saw so many flowers and such beautiful pieces as were there. There were over 6 truckloads sent out from the church.

Well, Bill how are you feeling these days? You must have received a lot of mail and mine is on the bottom list again since I haven't heard from you. It has been over 3 weeks since we heard from Gordon and I get a little anxious however he had planned to go on a 3-day leave and that may account for his tardiness.

It has turned somewhat cooler here and begins to feel like fall. Since I wrote you last I spent two days last week with my sister at Long Beach. Have you ever been at Long Beach? When you come down to visit us, we will take you down. I like L.B. better than any of the other beaches.

Well, Bill, good nite for now and I hope you are improving every day.

With kindest regards & love from Mrs. Mae Dawson

:: :: ::

Chapter Five

WALLA WALLA, WASHINGTON

W. H. Holt, S 1/c   (Post card)
U. S. Navy
Portland, Ore.
Nov. 6, 1944

Dear Mom,
Apparently you didn't get my wire. They didn't give me any warning either. They told me noon Friday and I left Saturday.
The trip has been fine. Will get into Walla Walla about 3:15 tomorrow morning. Will write then if I get caught up on my sleep.
I see Oregon hasn't changed - still raining.
Bill

:: :: ::

We didn't know or think to ask Bill which route he took through Oregon. If he came through Salem, he was just a few miles from us. Just a few miles from home.

:: :: ::

Mr. William H. Holt Sea 1/c
U. S. Veteran's
Walla Walla, Wash.

Salem, Ore.   (Post card – post marked at Dallas Nov. 13, 1944)
Dear Bill, Received your letter last Friday glad to hear from you. We are O.K. and hoped you are rested up from your trip by now. I am in Salem with Glen and Detta. It is cold this morning feels just like winter is around the corner. The sun is shinning. Will write you a letter later. Love Mom

:: :: ::

U S N
UNITED STATES NAVY
Nov. 23, 1944
Dear Mom,

It is about time I wrote you a few lines, don't you think?

Now that I'm here I'll tell you something. The last letter the Corona Red Cross wrote was very inaccurate. It made me sound sick but actually I wasn't. The Red Cross never did visit me either time they wrote those letters. The bunch they had when I first got there was swell. They would come around at least weekly. But the last bunch was lousy. The only time they came around was when they had to. The "Grey Ladies" (those who work without pay) were swell. They have some nice, Grey Ladies here too. They are in my estimation, better than they regular Red Cross.

You asked about my condition. My exact condition I don't know. But the doctor's reports sound good. As I said before, the hospital board has decided what treatment I need, and they started last week. Unless something unexpected happens, there is very little to worry about.

Do we have quite a collection of patients on this ward? Most of them are World War One Vets. The one next door is only half here. Have to keep sides on his bed to keep him from falling out. He is hard of hearing and is always taking shots. Speaking of shots makes me shudder. When my stomach was on the blink they gave me a vitamin B and C shot every day and they haven't stopped them yet.

I haven't seen much of this place. It used to be an old fort, and the hospital is built around the parade ground.

(Drawing)   Wards
              We are right on the edge of Walla Walla.
       Lawn   The surrounding area is flat
       Trees
I won't say what kind of dinner we had. I'll just send you the menu. And you can figure it out for yourself.

Everyone in this ward is army except for two navy men (I'm one) and one Coast Guardsman. Do we have a time. I haven't had much chance to talk but I guess it is easy to get an argument.

I'm at the end of the page. So I'll close.

W. H. H.   Bill

:: :: ::

Walla Walla, Wash
December 3, 1944
Dear Mom,

Will try to write you a few lines. First the Hospital you call McCall is McCaw. The McCaw is Army and is down the hill away from the one I'm in. It is known - just as the U. S. Veterans Hospital. If you want to get technical you could add 85.

Unless I'm mistaken, you will find out what is going to happen to me. You see, I wrote to a fellow in Corona, and I told him. He will tell another. He will tell Mrs. Witt and she'll mention it to you. And you won't know what to think.

At the present, I have fluid in my pleural space. When that is gone, I will have to under go probably two major operations. It will consist of taking out sections of ribs out of my back. It is painful but it doesn't take long to get over the effects. And too a person gets cured fast after then. So all in all it isn't too bad. I've seen more than one fellow get them. I don't know when I will get my first operation but

I'll let you know when I find out. Now don't go to worrying about it. They say they have an excellent chest surgeon here. I hope that will ease your mind some. Another thing my fluid is looking better. That sounds good too. So all and all things are looking better all the time.

That is all I can think of so I will close.

W. H. H.   Bill

:: :: ::

AMERICAN RED CROSS

France Dec. 4, 1944

Dear Butch,

Did someone say that you were a civilian? What is the matter are you 4-F or something. I have been expecting a change of address card or I would have written more letters. Mom wrote quite a while ago that you had been moved so I quit writing until I heard.

I am back here in rest camp and remembering the words of a certain little boy who said, "Charles stay home." Little Charles believed you but he talked his way out of a hospital to catch a trans-oceanic ride. He is now living to rue the day that he pleaded to get out.

We are having it pretty soft around here now. We are living in barracks, have showers, hot meals, and reading and writing rooms. This is no civilian's idea of heaven but for a front line man it is a heaven. I have seen combat. I say that I have seen because my company censor used that word. We have visited, and that word is true, several towns. Have you heard of Saarbourg, Baccarat, St. Blaize, and others in Alsace and Lorraine? All of this is interesting country but home will look good.

I have seen enough combat to receive the combat infantry badge – increase in pay of $10.00 and been instrumental in the capture of several Germans. I think the Germans thought that we were French. Everyone was in for a surprise.

Write soon and let me know where you are.

Your brother, Charles

:: :: ::

USN United States Navy
Dec. 6, 1944
Dear Mom,

What do I have to do - draw you a picture or something to get you to understand that I received an honorable discharge, and not a medical discharge as it came out in the Itemizer last week. In my first two letters from here I stated definitely and clearly I received an HONORABLE DISCHARGE.

Apparently I didn't tell you enough times. If I have to, I'll tell you in every letter that I received an honorable discharge. So from now on don't tell anyone I received a medical discharge because I didn't. As I said before, I received an honorable discharge. Now remember that because what the people don't know won't hurt them and when you say I received a medical discharge, it hurts me. Think it over and I believe you will see what I mean.

Now something a little more pleasant. It sure would be swell if Lewis would cut out war pictures, ship launchings, ships sunk, ships that have distinguished themselves, and new weapons, or vehicles. I don't have much opportunity to do it.

As for that eversharp. You can have that. I have one which matches my pen. If you receive any more of my checks, keep them but don't spend the money because as soon as they're notified they will send you a bill if they have over paid you. There shouldn't be any mistakes.

I hear from Elsie regularly. She sent me the measurements I asked for. I didn't expect her to send that book to you.

Where in the devil does Leeta live? I couldn't find Longview on the map, and I've never heard of it.

Received a letter from her today. (I think Longview had been misspelled and confused Bill.)

Also received a letter from Mae Winnecke. There isn't much change here. I can sit up and move around some. But for my own benefit I take it real easy.

I'll close now and write some more letters.

W.H. H.   *Bill*

:: :: ::

This was the only time that Bill ever wrote anything negative or in apparent anger. Evidently he had pride and wanted it to be known that he had an honorable discharge. It must have really touched a sore spot for him to react as he did.

:: :: ::

Wishing special happiness
for you at Christmas and
through the New Year

To Lewis and Arlie
With luck from Bill (over)
Listen you Bums, why don't you write? You haven't busted any arms or I'd heard about it.

Don't say you haven't time because I know better. Once, I went to school - you have time there too. You fool around quite a bit. Well, knock it off - once in a while and write. Lewis you like to play the piano. Leave it alone a few minutes and you'll have time to write me. Arlie the same with you except you can set aside your drawing and magazines, too. So you write too.

So let us have a letter now and then. It won't hurt, and it will do me lots of good.

A forgotten brother, Bill

:: :: ::

Reading this letter again over 60 years later, makes me wish that I had written more often. Writing has become so easy for me as an adult but as a teenager, it was not an easy thing to do. If only I had used my imagination!! I should have asked him about his experiences in the navy – where he had been and what he had done. It might have prompted him to write about those topics. They would have been interesting then and valuable years later.

:: :: ::

December 17, 1944   Pfc Charles H. Holt 19102881
                    Co K 397th Inf APO 447
                    % PM New York, N. Y.

Dear Butch,

Again I'll try to reach you through general delivery address. I haven't heard from you for over a month. Now darn you write a little.

I am in the same fix as you always were. I don't have a thing to say. Life goes and that is all that happens. If anything of interest takes place we can't mention it until it is old stuff and forgotten.

There is one thing that I like to remind you of in each of my letters. Remember what you said about the destination of my outfit. I'll be there but the weather is a little different than what you predicted.

Even the use of the outfit is a little bit different from what some one predicted because they don't give Combat Infantry Badges and Silver Star Awards away for just plain occupational duties. The other day I stumbled out in front of a truck load of armed Germans and luckily they gave up. For that another boy – I think he pushed me out in the road – and I received citations for the capture of them.

Just one other bit of news. I think that I have received another raise in pay. It isn't official yet so I can't put it in my address but the First Sgt. told me that it had gone in and should be back in a special order soon.

Write darn you.

As ever,

Charles

:: :: ::

Deer Island, Oregon
Dec. 18, 1944
Dear son Bill,

No doubt you will be some surprised to hear from me – our club, The Deer Island Woman's Club – wanted to adopt some soldier boy that was in the hospital. And we were lucky enough to have you chosen for our boy. I hope you won't mind. Maybe a letter once in a while, from some of us "old gals," will help you pass away the time. I say old – we aren't all old but I will be 53 Dec. 24. A heck of a time to give a child a birthday. I don't know how long you have been in the hospital or how long you will have to stay there, or what is wrong with you.

You see Bill I lost my only boy (only child) at Malta, he was an airplane pilot with the R.A.F. He enlisted in the R.A.F. before we were at war. He has been gone 2 yr Thanksgiving Day. His name was Carl Lee Johnson – from Kelso, Wash. He was 32 yr old & single. The boys at Malta called him "Johnnie." I get pretty lonesome some times but I have a "Belgium Son" like you. I've never seen him but he was a friend of Carls & he writes to me quite regular. He married last Nov. & he wrote me – "I would be grandma before Xmas. I'm very anxious to hear – he was in a plane crash & was in the hospital about 16 months. And I also have another "Son." A friend of Carls. I've never seen him either. At present he is in Kansas. They both (he & wife) write me lovely letters. So you see God has been good to me. He has given me 3 sons, with you.

I am keeping a little boy 5 yrs old – have had him 2 yrs in March & he sure is a darling. He calls me Mama. But he is going to Olympia to spend Xmas with his mother. How we will miss him. We will have our tree before he goes.

We live on a stump ranch 45 acres between Portland and Astoria. Now I think I've gabbed enough about myself. What I want to know – do you need shaving cream, tooth paste, writing paper, stamps & envelopes or are these things furnished to you? Do you like to read? If so, what kind of books. Now tell me & I'll see that you have something to read & tell me something about your self. How old you are? That is if you care to write to me or have me write to you. I know you are quite handsome – big black eyes & curly hair. (My boy's hair was curly). You see my mind always runs to him. But I love to talk about him; he was always so good & sweet to me. My little Jimmie sure is a live wire. He has a new pup & we have twin calves (Maud & Maudie) & of course they are his.

I'll bet Billie Boy! you are wondering when my pen will run out of ink – so I'd better quit, before the goat in the paper basket gets this. I would love to hear from you if you care to write. Merry Xmas & Love Your new mom

Excuse spelling.

At Christmas
These greetings come at
CHRISTMAS TIME
To bring you joy and cheer,
And wish you just the best of luck
Right through a
HAPPY NEW YEAR

Your foster Mom.
Mrs. Esta McCully
Deer Island, Oreg.
Dear Bill,

I hope you will enjoy eating these as much as I have making them, over,

They aren't like your own mother makes. No one can bake cookies like a boy's mother but they are like what you new mom makes. Merry Xmas Happy New Yrs

:: :: ::

THE WHITE HOUSE
WASHINGTON

Christmas, 1944

101

TO OUR VETERANS:

To all veterans I send a hearty Christmas greetings, with a hope and a prayer that the New Year may see those who are ill restored to health and the world at large to at least a measure of peace.

The way ahead of us still is arduous and continuance of our utmost effort together with that of our Allies is indispensable until victory is won and a stable peace is established. You, who have done your gallant share and have suffered in the doing, have the Nation's eternal gratitude and assurance of your country's lasting remembrance and appreciation.

Signed Franklin Roosevelt

:: :: ::

France Dec. 26, 1944

Dear Butch,

Come on old man and get up to date on the great world events. I was a Pfc. for a month and now have the title of Sgt. Yes, believe it or not I have finally received a rating and it is only a matter of time before I should get a rocker underneath the three stripes. It is about time; don't you think?

It is the same old story around here except that I am now back at a rest home. If I don't have one thing wrong with my feet, I have two. About a month ago I had a small infected spot on my heel and now – believe it or not – I have a boil on the back of my ankle. It rubs on my boot or I wouldn't have to be back. This is really a nice place to stay. It is a veritable mansion but very homey.

How was your Christmas? Where they could, a nice Christmas was given to everybody. We really had a good meal in every place. At this place they had a Christmas tree with ornaments and everything. The only thing that could have made it better would be home.

When you are going to have some kind of treatment, tell me the particulars or else don't tell me. You have roused my curiosity and I can't even guess what it is all about. You are almost insulting when you suggest that I might tell Mom. You know darn well that I keep from Mom as much as you do. Now give with some of the gory details.

I can't think of any more bull to fill in space, so take it easy. Chas.

:: :: ::

Sgt Charles H. Holt 19102881
Co K 397th Inf APO 447 % PM, New York, N. Y.
Dec. 31, 1944
Dear Butch,

It is almost that hour and here I sit at a table. Does that sound like a combat soldier? Well, to tell you the truth, I am not. As of a day or so a go I am one of those so and so rear echelon men. My job may be permanent or temporary.

I am back here because someone believes that some replacements need a little training. Why me of all non-coms, I don't know. The other non-coms from my regiment can think of some reason for being sent back; I seem to have been lucky.

What ever I have to do back here or have to undergo, I will enjoy part of it. Today I tramped around until I found a sign that read "Douche." I followed the direction indicated by the arrow and entered the door. The struggle that ensued resulted in a much colder but cleaner man. Boy did that shower feel good.

This evening after chow I strolled over to the Snack Bar and had coffee and rolls. After that I walked around and saw a GI stage show. I thought that I would laugh my head off. Some of the jokes were typical jokes like Mom says Lewis tries to pull but they went over big. On the serious side there was some very good music and dancing. Personally, I think that the talent was the best quality.

Brief intermission for lights out. I'll write a better letter when I learn something.

Why don't you give me a little more information on your self? I thought that you were well, when you were discharged? I figured that you were just recuperating before going home. When should you be released from the hospital? And what is the treatment that they are going to give you?

Your bud.   Chas.

:: :: ::

Jan. 4, 1945
Dear Mom,

I thought I had better get this money to you. This is all to be put in the bank for my future use. I have a $100 war bond too, but that will draw interest here just as well as there.

How much will I have in the bank after you deposit this four hundred dollars? I'll have a small nest egg with my bank account and war bonds.

I'll have some more money to send home in the near future. I am getting one check cashed now and I'll have one more to get then I'll be all square with the Navy, I think.

We sure are having some nice foggy weather. Just like California.

I am doing better now. I manage some how to keep my feet warm and that is quite a task for me.

I have a paper to read and, too, I want to get this letter out in this morning's mail.

Be sure to deposit this money in my account. And give me plenty warning before you come. Remember if you have a cold, sore throat, or sore chest, don't come. Your health is more important than your trip. The trip can wait if necessary.

Bill

:: :: ::

Doris Fiske
42 Summer St.   Jan. 17, 1945
Saugus, Mass.
Dear Bill,

I was so glad to hear from you. It's been such a long time and I was beginning to get worried. I'm sorry you are so sick but hope you are feeling much better now.

I imagine Washington would be a little colder than California. We are having a lot of snow now. It's about 8 inches deep. It's terrible to bother with overshoes, etc.

Nothing much for excitement around here. I'm going to a movie & dance this Friday night at one of the hotels, given by the bank.

My work is still fine. I play ping pong practically every night. Usually doubles. The American Institute of Banking is having its annual banquet and dance at the Hotel Statler in Boston Feb. 2. Something to look forward to.

Bill I have a surprise for you. Sorry it's not a picture of me in my bathing suit, but it's a picture of me I had taken a while ago. Maybe this summer I'll have that picture you want.

I saw a good musical show last week, "When Irish Eyes are Smiling." Went bowling last night with the bank. I'm doing a little better now or at least last night anyway.

Well I guess this will be all for now. Take good care of yourself and write when you can.

As ever, Doris

:: :: ::

WESTERN UNION

3 PRRO   14   4   EXTRA GOVT
WALLA WALLA WASH 927 AM JAN 17 1945

MRS VINTIE HOLT ROUTE 2 BOX 134 (OR OTHER KNOWN ADDRESS)

REGRET TO ADVISE YOU YOUR SON WILLIAM HOLT CRITICALLY ILL

BEATTY VETS ADMN 10:22AM

:: :: ::

On January 17, 1945 this telegram arrived at the Telegraph Office located on Main Street in Dallas, Oregon. A man from the Telegraph Office took it next door to Ruby Jones. Her step-father, Lewis H. Holt (I was named after him) was my father's half brother. The man in the telegraph office knew that Ruby knew us. She came to the high school to bring the telegram to Arlie and me. The principal came to my PE class to get me. I had to get dressed. The principal and I met Arlie in the hall by the office. Ruby drove us the 8 miles to deliver the telegram to our mother. It was decided that she should go see Bill. She quickly packed, gave Arlie and me instructions and rode back into town with Ruby and caught a train to Walla Walla, Washington to see Bill.

When Mom walked into Bill's room, he turned his back to her and asked, "What are you doing here?" She replied, "I received a telegram that you were serious." Bill told her not to come close to him because he was contagious. She was there only a short time when someone came to tell her that she was wanted at the main office. When she walked into the office, the man bluntly asked her, "Where do you want the body shipped?" Just that cold and that simple without any thought of her feelings. Mom never told Arlie and me that story when she got back home. She told us later after Bill had died.

Because Mom couldn't spend much time with Bill, she stayed only a day. Her visit, though, must have meant a lot for both of them. I now wish I could have seen him. Times were different then, money wasn't available, travel was difficult, I was in school and our nation was at war.

:: :: ::

The Harveys   Jan. 18, 1945
Rt. 2 Box 128
Dallas, Or.
Dear Bill,
Enjoyed your letter very much. As for catching up on my letters frankly I'm not doing as you see by the lateness in this answer. Yes Bill I think it was nice of that club and I really think our clubs could do more in that line instead of some of the things they do. Half of the

people don't really realize that our boys need all the nice things we can do for them. Some don't even write to boys in the service. I wish I had more time to write to them. We have 5 near relatives in and I write to them and then 4 others besides so far. We figure the boys are giving their all and we ought to be able to write a few letters etc. for them.

Jeanette is practicing here with her lesson and the radio is on and so I'm making a mess of this. I'm getting ready to entertain club next Tues. So have been cleaning a bit. I entertain in Frink's house so it makes me 2 houses to have presentable. The men are changing the barn so they can have horses and cows all in one barn now seeing they're not dairying. We had rain, sunshine, fog, and snow on the hills all in one day. The old woman must of been running things today. Seeing it was so changeable.

Went to Carm Teal's shower Tues. and had a lovely time and she got a lot of lovely gifts. Your mother wasn't there. Some one said why and it didn't sink in. She's O.K. tho.

So it was the Dr. and skipper that shipped you eh? Well guess that'll teach you to leave their nurses alone. You see they have special ones too ha ha!

Oh Bill am sorry didn't intend to tease you was going to ask you to forgive me as two on one and one that is down, isn't cricket you know. I think Elsie can keep you guessing. Without me bothering you but just couldn't resist my 2 bits worth ha! ha!

It's raining now. We'll be having hi-water if we don't watch out.

Reuben has gone to bed and I'm going to have done about 3 days work in one and feel sort of weary.

We had a grand time at the dance last Sat. nite. It was a nice friendly crowd and full of pep.

Don't those nurses know you'd naturally have a temperature when they came around or isn't she good looking or I should say easy on the eye. Please forgive I just can't help but try to tease, ha! ha!

Guess I have told you all the news I can think of so will ring off and go to bed and try to get some rest. There was some kind of explosion or crash last nite about 3:30 and I wasn't dreaming a very pleasant dream and so my rest didn't do too much good. So you don't like Wash. weather. It is pretty cool and snappy at that. The pup is making a racket so guess our rest is about done for or else take him and put him in the basement.

Nite and Best Wishes from us all.

The Harveys

P.S. If you can't read this, bring it down here and I'll try to help you with it. There I go again. Good nite.

:: :: ::

January 28, 1945
U. S. Veterans' Hospital
Walla Walla, Wash.

Dear Mom,

I am feeling much better than I was when you were here. I am still sleepy. It is lucky you were not here Wednesday because they worked on me and I slept all afternoon. Those shots they gave me which were supposed to help really left me nervous.

Charles gave me the devil for not writing. Now he can see what kind of a fix I was in. I wonder what his new job is.

I got a package from Mrs. Green, one from Aunt Gladys, and also one from May Wienke.

This is all for now.

Bill   Written by grey lady

:: :: ::

1844 Court St.
Salem, Oregon
February 2, 1945

Dear Bill,

Hi – how's every little thing? By now you're probably so tired of seeing this scrawl that you throw all this in the waste basket before you even open them. I'm getting to be "Heckler # I."

How's the weather up your way? Down here it's perfectly disgusting because you no more than get dressed for one kind of weather than it's changed again. So far we've had everything but snow and I've got my fingers crossed. The other day we had a fog that could beat any London fog. (listen to me – since I'm so familiar with London) anyway, it was just like pea soup. In fact I'm not exaggerating when I say you couldn't see two feet ahead of you. The only way people could drive was by trying to follow the yellow line down the middle of the street and when that gave out people proceeded to climb telephone and light posts. That fog certainly upset txhxe xfxoxg (now my brain is getting foggy) the schedule at the hospital because the buses were all off schedule and everyone was late to work. When the bus driver passed the Capitol Buildings he announced, "State House – I <u>think</u>." Well, now we're having some good old Oregon rain, which I'll exchange for London's pea soup any day. (Hmmmm, I did pretty well, didn't I – I filled up a whole page just about the weather.) But then you know me – I rattle on and on like a model T Ford. Oh, yes that reminds me – the other morning on a quiz program the radio announcer asked a lady what she'd be riding in if she were riding in a coupe and she answered "a Ford." ! ! Funny, wasn't it?

Now, I really am getting good – I've discussed the weather, the hospital schedule, bus drivers and Fords all in one paragraph. I hope none of your nurses are ex-English teachers because if they got a hold of this letter they'd be horrified at the structure. Still speaking of bus drivers – I really get amused at some of the fellows on the city lines. I live about ten blocks from the hospital so I usually walk to and from work except when I'm on night duty. Anyway, one of the fellows has gotten quite well acquainted with me and he just loves to tease so the other night I rode home just as the drivers were changing shifts and he was riding home on the same bus he had driven all day. When I got off – he waited until I got out the door then he yelled, "Hey, you forgot your violin." Of course I didn't even have it with me. One of the other fellows had some minor surgery and when I registered him I didn't even recognize him out of uniform. Did he ever rub that in. The one that drives in the morning is really a panic – he's short – fat and red faced and jolly as they come. If it's cold, he tells you to come on in out of the hot sun – or visa versa. On that run we always pass the

Catholic academy and pick up a lot of little kids. The other night some little six or seven year old boy got on with a lunch box about half as big as he was so Henry asked him if he had just gotten off work! I guess they have to be jolly to break the monotony of driving the same route day after day.

I'll bet you simply adore my stationery – half airmail & half typing paper. Heh, heh – such class.

Boy, the other day I sure had to laugh – one of the girls wrote on one of our admittance sheets – "Occupation of patient": <u>Trucking</u>. I guess I'll have to take up rumba-ing for my work!

Lets, see I'm about out of news so maybe I should sign off much to your relief. I hope you're feeling much better by now but if you don't feel like writing (which you probably won't after six of these) don't feel sorry about it – just be good, take your vitamins and don't do anything I wouldn't – heh – heh.

Clothes line _____

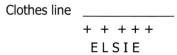

+ + + + +

E L S I E

P.S. Please excuse all the horrible mistakes in this letter but I can't seem to think tonight. Notice I said <u>tonight</u>.

:: :: ::

This next letter was un-opened for almost fifty years. It was post marked "Feb. 3, 1945" It no doubt arrived at the veteran's hospital in Walla Walla just a day or two before Bill died. He must have been very ill and nobody opened the letter for him so he never read it or had it read to him. When I opened it, I felt I was opening a time capsule and that I was infringing on their privacy. Here it is – Perhaps the last letter that Elsie Harber wrote to Bill.

:: :: ::

1844 Court St.
Salem, Oregon
February 3, 1945
Dear Bill,

Surprise! I finally graduated to some new stationery (it was only because I ran out of airmail).

Anyway, I couldn't fill up enough sheets to get my 3¢ worth and the Scotch in me really hurt ! !

In case I sound any sillier than usual, think nothing of it – my sis is practicing the piano again and nearly driving me nuts (two bags for a nickel) - Plink - plunk - plunk - bang -. It's too bad there wasn't some talent in our family.

Speaking of music – although I don't know why that plink - plunk should remind me of music – I went to a violin concert last Wednesday night and just about split laughing. He, the violinist, had rather a long hair cut and it was parted sort of in the middle. When he started playing some of the classics, he got to throwing his head around and swaying. (All good violinist do that so they tell me, however I haven't mastered the art as yet) I thought that he'd lose his hair for sure. I felt like offering him a hair pin. He was really a super - duper violinist and I enjoyed every bit of it. He played the Ava Marie by request. Remember? That's our song – my very favorite for string instruments.

Boy if you can read this scrawl you're a better man than I am (since I'm a girl.) They say the more education you get the worse your hand writing gets. To see mine – you'd think I'd had two or three degrees. What is really fun is to try to read a doctor's hand writing from the nursing chart. The other day we tried and tried to figure out something one of them wrote. Finally we gave up in despair and asked him what it was. He said he wouldn't even pretend to read it after the ink got dry.

Today I bought a new pair of shoes which is just like pulling teeth to me. I hate to shop in the first place and I especially hate to pick out shoes. It took all the courage I had but thank goodness that ordeal is over for another six months.

Do you have loose, ill-fitting plates? You don't? Well, if you do try – oh nuts – my teeth are so well "tied in" that my uppers can't slip. Today I went to the dentist – he didn't hurt me today but he made me hold my mouth open for a long time. He put his fingers in my mouth then gave a salesman an order for surgical supplies. I should have bitten him. Next time he is going to take my braces off and change them – which is very encouraging.

Say, how's your appetite? Would you like some more cookies? Or maybe a nice cream pie? Don't worry about how it would ship because I'm sure it would ship just like a rock. All my pies resemble rocks anyway to say the least.

The other night I was walking up the street past one of the Willamette University sorority houses when I saw some great big sparks coming from the chimney. There were two little boys standing out in front watching the sparks. One of them said, "Oh boy, just look at those big sparks coming out of the chimney." The other little boy said, "Don't be silly – those are gold fish, haven't you any imagination?" Talk about fish stories!

Don't tell me I'm running out of news. Not me - tsk - tsk - tsk. I am slipping!

I'll guess I'll tell you all the local news then get this in the mail for Postal Packen Papa to start on its way.

First, the weather is raining ! ! Very very unusual.

My sister is still running around to all the women's clubs in the county — eating fish.

And oh, yes – the little baby that lives next door cut his first tooth yesterday. Isn't that just too, too interesting? Boy, I should know, I walked the floor with him. Professional baby walker 10¢ an hour – two for 15¢. Oh, fer gosh sakes I'm getting so sleepy that I'm getting silly so I'd better sign off – to your relief. Be good and don't do anything I wouldn't you naughty boy ! ! !.

Lots of love, Elsie

:: :: ::

Elsie Harber's letters must have meant a lot to Bill. (He mentioned them in letters to others.) She wrote trivia, teasing, and entertaining letters but most of all, she wrote. Bill no doubt looked forward to each letter and when he was able, he must have written often to her. An early letter mentioned him writing several letters in one day to her. His letters would have revealed greater insight into their letter writing and add much to this document but perhaps they no longer exist. We can only use our imagination as to their disposal. Was it shortly after Bill's death? Or when she met her new husband to be?

In 1993 I called Elsie's sister, Mae. She told me that Elsie was very sad when she received word that Bill had died. She had put much into her letters to Bill – time and thought and emotions. One can only speculate as to her feelings for Bill. She joked about going to see him. I feel that she wasn't joking and would like to have gone. She knew that Bill was ill – seriously ill. Perhaps this is why she never wrote about the future.

After I moved to Salem in 1993, I was told by Elsie's sister that Elsie took ill and died suddenly leaving two small children. Her husband took her to the hospital one night when she became ill, she died the next morning. It must have been a terrible blow to her husband, to her parents and to her sister. Her husband later remarried. After several attempts I was able to contact the second wife. We talked on the phone. Bill's letters were not tucked away in a trunk as I had dreamed that they might be but knowing in reality that they would have been disposed of many years earlier. I volunteered Elsie's letters for her sons. The stepmother said that she would contact them but I never heard from them. The stepmother had raised the two boys as her sons. They did not remember their mother, I was told. But they were told about their mother.

:: :: ::

Mrs. Richard Witt   Feb. 2, 1945
1618 West 5th St.
North Platte, Neb.   (Valentine Card)

Hi Billy. Had a nice letter from your mother & your address. I wrote you a card at Corona but before I mailed it I found you had moved so waited to hear from your mother. Don was up & out of the hospital for a while but is back in there again. I bet you were glad to see your mother. I hope I can meet your mother someday. I plan to go to Oregon again some time & when I do I'll look her up. I enjoy her letters a lot & she thinks so much of all you boys. I know you have a good mother. Well good luck don't answer if you don't feel good. I'll write again someday.

Mrs. Richard Witt

:: :: ::

Mrs. John Riley   Feb 3, 1945
Timber Rt. Box 43
Vernonia, Ore   (post marked "Timber")

DON'T LET THAT ILLNESS
"BOWL" YOU OVER

A LITTLE "WOBBLE ON YOUR PINS'?
WELL, THAT'S TOO BAD – BUT THEN,
HERE'S HOPING TAIN'T
TOO LONG UNTIL
YOU'RE ROLLIN' HIGH
AGAIN !

YOU GOT TO GET WELL SOON
(Signed) Aunt Cassie   (Our father's sister)

:: :: ::

Bridgeport School   (Post marked Feb. 2, 1945)
Rt. 2
Dallas, Ore.

Get well card signed by: Glenna Gage, Jack Ryan, Kenneth Gardner, Betty Murphy, Wilda Sleighter, Happy Sleighter, Bobby Stewart, Billy Ennis, Jim Holfen (?), Pat Ryan, Ronald Walser, Larry Pitsenberger, Beth Hart, Marvin Dixon, Nancy Walser, Elsie Peterson, Larry Dixon, Bobby Trueax, Frances Peterson, and Betty Ennis

:: :: ::

M. Knudsen
1017 Frankland
Walla Walla, Wn

Dear Mrs. Holt,

Thank you so much for your sweet letter. Sometimes we wonder if our little visits to the boys are always appreciated but letters like yours reassure us and spurs our efforts to do all we can for them.

I came back by Bill's room, hoping I might see you and have a little visit with you on that Tues. evening you left but you had gone and then Bill said that you would be back at 7:00. I couldn't stay that long. I'm so happy you came – Bill hasn't been in very good shape since he came to this hospital and since you hadn't seen him for so long – I wanted you to see him and for him to see you. He's such a sweet kid – so uncomplaining – so kind and tho'tful of every one – everything is just right so far as he is concerned – and surely you know that those kind are few.

I visited with him Tuesday and wrote a letter for him to a friend who had sent him a gift package – someone at Deer Island. Then Friday I went out again and don't think he was quite as strong. They are giving him sleeping medicine or drugs of some kind which make him very sleepy – altho he said he had not been sleeping very well at nites and they seemed long to him. They bro't his supper while I was there & when the nurse raised his bed he complained of not being able to see – this must have been the influence of the sedative. Anyway I stayed & helped him eat. He drank the tea and soup – ate a cracker and a few bites of the jelly roll but said that it was too sweet. I ask him about drinking his milk and he said he couldn't with so much fever – as it made him sick to his stomach.

I told him I had had a nice letter from you thanking me for doing things for him, etc. but I didn't let him know of your real concern for him or that I would answer. When I told him you said the boys had gotten along nicely while you were away he said, "That is a wonder – they must have changed in 3 1/2 years. I'll be out again Tuesday & will drop you a card after that. Thanks for your nice letter.

Sincerely,

Marguerite Knudsen

Mrs. Ralph Knudsen
1017 Frankland
Walla Walla, Wn

:: :: ::

Chapter Six

A Telegram

On February 6, 1945 the principal at the Dallas High School came to me in my PE class. I was fifteen and a sophomore. He told me about the telegram. I got dressed, went upstairs where I met Arlie and our step cousin, Ruby Jones, in the hall near the office. She had taken us to our mother in January when we received the telegram that Bill was seriously ill. She drove us quietly eight miles to our home. She parked, we got out of the car. Mom opened the front door and came out on to the front porch. Before we said anything, she asked, "Is he dead?" We nodded to say that he was. We went into the house to decide what we should do. It was a sad time.

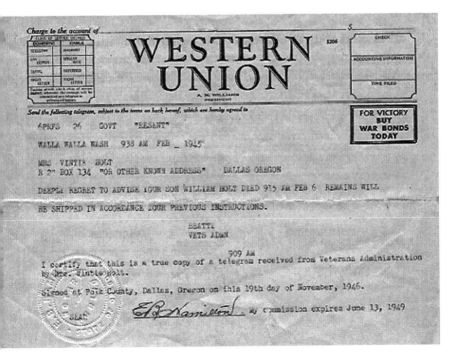

My mother knew Bill was going to die. He must have known that he was going to die. Neither of them let on to the rest of us. Arlie and I never grasped the implications of Bill's illness and looked forward to him getting well and coming home. Our mother must have spent many hours of the day and sleepless nights thinking about her sick son she had visited in the Veteran's Hospital in Walla Walla, Washington and knowing that he was going to die. She had lost her husband, our father, just six years earlier through a logging accident. Now she had lost a son. Her oldest son was in combat in Europe.

Bill did not die as a hero on the battlefield from an enemy's bullet. There was no glory in the way he died; nevertheless he died as so many young men and women have done before him in wars. He was taken from us because of the war. He and many others were denied a future because of the war. His death was from an illness, tuberculosis. It was slow and deliberate. Others, also, contracted tuberculosis. Some died and others recovered from their illness to lead normal lives. That was not to be for Bill. He showed bravery during his illness – always positive, never complained, never asked for sympathy.

Perhaps an even greater irony is that the USS Phoenix survived the attack at Pearl Harbor and went through the war in the South Pacific with only one war-related casualty but Bill was to die of a disease that had nothing to do directly with the war. No death "has to be" or "needs to be" or can necessarily be justified, but how simple it would have been for Bill not to have contracted tuberculosis and to have returned to live a normal civilian life after the war. The odds were certainly in his favor as compared to a marine on the beaches of Iwo Jima or a foot soldier on Saipan. The odds were against his brother, Charles, in combat through France and Germany as a foot soldier. Although wounded twice and having other close calls, Charles survived many months of combat. Historically, disease has caused the deaths of many military people – often even more than battlefield casualties. Bill was one of those casualties.

After Bill's death, his body was shipped to the funeral home in Forest Grove, Oregon. When we received word of his death, we took a bus from Dallas 60 miles to Forest Grove, where we were met by relatives. Several days after we arrived, his funeral was held at the mortuary in Forest Grove. Because he was a veteran, his casket was draped with a flag, which was folded and presented to his mother.

After the services in the funeral home, we all went with the body 15 miles to a little country cemetery near Buxton, Oregon. After a few words, Bill's casket was lowered into the ground just a few feet from his father's grave. We have returned, at the time of this writing, almost every year for more that 60 years to place flowers on his grave and to stand silently for a moment thinking about him and what might have been. Bill's 89 year old mother was later buried between Bill's grave and his father's.

Wars take away young men and women for a variety of reasons, i.e., battles, diseases, accidents, etc. If there is such a thing as being "fortunate" in death, we were fortunate to be able to have a funeral for our casualty of the war. We did not have to wonder how he died or where he died or know that he died some horrible death in a battle. Or that his body was to sink to the bottom of the ocean.

The many years that have passed have helped put Bill's life and his death in a different perspective because now we know, had he lived, that he would have contributed something to all of those around him. At the time of Bill's death I was a young teenager, I had my own life to live – with high school, college, still later marriage, a family and a job. It is only now that I wonder about and question his death. If it were not for my research and the results of my research, I would have continued to accept his death many years ago as being an event in our family that happened because of the war and disease. I would continue to look at a picture of him in his uniform, think about him, admire him and then wonder for a moment about him and put the picture aside. Our letters to him and his letters to us only now better reveal the actuality of the times. Now they can be read and seen in one short segment of time. We experienced these happenings from the day he joined the Navy in June of 1941 to his death on February 6, 1945. At that time we were unable to put the pieces all together as they happened and know the outcome as we do now. Better knowing the story of Bill allows us to read letters he wrote and the letters to him and better understand the people in his life and the events that lead to his death.

Had Bill not saved letters written to him and if his mother had not saved his letters, this story could not have been written. They read as a novel but as readers we know what the ending is going to be before we read the first page. We know how the story of Bill ends but the participants did not let on at the time. There was no hint of Bill's impending death. There was always hope that he would get well. This makes the letters even more meaningful, adds a touch of irony and perhaps makes them a bit sadder to read. The reader cannot hope that a miracle will happen that Bill will get well and that he would get to come home.

We were either given or purchased a banner with a Gold Star to hang in the living room window. It represented that someone in that house had died in the war. We, also, had one with a blue star which represented someone from the house was in service. Our living room window had both a blue star and a gold star. The blue one for Charles and the gold one for Bill. These were times of great patriotism and this was one way families had of displaying that they had sons or husbands in service. A gold star indicated the supreme sacrifice – a family member had died in service.

:: :: ::

THE POLK COUNTY ITEMIZER-OBSERVER (I include other news to better show the community and the small town newspaper.)

BRIDGEPORT

February 15, 1945

Dora Mae Hart was brought home Saturday from the Bartell hospital following a minor operation. She is reported as improving.

Mrs. Chester Gardner has been quite ill again. A doctor was called out to see her, and her daughter Mrs. Claude Hoisington has been coming out regularly to help with the home duties.

The basket social Saturday night at the hall netted the Woman's Club $50.05 due largely to the selling power of Auctioneer Reuben Harvey. What to do with the funds had not been definitely decided, though sending some child to the 4-H summer school is being considered.

Mrs. Vintie Holt, after returning from Walla Walla where her son Billy died, left last Thursday for Buxton to attend the funeral. Buxton was the Holt family's former home. Billy had been ill with tuberculosis for a long time and was only recently transferred to the Veterans' hospital in Walla Walla. Mrs. Holt's eldest son Charles is also in the Service.

World War II Veteran Dies

William Holt, 21, son of Mrs. Vintie Holt of Dallas, died February 6 in the veteran's hospital at Walla Walla, Washington, where he had been undergoing treatment for some time after his honorable discharge from the navy on November 7, 1944.

Funeral services were held in Forest Grove on Saturday at the Forest Grove Undertaking chapel and burial was in the Buxton cemetery at Forest Grove. **(At Buxton actually)**

He was born July 5, 1923, at Claflin, Kansas, and came to Oregon with his parents when a baby. They lived for a time in the Vernonia district. The father, Charles Holt, was killed in a logging accident at White Salmon, Wn, in November, 1939. The family moved to the Bridgeport district in 1940.

William graduated from Dallas high school in 1941 and entered the navy in June of that year. He was at Pearl Harbor during the Japanese attack and remained overseas until May, 1942 **(March, 1943)**, when he was brought to the states suffering from tuberculosis. He had been in navy hospitals until last fall when he was discharged and sent to the Walla Walla Veterans hospital.

He leaves his mother and three brothers, Charles in the army in France and Lewis and Arlie at home.

121

VETERANS ADMINISTRATION
                    WALLA WALLA, WASHINGTON
                         February 6, 1945

    Mrs. Vintie Holt   HOLT, William H.
    Route #2, Box 134
    Dallas, Oregon

    Dear Mrs. Holt:

    May I express my sincere sympathy in informing
    you of the death of your son, William H. Holt,
    which occurred 9:15 A.M., February 6, 1945, while
    he was a patient in this facility.
        I trust it will be a comfort to you to know
    that your son received every attention during his
    period of treatment here. You will have the further
    consolation of the thought that he served his
    country, and died honored and respected by all of
    us.

        Very sincerely yours,
        J. J Beatty,
        Lt. Colonel, MC
        Manager

                         :: :: ::

I have box of "sympathy cards" we received after Bill's funeral.
They are interesting but I chose not to include them.

                         :: :: ::

After Bill's death the following material was taken from a little black
note book that he had in his duffel bag. It was sent to us from the
Veteran's Hospital in Walla Walla with his other possessions.

William H. Holt, Sea 1/c U. S. Navy
PT B. 88
C4 544 638 502 035

Jimmie Rice   (autograph)
For Bill Good Luck! Ann Rutherford   (autograph)
The best of luck! Frances Raeburn   (autograph)
(These must have been visitors to the hospital. Many were well known actors and actresses.)

Ava Gardner	Elsie Eunice Harber
Jane Wyatt	Birthday Feb. 13, 1926
Martha O'Driscol	Waist 26
Don Ameche	Bust 34
Olivia DeHavilin	Neck – yes. Oh, I mean 13
Ronald Coleman	Dress size 16
Spencer Tracy	(USS Phoenix)
Bob Hope	Ordered Aug. 22, 1934
Jerry Calona	Keel Laid April 15, 1935
Martha Scott	Launched Mar. 12, 1938
Helen O'Hara (big picture)	Commissioned Oct. 3, 1938
Eleanor Counts	(autograph)

1-9-43   **USS Phoenix** (The day he reported sick)
1-26-43   **12th Stat.** (Left Phoenix this date)
3-23-43   **Transit**

3-27-43	**118 Gen.**
4-10-43	**USS Mizar**
4-14-43	**Crossed 180th Meridian**
4-28-43	**U. S. N. H., Oakland**
10-16-43	**Corona**
11-4-44	**Transit**
11-7-44	**U.S. Vets' Hosp. Walla Walla**

Bill kept a log regarding his medical condition from 4/8/43 to 12-8-44 when he became very ill. Here are a few examples from the records he kept: (1943)

4/28 Admitted to 63-B   10/21   Weight 140 1/4

4/29 Fluoroscope and moved to 63-A 11/16   Went   before   the survey board.

6/16 Fluoroscope weight 124 1/2 attempted tap   12/17 Survey approved

7/9   Numo 200cc Fluoroscope   1/22/44 Hemorrhage   Numo 50cc(/)

8/4   Weight 140   (In 2 weeks from today 2/26) remind doc about

10/1 Fluoroscope Numo 50cc   my transfer.)

10/20   Sed Rate Kahn Teeth Checked   4/5/44 Weight 144

10/19   Fluoroscope Weight 138   9-26   Trouble

This was a sad section. It shows the specifics of his illness and his concern for his illness. Bill was young – as were many military people at that time. He had to face his illness by himself – without loved ones for comfort and support. He had letters and cards, other men in the wards, the nurses, the Red Cross, Grey Ladies, community volunteers and visiting dignitaries but he lacked the main support that a young man of 19, 20, and 21 should have had when he was ill – his family by his bedside. Today we would be there but the times were different then. Communications, transportation, experiences, obligations, money, the war itself and other limitations of the times set different standards for us. We were a victim of those times

:: :: ::

Chapter Seven

Following Bill's Death

Over the years we had received several telegrams that Bill was sick with tuberculosis. One from Australia in 1943 when he first became ill. Another one in the fall of 1944 when he was sent to Walla Walla, WA. Another in early January, 1945, telling that he was seriously ill. And then the one telling of his death in February 1945. The winter and spring of 1945 brought the reality of war and death to us with four telegrams. The first came early in January when Bill became seriously ill at the Veteran's Hospital in Walla Walla, Washington. Less than a month later the next telegram told of us death in February. That spring we received two telegrams from the war department. Each telegram added to the stress of war. The first was on March 11, 1945.

```
WESTERN UNION
PR 19 29 GOVT=WASHINGTON DC 11 214A

MRS VINTIE O HOLT=1945 MAR 11 AM 9 49
:ROUTE NUMBER TWO DALLAS ORE=

:REGRET TO INFORM YOU YOUR SON STAFF SERGEANT
CHARLES H HOLT WAS SLIGHTLY WOUNDED IN ACTION
TWENTY THREE FEBRUARY IN FRANCE MAIL
   ADDRESS FOLLOWS DIRECT FROM HOSPITAL WITH
DETAILS=
   J A ULIO THE ADJUTANT GENERAL
```

On a Saturday morning a car pulled up in front of our house. There was a knock at the door. We went to the door to see a man standing there with a telegram in his hand. It was obvious that he was nervous. Our hearts pounded, fearing that the telegram might tell of Charles's death in Europe. He handed the telegram to one of us. I don't remember now who opened it. When we read the telegram and it said that Charles was slightly wounded, we gave a sigh of relief.

:: :: ::

Sgt Holt Reported Slightly Wounded
(Dallas Itemizer Observer)

S/Sgt Charles H. Holt, with an infantry regiment in General Patch's Seventh Army in France, was reported slightly wounded in a telegram received by his mother Mrs. Vintie Holt of the Bridgeport district Sunday. The date of the wound was given as February 23.

Holt's outfit is near the southern end of the German front. He has been in France since last fall. A brother, William Holt, died last month in the Veterans' Hospital at Walla Walla from disease contracted while in the Navy.

A letter was received Tuesday by Mrs. Holt from her son, dated February 24 and stating he had been slightly wounded in the hip but was able to walk. He also related that while he was having his wounds dressed at a first aid station his cousin Claude Keller of Kansas looked him up. The boys had not met since they were very small, but Claude had learned of his whereabouts from an exchange of letters between the families.

:: :: ::

Another telegram was delivered later that spring stating the same text – another wound. One was a bullet through an ear. The first one was a piece of hand grenade shrapnel in his rear.

(After the war, in 1946, when Charles returned home, he showed us a roll of film that had in his coat pocket. A bullet had gone length wise of the roll of film almost cutting it in half. It was a close experience.)

:: :: ::

(Some notes from the fall of 1991.)

Unless more letters turn up in a box, in a drawer, in other letters, or in some unexpected place, this is the end of the letters from this time – extending six months before the attack on Pearl Harbor to after the war. Mom, Arlie, and I experienced the inconveniences on the "home front" and were involved in thinking about the health and welfare of Bill and Charles. We did without extra candy bars, bananas, gasoline, sugar, shoes, and other rationed and scarce items that were often not available. Arlie and I were important in the workforce of the community because of the older boys/men being in the service. We did the work of men. Our sacrifices "on the home front" were nothing in comparison to the sacrifices of men and women in service.

Early in my childhood Mom talked often about "The World War. (WW I) To me, at that time, it was so long ago that I could not fully understand its relevance and importance but now looking back, it had been only a little over twenty years before. It was just "yesterday" in her life as are so many events twenty years ago are in our lives today. She knew the horrors of war through people and the newspaper and being a young person concerned "about the boys in France."

After we got electricity in 1943, the radio was our entertainment in the evenings. Some of the programs were based on a service man being reunited with his family. The family might not know that the son was in the states. Mom would shed tears as she heard the drama on the radio of the family and the serviceman being united. Perhaps she was shedding tears for herself and for her sons (and all mothers). As teenagers Arlie and I did not understand her emotions. Now I feel that I do. And I could shed tears with her.

We will always wonder what Bill would have contributed to our lives had he lived, gone to college perhaps, and grown old as our brother. We will never know.

The USS Phoenix went to Philadelphia in 1943 for repairs. Before the ship returned to the Pacific it took Secretary of State, Cordell Hull, to the Mediterranean for a conference. (Cordell Hull would not fly.) If Bill had not gotten tuberculosis, he no doubt would have come home on leave at that time. His stories of Pearl Harbor and life in the South Pacific would have been of great interest to us.

Bill's letters show his pride in the Navy and affection for the Phoenix. Many of his letters were signed "U.S. Navy" and then his name.

The media coverage of the 50th anniversary of the attack on Pearl Harbor has made all of this more real. If I had written most of my letters to veterans of the Phoenix in July, 1991, there would not have been the same emotional involvement from me or perhaps from them. A number of them have stated that they will be attending reunions in Pearl Harbor in December (1991)and will be talking to others about

Bill and my letters.

Since I originally wrote the paragraphs above, the 60th Pearl Harbor reunion has been held. And now the 66th.

:: :: ::

Chapter Eight

Remembering Bill

Bill's mother, Vintie Holt, writes many years after Bill's death –

Story about Bill

In June 1941 after Bill graduated from high school in Dallas (Oregon) he went into the Navy. Bill, Lewis, Arlie, and I rode in Mrs. Harvey's car to the Guthrie Road (four miles from our place and four miles from Dallas) where we turned up the road to go pick boysenberries. Well, Bill got out there and walked into town to go join the Navy. That was the last time I saw him except on his deathbed at Walla Walla, Wash. (January 18,1945)

It was in January, 1945, when Ruby Jones brought Lewis and Arlie out to my place with a telegram that Bill was ill. I can't remember whether I went back into Dallas with her to go to the bank to get some money and to take care of how I was going or traveling. I was busy washing and I left it for Lewis and Arlie to take care of and the Murphys stopped by and the boys told them so Larena took the washing home and took care of it herself. I can't remember too much about anything but I can remember traveling on the train to Walla Walla. I got there at 4 o'clock in the morning. It was dark out yet. No one on the street. So I set there waited till day light. There was a man sitting in the depot alone so we talked. He helped me some of what to do.

Then I went out side walked around stopped in a restaurant and asked for the way to the hospital. Was quite a ways but I walked. I stopped at a home asked if I could find a room to stay over nite and started to walk away and this lady stopped me told where I could go. So I did and I stayed there. I pd for the room but she wouldn't take any pay for meals so I bought some food of different kinds.

Then I walked up to the hospital. And when I got there I saw a woman crying and it made me feel sad and then to think what I had to see. Well, I went in the hospital. Found a nurse asked where was

Bill Holt's room so she took me to him. Bill knew me but asked me not to come close to him. When I walked in Bill's room, he turned his head and his eyes filled full of tears. He asked why I came. I told him I received a telegram from the hospital.

I was only in the room but a short time a nurse came in said one of the head guys wanted me to come to his office. I just walked in and he just said, "Where do you want Bill's body sent to?" So I said to Forest Grove and he is to be buried at Buxton graveyard. So he asked some more questions and that was all.

I was there (Walla Walla) about 3 days. Bill was sinking. The Dr told me I better go home for he wasn't going to last long and I was home only a few days when I got word he had died on Feb. 6,1945. He was going to be 22 years old. (July 5)

The services were at Forest Grove and then we all went out to the grave yard. His body was taken to Buxton graveyard. Sometime later the Navy sent a tombstone. All it cost me was the freight.

Just a few months after he went in the Navy he was at Pearl Harbor when it was bombed so the ships all went out to sea. U.S. Navy Arizona was sunk. Bill was on the Phoenix. It was a cruiser and was sent out to sea with other ships. I never heard from Bill until I got a card from the government that he was OK. Then months afterward got a letter from a girl in Australia saying she had seen Bill and he was fine. Then a year later got a telegram he was ill and had been sent to a hospital in Oakland, California. My aunts went to see him. Then later he was sent to Corona. There he wrote a story about the battle at Pearl Harbor. Then he was sent to Walla Walla, Wash. where I saw him a few weeks before he died.

Mom

:: :: ::

Lew Holt 1992

I do not remember much about Bill's life. He was six years older than I. Bill joined the Navy when I was twelve years old. I best remember Bill through the many things he did for Arlie and me as our "big brother." When we moved to Bridgeport in May 1940 he helped us build a toy logging camp. We used adhesive tape spools for the drums on the steam donkey, an Ovaltine can for the boiler, string for cable and bent shingle nails for chokers. He converted a toy truck that Arlie and I got for Easter, 1934 into a logging truck. I still have it. I realize now as I write my own memoirs that many of the little things that I learned in my early years I learned from Bill (fishing, guns, kites, bean shooters, "dog trotting," playing cards, swimming, etc.)

After we moved to Bridgeport in May of 1940 Bill found two old 22 rifles above the root house in the woodshed. He did not know if the guns were safe to shoot. He took one to the front yard. To be safe he tied a string to the trigger and pulled the string from a safe distance. The gun fired safely. One gun did not have a firing pin so Bill made one by filing it out of nail.

The first summer we were in our new home, 1940, Bill had a chance to work for a family several miles away. Our oldest brother, Charles, took him to the farm to board with the family. We heard that Bill had to work long hours for only his room and board and $10.00 a month. Charles went to the farm and brought Bill home. We all felt happy to have him back home.

Our cats were great hunters. Sometimes they would bring in live chipmunks. One time I grabbed the cat with a chipmunk in his mouth and forced his mouth open. I let the chipmunk fall into a rubber boot. Bill built a cage along side the woodshed for the chipmunk. He built a wheel for the chipmunk to run in.

Bill, Arlie and I would cross Oscar Smith's hop yard, crossing Teal Creek to cut small ash trees for firewood. Bill taught Arlie and me to play pinochle. We would play cards and then quickly cut down trees before we went home. Our cat would follow us across the fields to where we were working. We often ran home (dog trotted). The cat would run along with us. The weather was hot so the cat would pant with his little red tongue hanging out. We thought it was funny.

When Charles went to college in Monmouth 9 miles away, Bill was the oldest son at home. It became his chore to milk the family cow. Milking the cow intrigued me and I asked Bill to teach me how to milk. Daisy was a gentle old Jersey cow so Bill obliged me. That was a mistake on my part. The job became mine for many years.

I remember the time that Bill shot a rock from a bean shooter at a small bird. He was standing on the road across from the house and the bird was on a hop "dead man" wire at the end of a row. The rock hit the bird and killed it. Bill was sad that he had killed the bird.

Bill attended four high schools. His freshman year 1937-38 at Kalama, Washington, part of his sophomore year 1938-39 at White Salmon, Washington and completed in Colton, Oregon, junior year 1939-40 beginning at White Salmon and ending at Colton, Oregon and his senior year 1940-41 in Dallas, Oregon. I never heard him complain. At White Salmon he made a cribbage board out of cherry wood. We were proud of it and used it when we played cribbage. We still have it. Bill was short but he enjoyed basketball. Charles tells me that Bill was a pretty good player.

It was during his senior year at Dallas that he decided to join the Navy. Mom had to sign papers to give her permission because he was only 17. He turned 18 on July 5, 1941 – when he was in boot camp in San Diego, California. I don't remember Bill going to "Mama" to tell her that he wanted to join the Navy and that he needed her permission. I wish I could remember the night before he left.

It would have been nice had there been more letters from Bill and from Mom to him. If there were more, they evidently have been lost. I particularly enjoy Mom's letters because they often give details about an event that I did not understand as a twelve year old or later as a teenager. They are very representative of our lives at that time – at least from Mom's viewpoint.

Bill's letters always show hope and encouragement. Perhaps his purpose was to be positive for Mom's sake. But then perhaps at the same time, the letters gave him hope.

:: :: ::

Chapter Nine

The Beginning of a Book

Bill died and was buried. We grieved and went on with our lives. This could have very well been the end to Bill's story; just his letters and Mom's letters to him. Our memories of him continued to live in our hearts and in the pictures on a shelf and in the other pictures and letters tucked away in Mom's many boxes. His story did lay dormant for almost 45 years. In April 1988, I attended a fiddle contest in Crescent City, California. During a break I purchased a hamburger and went outside to eat in the warm sun. I sat down at a table opposite two couples who were eating their lunch. I overheard their conversation about a naval reunion one couple had attended recently. It caught my attention. I stated that I had been thinking about trying to locate someone who had served aboard the USS Phoenix who might have known my brother. I commented that if I knew when his ship was having a reunion that I could have a note posted and perhaps locate someone who remembered my brother, Bill. One of the ladies suggested I give her my name and address and that she would try to find out when the Phoenix was having a reunion. I was pleased, but never thought that I would hear from her. To my surprise and pleasure, six weeks later the lady called me from central California. She gave me Andy Wilson's address in Washington – the chairman of the Phoenix Association. All of my motivation, research and material have come from that chance conversation. It opened many doors. As I have gathered material to record Bill's story, I have been fortunate to have many opportunities that have allowed me to go far beyond the story of Bill joining the Navy.

I sent Andy a letter asking if he would print it in the Phoenix newsletter. I didn't know for sure if my letter had been printed until Johnny Dollar in Florida sent me a copy of the April, 1989 issue. Johnny didn't know Bill but he was on the Phoenix at the same time. He shared stories with me about the Phoenix.

In the newsletter there were comments about individual seamen who had served aboard the USS Phoenix. Three had been on the Phoenix at Pearl Harbor. I knew they had been on the Phoenix with Bill. I wrote to them telling them of my search for somebody who might have known my brother and enclosed S.A.S.E.

When we returned on July 26th from a 13-day fiddle trip, there was a message on the answering machine from Horace B. Hamilton in Texas. He was one of the three that I had written to. I returned his call. His wife called him to the telephone. (They both had nice southern accents.) Horace was very friendly and willing to talk. He had read my letter in the "Phoenix Flame" and was going to write to me but had put it off "until tomorrow." Tomorrow was a long time coming.

He told me that he had a picture of William taken on December 2, 1941. They had gone to town on a shore leave and while they were there, they had their pictures taken. "They went on shore leaves together and were shipmates." "They palled around together and were friends but were not bosom buddies." Besides the picture of Bill, he also had a picture of a girl in Brisbane, Australia they both liked. He described Bill as being a quiet sailor – not like most who were rowdy. He was very complimentary about how nice Bill was. He remembered Bill as being small and "sickly."

Horace said that he would send me the pictures and that he would write down all that he could remember and send me information about Bill. It was asking a lot for someone to remember back 50 years ago and to go into detail about somebody he did not really know well.

Late in September I wrote a letter to Horace asking him questions and reminding him of his letter to me. On Monday, September 30, 1991, the long anticipated envelope arrived with his reply. It included the two pictures – one of Bill taken on December 2, 1941 and one of a girl in Australia. This was my first letter that dealt specifically with Bill – exactly what I had been hoping for. It was exciting. But little did I realize that many opportunities were yet to come.

:: :: ::

Horace B. Hamilton   July 29, 1991   (Mailed Sept. 30)
Caldwell, Texas 77836

Lew,

Well I finally got around to writing to you. Sorry that I took so long. I know that you are anxious to hear from someone who was with your brother aboard the Phoenix. I hope you can hear from someone else to talk about him.

I am enclosing a picture of William that was taken in Honolulu on December 2, 1941 while we were on "Liberty." I knew that I had his picture when I talked to you on the phone so I took it out of my album and want you to have it. If you look on the back you will see that it is written Honolulu, T. H. Dec. 2, 1941. We were ashore together and gave each other our pictures. Neither one of us had much money (we only made $21 a month) so we couldn't get into too much trouble. We sure got into a lot of trouble a few days later on Dec. 7th though. I should have said, that trouble found us!

My experience that day was basically the same as Williams but a few things were different. It was a terrible experience to go through but thank the Lord we made it. I'm sure that you have read several articles on the attacks so I won't go through it again. However if you have any questions or comments for me I will tell you what I can remember.

Talking about remembering, I remember William very well. We were both in Division 3 aboard the Phoenix. He was a Seaman – I was a Gunners Mate. However, we bunked close together and were good friends. We went ashore together and even dated the same girl for a while. I am sending her picture along, too. I am sorry that I don't remember her name but we met her in a city in Australia by the name of Perth. Fremantle was the Port of Call for Perth and that is where we anchored. I am not sure why I wound up with her instead of William. Maybe I just told her a bunch of lies. Sailors do that you know.

I'll say one thing for William though. He didn't drink and run around like me and the rest of the guys. He was kind of quiet and reserved. He was not loud or rough talking but just a nice guy.

135

Sept. 24, 1991

Dear Lew,

Enclosed is a letter that I started to write you a couple of months ago. I hope you forgive me for not sending it to you before now. I am not much of a letter writer like you. I realize that this is so important to you and I am ashamed that I have not answered sooner.

Now that I have received your second letter I just have to answer it. To answer your questions in order that you asked I'll start with "who else knew him?" Well, anyone that was in the 3rd Division should have known him. There were not that many of us in that one. I think that in the Roster of the Phoenix Flame that you ordered there will be someone who was also in the 3rd Division and you might write and ask him.

I met Bill aboard the Phoenix and worked with him for a while on Deck as we were both Seaman 1/c. I then "struck" for Gunners Mate and left the Deck force while he remained. However, we were both still in the 3rd Div. and still bunked in the same compartment.

We went ashore together in Pearl Harbor as we were both new to the ship and other shipmates. We had our pictures taken and exchanged them as you can see from the picture that I am sending you.

Yes, we went to the bars there in Pearl Harbor. Neither of us had much money or experience with girls and we learned a lot in a short time from the girls and from listening to our older experienced shipmates. Of course our shipmates always told more than the truth because they felt that they had to impress us "Boots." Bill did not drink hardly any – there in Pearl but later on when we were in Australia we both drank more as we fell into the routine of being a sailor and getting in with the crowd. But Bill never was a heavy drinker tho.

My account of the Bombing of Pearl Harbor has been on my mind all along and I have told my story to a lot of people in the past 50 years. It is basically the same story that I have read in the papers and from other accounts by survivors that I have met and have worked with in the past. I can't add anything of significance to Bill's story. It was an exciting and an awful awakening to the facts of life and death for us innocents. Manhood comes early from experiences like that. It did prepare us for the following 4 years of War after we got over the shock and grief of such a terrible atrocity.

After the Attack, a small Convoy of us – Cruisers and Destroyers – went out after the Japanese and after 3 days we turned around and came back to Pearl Harbor. We were almost out of fuel and ammo and knew that the Japs were a much larger fleet than we were anyway.

We then headed for San Francisco and had our guns that were damaged (split barrels) repaired and took on provisions for the trip to Australia.

We formed a convoy of ships and escorted them to Melbourne, Australia, after stopping on the way at Pago Pago for fuel. Those people treated us royally, treating us like we had never been treated before – nicely! Before no one had a good word for a sailor. In fact, in Norfork, Va. there is a sign that says "Sailors and dogs stay off of the grass."

After Melbourne we sailed for the western coast of Australia and patrolled the Indian Ocean. The American submarines were stationed there and we also went over to the Christmas Islands on a convoy. We sailed with the Royal Australian Navy and were under the Command of The Seventh Fleet Admiral.

Bill and Horace Hamilton both dated this girl in Australia.

While we were stationed in Fremantle - Perth on the western coast that is where Bill and I dated the same girl for a while. I'm sending her picture and am sorry to say that I don't remember her name. I really don't remember any of the girls' names to be honest about it.

The Phoenix then returned to the east coast of Australia and the war really began for us. As you can see from the copy of a certificate that I have enclosed Guadalcanal came next and then the rest of the "engagements."

Along about here I don't remember Bill. I do know that from the beginning back in Pearl Harbor that he was not a real robust type of fellow. Not that he was puny by any means but he was just not the "strong arm" type. As for him contacting TB from a bunkmate that is not true. No one in the third Division had TB. We all stood watch top-side in good and bad weather and I know that it didn't help anyone's health. I don't think Bill worked below deck except in our regular clean-up and repair because the 3rd Division was a deck division. We all had to work below some of the time. And we did have lots of torpedo attacks and alerts. If we were below decks when the attacks came, then we had to stay there and lock ourselves in our little compartment so if the torpedo hit, then the damage would be contained to that place. It was not comforting to lock yourself in way down below knowing that if the torpedo did hit then you were a "gonner."

I only knew Bill for a short time and I wish that I could tell you more than I have. He was a good person – never got into trouble and everyone liked him. He was quiet and kind of a loner. If I had known how things were going to turn out – Bill getting sick and leaving – I could have gotten closer to him and could tell you more. But you can be proud of him. He gave his all – while he could and that's all any of us did. He is as much of a hero as anybody else.

Those really were sad times for you. Losing your father and then Bill. And worrying about your brother Charles being wounded. You must be a very strong person to stand up under all those burdens. I hope life has been kinder to you since then and that your times are better now.

You really are a letter writer. Writing to your Mother all those years. And now getting together all you can for Bill's records. My hat is off to you. We like Country Western type music. Of course, Polkas and waltzes are great too. That "fiddling" keeps you out of "meanness" too.

I stay busy, too. I'm the Adjutant & Quartermaster for the VFW Post here in Caldwell and also the Quartermaster for the District here in central Texas. I didn't have enough to do so they elected me the County Veteran's Service Officer for Burleson County where I live. It keeps me out of "meanness" too.

I'm sure there're other things that I should have said but I'll close for now. Please answer and ask any other questions that I may be can answer for you. I hope what I've said will help some. You can be proud of Bill.

Respectfully,
Bill's shipmate Horace B. Hamilton

:: :: ::

Chapter Ten

REPLIES TO MY LETTERS FROM VETERANS

Names from Phoenix Roster of DECEMBER 31, 1942

During the summer of 1991 I ordered a microfilm from the Naval Archives of the crew of the USS Phoenix from 1938 through 1945. The Phoenix Association roster contained about 650 names and addresses. About 250 of those were on the Phoenix on December 31,1942.

In November of 1991 I mailed letters to three groups of Phoenix veterans. In a box of Bill's I found a picture of "Bill and Wally." I wrote to three "Walters" asking if one of them might be "Wally." I included a copy of the picture. None were the Wally I was looking for. I wrote to those in Division 3 who were on the Phoenix on Dec. 31, 1942 – whose names and addresses I had. I wrote to those who were transferred from the Phoenix on January 27, 1943 – the same day as Bill. And then I wrote to the rest of the crew who had been on the Phoenix on December 31, 1942 – whose names were in the Phoenix Association roster. I sent out over 300 letters. About 50 letters were returned – marked "deceased" or "no longer at this address." About 50 men or their widows answered my letters. The replies were interesting. Rather than trying to put the replies in context, I have included the replies in the order that I received them.

:: :: ::

Also earlier in 1991 I had received letters from others to whom I had written. In April of 1991 I checked the North Bend City Library for books about Pearl Harbor. I checked out *A DAY of INFAMY*. The author quoted four sailors who had been on the USS Phoenix during the attack at Pearl Harbor. I found three of their addresses from the Phoenix Association Roster and wrote to them. James "Johnny" Dollar called me from Florida to talk to me about his material. He did not know Bill but was willing to share his own material about the Phoenix.

He sent the following letter and later sent a packet of information.

:: :: ::

James Wm. Dollar   April 30, 1991
Jacksonville, FL 32210
Mr. Lew Holt,

Para. # 1 Yes, I was on USS Phoenix (CL-46) from commissioning in Oct. 1938 until mid 1943. Your brother, yes was on Phoenix and remembered. Due to age difference and different divisions of ship, I can say we were known to each other but not really too close. He was in 6th Div (A.A.) and I was in 1st Div. (Turret # one), a gunner's mate.

#2   I have not read of the book *A Day of Infamy* but someday I will, if I live long enough. I have met Andy Wilson, but he came on the Phoenix after I left in mid '43. In the days we are talking of, unless you were really close to one another, most of your shipmates were known only by last name or "nick name." Home towns, same. I wonder what other names, mine, (Johnny Dollar) and D. C. Christensen were given. I knew "Chris" – he was a signalman and I was also at Great Lakes Naval Training Center with him. Still only now finding out his name was "Donald C. " Christensen. Small world. Recently on the ship I was on in 34/36 had a reunion at Tumwater, WA. My wife and I had a "U-drive" and toured Oregon's border down to the cheese city – enjoyed it. By the way in 1939/1940? during the fleet week – Portland, OR., our cruiser Div. went up Columbia River to Portland. Very enjoyable. USS Phoenix, Honolulu, Boise, Helena, St. Louise (cruiser div. nine – Cru. Div. Nine.)

#3   Yes, the Xerox copies helped me to place Wm H. The A.A. area was approx. mid-ship – from fore/aft. The gunner's mates in the A.A., a lot in common with the turret captains and turret G. M., was headed by chief K. L. Winchell, a fine man and very knowledgeable about T's and other A.A. guns. He was a very caring and likable person. As fine as they came. See my book. I have many stories & anecdotes concerning the "old Phoo-Bird" – USS Phoenix. I loved that ship.

#4   Do I know of a list? I'm sure somewhere there is but where? If you ever find one, please share. If you wrote every one (time is taking its toll) there are still a few around.

#5   How many served on Phoenix at one time. From 900 to 1400 – when all billets and stations were manned. About 1200 average.

#6   My reply. Yes, I have various items that you may or may not want. My first thought was to go down to an Insta-print or Xerox shop and mail you copies. However, it got to be too many and I don't know of your desires. My proposition – box up what I can find, mail out to you – go through what you want printed – do same – then mail all material back to me. Know it will take a little time and if you have a different idea let me know. I do want it all back , if you use this plan – OK? Let me know what you want to do. One copy of 100 different papers is much more, here in Jacksonville. Awaiting your decision.

J. W. Dollar   (We had several excellent phone conversations.)

:: :: ::

(Got this name from *A Day of Infamy*)
Tom F. Shook   April 30, 1991
Boone, NC 28607
Dear Mr. Holt,

Received your letter yesterday. Nice to hear from someone whose brother served aboard the USS PHOENIX.

Even though I served aboard the PHOENIX from April 1, 1940 until September 19, 1945, I did not know your brother, William. I do have a faint recollection of a man leaving the ship with suspected tuberculosis. I may have this person confused with another man by the name of Skaggs who also developed tuberculosis. I worked in offices aboard ship and had little direct contract with deck and gun crew personnel.

From what you write, William was most likely in the 4th, 5th, or 6th Division, and I would suggest, if you have a directory of PHOENIX people, write to some of the people who have indicated their divisions in the booklet.

I cannot add anything to the Pearl Harbor attack except a passage from the movie that was shown the night before the attack. One of the stars in the movie, *THE LITTLE FOXES*, said, "Take us the Foxes, the little foxes that spoil the vines, for our vines have tender grapes." Not until much later did I learn this passage, though it may not be exact, came out of the Bible. Approximately 2,128 young men lost their lives there.

I wish you well, and I am sorry to learn of William's death.

Sincerely, Tom (Tom F. Shook)

:: :: ::

(Name from the Phoenix Flame)

Harry A. Rogucki   Sept. 13, 1991

Bloomfield, NJ

Dear Mr. Holt:

I have received your letter and copies of the newspaper clippings regarding your brother, William Holt. I apologize for the delay in answering your letter. I was in the Ship's Personnel Office during your brother's attachment to the USS Phoenix, however, I cannot recall the face or the name as per the newspaper clipping at this date.

If you know what division your brother was assigned to while serving on board the USS Phoenix, I suggest that you have such information published in the USS Phoenix Flame. It is possible that somebody who was in the same division at that time may recognize the name.

I am sorry that I cannot render any further information regarding your brother. The best of health to you and your family.

Yours truly,

Harry A. Rogucki

:: :: ::

Microfilm records indicate that Verlin Wyatt left the USS Phoenix in January 43 the same date as Bill – or the record was entered the same day as Bill's.

Verlin D. Wyatt   Nov. 23,1991

Golden, CO 80401

Dear Mr. Holt,

I'll try to remember correctly as possible. I don't remember your brother, William Holt but I will try to relate the travels of the Phoenix while I was on board.

I boarded at San Pedro in Dec. 1939. Most of 1940 was spent on a good will cruise to Valpariso, Chile and Callao, Peru – then to Pearl Harbor for endless exercises, drills, night battle simulations, etc. In Nov. 1941 the Phoenix took three shiploads of army troops to Manila, P. I. then back to Pearl. I was a signalman at the time of the attack and had the watch at that time and was on a 36 power long glass watching for Prep (a flag denoting the letter "P" to be hoisted by the signal tower for colors.

Prep is hoisted 5 minutes prior to 8:00 AM and executed at 8 AM and all ships hoist colors at the same time. Your brother's experiences were essentially correct but you must remember that many differing stories have been told by eyewitnesses. My recollection is that the Captain and Executive officer were ashore. The 1st Lieutenant was the Sr officer aboard. (He was a Lieutenant commander) It took only 20 minutes to heat the boilers to get underway. Our usual route out of the harbor was by the battle ships tied up at Ford Island and we started out that way but we got a signal that informed us that the battle ship Oklahoma was lying on her side and blocking the channel so we turned around in the channel – a feat never tried before as the channel was only about 5 times our length. All this time the dive-bombers were attacking the battle ships and coming out of their dives over us and our 50 caliber machine guns were giving them a bad time. We were credited officially for knocking down seven planes. We then started out the west channel but the signal tower again informed us that there were midget subs in the west channel. So, again we turned around in the channel and by this time our B29s (B17s) were trying to land at Hickam Field which of course was all torn up from bombing so they were trying to take off again at slow speed. And our fleet was trying to shoot them down. I didn't see any of them get hit though.

So now we are turned around again in the channel (all this happened near Aiea – Landing at the north end of the harbor) and started out over the Oklahoma, the Arizona had already been fatally hit and we could see men on her foremast in a lookout nest who were trying to get off a burning ship. One did a perfect swan dive into the burning oil. The second hung by his hands from the mast for a while then just turned loose and fell on to the burning deck. We went over the Oklahoma without touching her. We were not at full speed but we were creating a good wake at the speed we were going. After we were outside the harbor we joined up with the Raleigh (4 stack cruiser) and several destroyers and started around the island of Oahu to attack the Jap fleet which was reported to be landing parachute troops on the north shore. Which proved to be false then we received a message that informed us that the Jap fleet was at Lahaina Roads. So we rushed over to battle and found nothing. We stayed out for three days before re-entering Pearl, what a mess. We again anchored at Aiea Landing and the pier at Aiea was stacked with coffins 5 high and 100 yds long.

Next day we left for San Francisco where we went to Mare Island for a new gun barrel for a 5 inch which was split due to too much firing, 50 cal. AA gun. Then we went in to Frisco Bay and anchored just north of Alcatraz and took on stores all night. The next day we set sail for Melbourne, Australia with three Matson Lines loaded with army personnel – over 7000 miles. We then joined the fleet but we had no radar or "AA" guns except 50 cal machine guns and 5" 50 AA guns so we were to receive radar and "AA" 1 point 1 gun mounts at Sydney and also repair our steering.

So after Guadalcanal we went into dry dock at Sydney but we were only there for 12 hours before the USS Chicago who had her bow blown off at Guadalcanal took over our berth in dry dock. We had to leave with out steering and the pilot ran us aground in Sydney Harbor. But eventually we did get our radar and "AA" guns and took off for the Indian Ocean where we were to stop a Japanese battle ship from destroying shipping. We were operating out of Perth. We were escort for a tanker and two destroyers – at one time – to deliver P 40s and fuel and spare parts to Chennault in Burma. But a couple of subs got the tanker and one destroyer and we just picked up survivors. Shortly after that we ran full speed up to the East Indies to help the evacuation of the Philippines. The Boise (our sister ship) had taken another bunch of troops to Manila and got caught there and was trying to get down to Australia but she got sunk before we got to her. The USS Isabell, a luxury yacht was the only ship we found.

We stayed in the Indian Ocean for about 8 months then came back over to Sydney where we were assigned to the Australian fleet – H.M.A.S. Australia – Hobart and several destroyers. We had to send some of our signalmen and radiomen over for duty on the H.M.A.S. Australia for better communications. We then operated in the Coral Sea and at one time stayed out continuously for 90 days without reprovisssioning. That's when we ate a lot of spam. When we did come in we came in behind the Great Barrier Reef. What a beautiful place.

It was at one of these reprovisionings stops that we were transferred off. I only remember 8 men leaving when I did. We anchored off Townsville and were sent ashore in a boat where we spent one night with the Australian army then sent by train down to Brisbane. Thence by ship to Neumea New Caledonia where we lived in tents for a week or so before we boarded a merchant vessel called the Sea Witch and sent to Frisco by way of Pago Pago. It took 30 days.

I was given 30 days leave and sent to Miami where I instructed for 18 months before being shipped out into the Atlantic on a destroyer escort. I made two trips with convoys to the Mediterranean. Then back to Miami where I was sent to Melville, R. I. to pick up a net tender. I was there for about 6 months and the skipper of the base transferred me from one ship to another till I finally got the last one built – the "Tonawanda" and had to go to Sturgeon Bay, Wisconsin to commission her. We sailed out (of the) lakes thru the Welling Canal – then thru the St. Lawrence River and into Boston where we outfitted before going thru the Panama Canal then around to San Pedro. The war ended while we were off San Diego and they changed our orders to pick up the submarine nets in San Pedro Bay. I was discharged in Nov. 1945. Married June 46 had two children, joined the reserve and was called to active duty in May 1950 and assigned to a tanker "USS Kennebec" for two long years.

I have been a painting contractor for 40 years. Had a triple by pass in 85 causing semi retirement. I blow the Bag pipe in a Shrine Band for enjoyment. I am now 72 years young. I did not attend any of the Pearl Harbor festivities this year.

I belong to both the national and the state organizations but I do not attend much. We did receive a medallion this fall from the nation in thanks. It reads – "Remember Pearl Harbor, December 7, 1941. Is about the size of a silver dollar and comes in a nice case. You are entitled to one in your brother's name. All you need to do is apply thru your Pearl Harbor Assn.

I have a USS Phoenix history and list of battles, etc. I will send you.

Did you know the Phoenix was sold to Argentina and sunk during the battle for the Falkland Islands? Renamed General Belgrano.

Also in 1980 a nuclear sub was commissioned named Phoenix. My wife and I attended the launching in 1979. There were about two hundred ex Phoenix sailors attending.

I'm sorry I couldn't be more personal about your brother but I was in the "C" Division (communications) and I assume your brother was in a deck Division. There being nearly 1200 men on board, we didn't know very many from other divisions.

The battles we were in while I was on board were Pearl Harbor of course, Guadalcanal and Coral Sea. We were never hit except by a little machine gun fire from dive-bombers coming out of their dives at the battle ships. I know this will only make you want to know more but hope it will help a little.

Yours – Verlin Wyatt

(Bill and others may not have been transferred the same day but perhaps were written up in the same transfer records.)

:: :: ::

I received many letters from Phoenix veterans who were on the Phoenix at the time of the attack on Pearl Harbor. I have chosen not to include all of them. Each one was interesting but basically they said the same thing, i.e. they did not know Bill, they were sorry he died and that they couldn't add anything to his account of the attack. When I sent out my first 300 letters, I included a letter of introduction from me, a picture of Bill and his account of the attack. I thought that his account would stimulate them to write their account but it was just the opposite. They wrote that his account pretty much covered the attack. Perhaps I would have received more accounts of the attack from the Phoenix veterans had I not sent Bill's account of the attack.

Several wrote that they came home after the war, got jobs, got married, had families and basically erased the attack from their minds. Others remembered the attack, gave talks and continued to make it an important event in their lives. Others were not letter writers. They stated that their wives wrote the letters in their families so they had never written anything down about the attack or their later war experiences.

:: :: ::

Joseph H. Brillant   11/30/91
Topsham, ME 04066
Dear Mr. Holt,

Reference: William H. Holt, Sea 1/c Div. 3 or 4

First of all, I was stationed on the USS Phoenix from 10-5-38 to 5-23-45 "F" Division. Right now, the name Holt does not come to my memory. I looked back into my shipmate's pictures & album which I have and I was almost sure that he was in one of the pictures taken on the Waikiki Beach in Honolulu. The name was Hope as listed on the picture. So, evidently it was not William Holt.

If his battle station was on the starboard side of the forward machine gun platform, then I must have known him then because my battle station was the forward A.A. Director which is located almost above the machine gun platform and I was pretty well known by all the machine gun operators.

I am now discovering that evidently many of us contracted tuberculosis, because I too had contracted T. B. as well as three other in my Division "F" that I know of.

After 18 months of rest and hospitalization I fully recovered. My doctors at the V.A. Hospital seem to think that it was a miracle that I was cured. I have lived a normal life had five children, 4 girls, 1 boy and have been very active in my own town activities as well as in my work. Went to college and became an accountant for an automobile GMC-Pontiac agency.

I have also been very active and volunteer to my Credit Union here in Brunswick. I am now Chairman of the Board of Trustees. It is a 55 million credit union. I've been retired for the last 6 years and have been vacationing in Arizona and Florida 6 to 8 weeks at time with my wife Lorette.

I do belong and am in touch with many of my shipmates who belong to the USS Phoenix (CL-46) association. Especially those of the "F" Division.

Joseph H. Brillant

:: :: ::

[From my journal LH]

December 1, 1991

I went to the store, when I got back Alice told me that Jesse Sisk from Manchester, Tennessee had called. I called him back. He had received my letter that day and had cared enough to call me on the phone. He said that he had known Bill and that they had called him "Tim Holt" after the cowboy movie star of that time. Jesse was on watch on gun 8 and Bill was in the "cleaning station" just below him. They use to talk when they had watch. He did not know Bill well – they were not buddies who went on leave together.

He spoke of the Phoenix being the first ship in the harbors of Australia. It served as an air defense for the Australians who had no guns or any way to counter an attack by the Japanese. The Phoenix was their only defense. The Phoenix spent a lot of time escorting ships around Australia. The Phoenix carried seaplanes – single pontoon, two wings – SOC and OS2U. A five-inch shell would launch the plane. (Dick Hans later told me that one would go from 0 to 120 mph in 60 feet.) When the water was too rough to pick the planes up, the Phoenix would make a sharp, fast turn and the water would be smooth on one side. The plane would come into the smooth water and make its way on to a rope sled – a canvass sling that would be used to pick the plane up.

Profile of the USS Phoenix in camouflage paint clearly shows the seaplanes and crain used to retrieve them.

He suggested that I buy the book *Sinking of the Belgrano* by Gavshon and Desmond Rice. It tells of the Phoenix as an Argentine cruiser after the war.

Jesse was transferred from the Phoenix to the USS Cabbot – an aircraft carrier. He said that on the Cabbot he had a rating and a responsibility and felt better about being aboard it. On the Phoenix he was a seaman without any direct responsibility and never did develop a loyalty as he did on the Cabbot.

I invited him several times to write information down and mail it to me but he said that he had 13 invitations to give talks to schools about Pearl Harbor and that he was very busy. He mentioned that the Cabbot is having a reunion in Portland in August and that he would be glad to meet with me to talk about the information. (I had surgery that summer and couldn't make it 220 miles to Portland.)

:: :: ::

Ref: Dick Hans   (From my journal)
December 4, 1991
Oregon City, Oregon

Last evening when I came home at about 5:00 Alice said that I had received a phone call from Dick Hans. He was in Lakeside (13 miles north of North Bend) visiting his brother-in-law and family. Dick was aboard the Phoenix the same time as Bill. I had written to Dick several days earlier requesting information. The letter went to his old address in Clackamas. (He now lives in Oregon City, Oregon.) The people who live at the old address received my letter and called his daughter who lived next door to them. She called her Dad and read my letter to him. He told her that he was going to North Bend in a few days and that he would give me a call.

I called him back. We made arrangements to meet the next morning at 6:45 at the Humbolt Club in North Bend. His brother-in-law, Bill Jones, often comes in to have coffee with the gang at that time. (He is a retired longshoreman.)

I organized the things that I wanted to take with me, got up early, and was at the Humbolt Club at 6:45. I walked up to two men sitting at the bar having coffee. They were Bill and Dick. We introduced ourselves and then went into the other room to a table. We ordered breakfast and started talking. Dick went aboard the Phoenix from boot camp in 1940. He had been aboard the Phoenix for 14 months on December 7, 1941.

I asked him about coming to San Francisco right after the attack on Pearl Harbor. He said that a five inch gun had a bulge in it like a lemon. (Others have written this, too.) If he remembered correctly, the replacement gun was hanging on a crane ready to go aboard. They took the new gun and supplies aboard and left. I asked him why Bill might not have written us a letter from S.F. or made a telephone call. He said that they were all caught up in the excitement of the war.

Dick told us that just before 8:00 on December 7th he started to the deck of the ship to catch a boat to go to mass on the Nevada. He had a knife, a long knife, on his belt that he was going to leave at his station so he could sharpen it when it got back. When the attack started he grabbed his knife and started cutting the awnings covers off the guns. He was skimming Bill's account of the attack so I told him to read on. Bill wrote in the next paragraph about somebody getting a knife from the galley and starting to cut the canvas covers off the guns. Perhaps he was writing about Dick. Dick said that others were cutting canvas covers, too.

He enjoyed reading Bill's account of the attack – shaking his head in agreement. He was curious about the two cruisers that Bill wrote about and wants me to find out their names if I can. He doesn't remember there being any cruisers. When Dick read that Bill was on the boat deck, he said that he must have known Bill because that was the area that he worked in.

Most of the action of the Phoenix came later in the war after Bill had left. Often as they entered a port in Australia they were the first American navy vessel that had called since Teddy Roosevelt's fleet had toured the area. The girls lined the docks waiting for the sailors to come ashore.

One of their main duties in the Indian Ocean was to harass the Japanese fleet. They would go close to the fleet and then run. The Japanese would chase them but couldn't catch them. If the Japanese destroyers were to go to the sides, the Phoenix could out shoot them. The cruisers couldn't catch up with the Phoenix and could not shoot straight ahead – as the Phoenix could. Dick said that sometimes they would be traveling so fast and so long that there would be up to 1 1/2 inches of salt collected on the funnels.

One day a garbage can that had been welded shut was brought to the ship. It was loaded aboard the Phoenix. They sailed to the Red Sea where they put the garbage can aboard a British ship. They never did learn what was in the garbage can.

The Phoenix escorted the Queen Mary on one trip but had a hard time keeping up with it. The Captain had a shot fired across Queen Mary's bow telling it to slow down.

The Phoenix was known as "The Galloping Ghost of the Aussie Coast" during the early part of the war when it was patrolling the Australian Coast. It was a fast ship. Dick told of it going to different cities but no great detail. One time he was dating a girl whose father did not like American sailors so he met her down town. One day he was killing time waiting for her in a bar and got to talking to one of the local people. The man insisted that he come up to the house. He did – and there was his date. The man was her father. Later he was invited to go inland to hunt kangaroo with the father. He asked permission from the captain who said that he had to be back in two days or he would spend the rest of the war in the brig at Mare Island.

The girl's father and Dick boarded a train and rode out into desolate country. About 40 miles out the train stopped and dropped them off. They watched as the train left them standing there. The fellow had brought a canvass bag of water, a couple fruits, and a couple sandwiches. All he had were three shells so they each had to count. He shot two kangaroos and skinned them. Dick said that after the man shot the first one, he told Dick to watch the brush around them. He did and after awhile he saw black heads peeking through the brush. Dick had thought that they were all alone.

Later that summer when we were visiting our daughter, Patty in Salem, Patty and I visited Dick in his home near Oregon City and went through all of his Pearl Harbor and navy material. I was pleased that Patty had the opportunity to meet a Pearl Harbor Survivor.

:: :: ::

Tom A. Brown   12-9-91 Monday
Boise, Idaho
Dear Lew,

I'm answering your letter, although I can't remember if I knew your brother or not. As I was in the 1st Div. and our duties were in the bow more or less of the ship, and I think he was at the mid ship or stern port of the ship. Although I knew quite a few shipmates aboard; it was hard to know them all. I think we had about 11 or 12 hundred men aboard; our capacity was supposed to be 600. But I remember a fellow who had TB – seems to me he was kinda husky and had kinda blond hair – and was transferred off to a hospital or Ariz. It's been so long, and my memory is really getting bad.

When we went to San Francisco for several days; we had some good times there. I was 19 then. If he drank I don't know. But there was a lot of fun places "Streets of Paris" etc. – and being service men we were treated like "we were heroes" already. Remember it was colder than hell waiting on the dock for our motor launch to take us back to our ship (all bundled up in our Peacoats.)

Anyhow – loaded up and headed for Australia. We crossed the equator on the 19th of Jan., and us recruits (pollywogs) we were called – really got the treatment – hair shaved off, washed downed with fire hoses, beat on with canvas clubs, soaked with water – kinda rough treatment. But going to Australia was worth it – war or not.

I think we were the first war ship to hit Melbourne in 17 yrs. We were like movie stars – what a reception. I think everybody loved it. We stayed there about 2 wks – then headed for Fremantle, on the other side of Australia; as they thought the Japs may try to invade over there I guess. I forgot if we stopped at any other ports on the way there or not. I remember we were at a place called Townsville – but when?

We stayed at Fremantle for a long time, we had that place and 6 miles away Perth, a real nice place. We rode the tram there. We were treated like kings. Every one loved it. We were in & out of port operating. When out on patrol, we would stop here and there – one island where we would lay in the sun, swim – had a ration of 4 cans of beer and pop. Some would buy beer from the shipmates who didn't drink for $1.00 a can or more. I think how lucky we were that no one got attacked by a shark. A lot of them over there. One guy did dive into sand bar and break his neck. Also a guy got a "Portuguese man of war" on his face (a very bad jelly fish) that can paralyze you for a spell (which could cause one to drown – don't remember what happened.

Also, we escorted the "Langley" an "old carrier" loaded with P 40's that was going to Java. At that time the heavy cruiser "Australia" & light cruiser "Hobart" were operating plus destroyers with us. We took them half way there and were met by another force to take them the other half of the way. They were on the way to Java, when they encountered the Japs. I think that was the "Coral Sea Battle." The

Langley was sunk – plus some others, can't remember them all.

We were in & out so many times, then headed for Brisbane; had a good time there (a lot of marines were returning from Guadalcanal; we were also there for a while. I remember the marines had a lot of Japanese swords & Jap gold teeth. A lot of stories there. We were all making the best of it, as you didn't really know if you were going to get through all this, alive or dead.

After there we hit Sydney, Aust. for a while. I think we were in Cockatoo dry dock a while. I think we saw the heavy cruiser come in from the battle of the Coral Sea with its bow blown off. After we left Sydney we headed for the states – pulled into Philadelphia Navy Yards for an overhaul and leave.

God, I didn't know I could write so much I haven't written this much for a long time – so many things; you can't remember them all. Too long ago, after we came in 1943 – after that I went on the heavy cruiser "San Francisco" for another tour of the Pacific till the end of war. I signed up 1941 April 17th for 6 yrs – got out in 1946. Many times I wished I'd just stayed in.

I hope this will help a little, maybe you'll find someone in his div. that could tell you much more. We're all getting a little old. I'll be 70 this month. I'm sorry I'm such a messy writer – probably you will decipher enough out of this to know something.

Yours truly, Tom A. Brown

I wish I could remember more about your brother. We were all young kids going out into a new world and found excitement all of a sudden – Pearl Harbor. Write anytime.

:: :: ::

Walter Premo   Dec. 15, 1991
162 Pawnee Ave.
Dover, PA 17315

A few lines to let you know I received your letter. I'm not too good at names, but the more I think of it I do remember when your brother was sent back. I don't remember too much about the ship and crew, except most of the time it was a good and happy crew. It was the type of environment where everyone got along good. You didn't have to lock your locker, no fights, friendly competition between div.

I was in the 6th Div. My duty sta. was the quarter deck, battle station # 5 port side under the wing of the bridge.

I have some clippings from the paper they had about a week ago on P. H. 50th. Things like where you were, what your thoughts were. To most the only time they think about it is some thing like now the 50th anniversary. Some of us it's an on going thing.

I wish I could help you more but that is about it.

Good Luck

Walter P. Premo

:: :: ::

Walter Zbyzenski   Dec. 15, 1991
Fremont, CA 94539
Brief log on USS Phoenix from Nov. 16, 1940 when I reported for duty at Mare Island shipyard – Vallejo, CA.

Left Mare Island Nov. 28, 1940 for Long Beach. Arrived LB 12-1-40. Left LB 12-6-40 bound for Pearl Harbor. Arrived PH 12-12-1940. On operations training in Hawaii area. Left PH July 1940 bound for LB. Arrived LB July 10, 1940. Left LB July 24, 1940. Back in PH early August 1940. Sept. 6 left PH on Convoy USS General Henderson with 3000 troops on board bound for Manila, PH. Arrived Sept. 16, 1940. Visited Manila, Iloilo, Zamboanea and Cebu. Left PH late October 1940. Back in PH mid Nov. 1940. (I wonder if he should have written "1941" for the trip to Manila. Bill and others wrote about such a trip?)

In PH Dec. 7, 1941. Convoy to USA with dependents from Hawaii. No visits in SF. Back to PH. Early Jan 1942 from PH to SF. Jan 12, 1942 left SF with troop convoy bound for Melbourne, Australia – arrived 2-1-42. Left Melbourne 2-12-42 for Fremantle, Australia. Operated around Australia until July 1942. Indian Ocean duty. Convoy USS Langley and Dutch Ship Sea Witch for India. Relieved of convoy duty to join our forces at Java. Shortly after we left Langley and Sea Witch sank. July

1942 left Fremantle for Sydney, Australia. Couple weeks' liberty at Sydney. Left Sydney August 42 on operations various islands, etc. April 1943 to Sydney for liberty. Left Sydney for Brisbane. 4-19-43 left Brisbane, Australia bound for Panama Canal for extensive work at navy yard in Philadelphia.

Hi Lew

I hope the above info helps you in trying to trace his movements. I was in the "C" Division (radioman) when I was on Phoenix. On board Phoenix 11-16-40 to May 12, 1945.

I do not recall knowing your brother during his tour on Phoenix. If I can be of further use, let me know. The very best to you. He – as well as all other shipmates called me, "Ski." My apology for not getting back to you sooner.

Sincerely,

Walter Zbyzenski

:: :: ::

Wesley G. Singleton   Dec. 15, 1991
Goldsboro, N.C.
Dear Lew,

I received your letter asking about your brother that was on the Phoenix. I recognize him from the picture but didn't know him well enough to help you with any personal info. The story he told about Pearl Harbor was a very good and true story as to what happened that day. There is a man here in N. C. that was in the 3rd Div. , Charles B. Conley. He went to the PH event in Hawaii on Dec. 7th so I didn't see him at our PHSA meeting so I didn't see him to ask if he remembered William. Hope you will find someone that is more help than I. Charles may be able to give you more names of 3rd Div. men.

So now let me ask you something, did your ancestors pass through Va or N.C.? There are a lot of Holts in N.C. My great grandmother was Sophia Holt Hollowell, her father was William Holt who owned Holt's Lake and his father was Lt. James Holt that was a Rev. war vet and moved from Southhampton Co. Va to N. C. I haven't been able to find out who James's father was. Holt's Lake is still owned by a Holt and am enclosing this heading from our paper today. Thought I would tell you all this just in case by chance it looked interesting. (A.F. HOLT & SONS INC. TRUE VALUE HARDWARE)

If your brother ever got sea sick he must have on our way out to the Philippines in Oct. 1941 as we were in a very bad typhoon for three days. It was very hard to go out on deck in the forward part of the ship where the 3rd Div. was. Most of the 3rd were in no. 3 turret which would not be used against aircraft. Some in the 3rd were on the bridge and gun deck. Anyway we got through the typhoon and into Manila harbor. We spent about a month going to different ports, Ilailo, Cebu, Zamboango, and then went back to Hawaii and hadn't been at Pearl Harbor very long before the attack. I'm sure your brother could have told you some interesting stories about such trips. The Phoenix was a very good ship and the crew was a good bunch of men. Anyone who served on it has great praise for the officers and crew. I was on it for 5 1/2 years and will always remember it as a wonderful place to be.

Well Lew take care and good luck on your search.

Yours truly,

Wesley G. Singleton

:: :: ::

James G. Watson, Jr Dec. 20, 1991
Yarmouth Port, Massachusetts

(from Bill's writing)
". . and they both hit the water in one, two order. Two – A plane made his run over the battle wagons and pulled out right by us and a machine gunner began to pour lead into him on the quarter and continued till he was on the bow. Apparently the pilot was killed because the plane continued on in an even climb. He cracked into the side of the hill and burst into flame."

(Jim writes)
I recall this in detail. Carl Wolfe 4th Div. was on the gun. I was beside him & I believe your brother Bill was also handling 50 cal ammo boxes.

History of Phoenix enclosed.
Jim Watson GM 3/c
5th Battery

:: :: ::

(I feel this is perhaps the most important letter I received from a Phoenix veteran.)

Sam P. Bailey   Dec. 29, 1991
Cary, North Carolina
Lew,

I remember your brother aboard the USS Phoenix. I was in "H" Division. "H" Division shared the sleeping compartment with 3rd Division. When your brother came aboard, the "H" Division was composed of a doctor, a dentist, seven-hospital corpsmen and one striker. You can see our Division was a small one. The "H" Division took care of the health needs of the ship's crew. My rate was Ph.M. 2C (Pharmacist's Mate 2nd Class). I was in charge of the Sick Bay Ward and Sick Call.

William came to sick call complaining of loss of weight, night sweats, and feeling very tired. The young Dr. we had received aboard just before Pearl Harbor thought William was gold bricking. I took William to the Senior Medical Officer and explained his symptoms. He ordered a chest X-ray and microscopic examination of William's sputum. The chest X-ray revealed lesions on his lungs. The stained smear using Ziehl-Nielsen or acid-fast stain showed acid fast bacilli morphologically resembling tuberculosis bacilli.

The ship was operating in the Coral Sea area and Milne Bay in New Guinea. One of the destroyers was periodically sent to Townsville for mail, supplies (emergency), etc. Our Senior Medical Officer requested transportation for William and a Lieutenant that had suffered a ruptured appendix to be transferred to the Army Hospital in Townsville. Due to the seriousness of the lieutenant's condition, myself and Tommy Kingsley were sent with the patients on board the destroyer since there was only one Hospital Corpsman aboard the destroyer. We went along to take care of our patients. I saw both patients admitted to the Army Hospital in Townsville. That was the last time I saw William. I returned to the destroyer immediately. We got underway and returned to the Phoenix in Milne Bay.

William Holt was well liked by his fellow shipmates and the Petty

Officers in the 3rd Div. We were a close knit crew aboard the Phoenix. We knew one another, each other's problems, and all good points. We had a good group of officers and watched out for one another on ship and a shore.

I believe William received the Commanding Officer's commendation for his actions on Dec. 7, 1941, Battle of Coral Sea, Capture and Defense of Guadalcanal, and the Battle of the Dutch East Indies. Entries should have been entered in his service record to this effect.

Sorry I can only relate to you how I took care of William in the sick bay aboard ship & his transfer to the Army Hospital in Townsville, Australia. I hope men from the 3rd Division will get in touch with you with more information.

Sincerely Yours,
Sam P. Bailey

:: :: ::

January 4, 1992   (From my journal)
I called the Baileys about 1:00. Mrs. Bailey answered the phone. Sam was working at a bowling alley. She was friendly, knew my name, and was pleased that I called. She said that my letter was on the kitchen counter. After Christmas she told Sam that it was time that he answered their Christmas cards. He sat down at the desk – upstairs, I believe. She checked back with him several hours later and asked him how many he had answered. He said, "One – just the letter to Lew Holt." They have a daughter who lives at Underwood, Washington near White Salmon and they come out every year to see her.

Later in the afternoon I called back to talk to Sam. He is 73 years old and was 23 during the attack on Pearl Harbor. He served on the Phoenix for 53 months. Because he dealt with the records and talked to many of the men, he was able to recall Bill. Sam spent 20 years in the Navy and in civilian life he worked in the health care industry until he retired. Now he works several afternoons a week at a bowling alley.

He took several courses in microbiology. He told me that he was to be transferred on Monday, Dec. 8, 1941 to the States and then be discharged on January 6, 1942 at the end of his enlistment but the attack on Pearl Harbor changed all of that.

A Lieutenant who had tuberculosis slept in the same compartment as Bill. He may have been the one who infected several others. A Lieutenant Williams was on the Phoenix and transferred before Pearl Harbor and left the ship maybe in November. Sam met him after the war while working in a TB ward in a hospital in San Diego. Lieutenant Williams had TB and had done some research into all of the documented cases of TB – hoping to find the reason why there were so many cases of TB in the 3rd Division. Sam felt that the first person who had TB and who in turn gave it to others probably contacted it in China or Asia someplace.

Eugene Meitl was a Pharmacist's Mate on the Phoenix and was a friend of Sam's. I have written to him but Sam tells me that he is deceased. He might have been a good source, too.

Sam is not sure that Tommy Kingsley was the actual one who went with him when he took Bill and the lieutenant on the destroyer to the Army Hospital at Townsville. I wrote to Tommy today (1/3/92) quoting Sam so it will be interesting to hopefully hear from Tommy soon with additional information.

:: :: ::

C. K. Keefe (Clellen)   January 7, 1992
Lusby, Maryland
Dear Lew,

First thing I want to do is apologize for being so damn slow in answering your letter but then I guess I'm the worst guy in the world when it comes to writing letters!

Sorry I can't give you any useful information on your brother. I remember the name but can't place the face in my memory. I'm getting so damn old my memory is slipping a bit. I'll be 79 on my next birthday.

When I left the Phoenix in '43, the chief master at arms told me that the captain wanted my scrap book so I told him he could have it – now I don't have a single picture of the Phoenix or of the crew.

I was in the Walter Reed Army Hospital getting over a stroke when the news came on about the Phoenix being sunk by the British Navy down in the Falkland Island off South America. It sure made me feel bad because I was real proud of that ship.

Did your brother get his Pearl Harbor medal? I got mine when they gave them out at the Naval Academy. They had a special ceremony that day.

There are four or five of us survivors that live in this area and the newspaper wants us to come up and be interviewed. I would like to show them the letter you sent me if you don't mind.

After I left the Phoenix I went to Boston and put a DE-261 in commission. In a very short time I was back down in the South Pacific.

If I ever run across any papers or pictures that I think you might be interested in I will send them to you.

Sorry I can't be of any help to you but God Bless you and your family.

Respectfully, C. K. Keefe

:: :: ::

M. J. Cagley   Jan. 20, 1992
San Diego, California
Dear Mr. Holt,

I am finally responding to your letter of November 18, 1991. It took a bit of searching but found a couple of pictures that you might like to have.

I realize that the ones of General MacArthur were taken after your brother left the Phoenix but thought they would be of interest knowing this was the ship your brother was part of the crew.

I went aboard the Phoenix in 1939 and was an electrician's mate, but regret to say that I did not know William Holt. I was also the one who ran all the movies aboard the ship.

It was late August 1944 that I left the Phoenix as a Warrant Officer and went to new construction of the USS Lake Champlain. I continued with the Navy and retired in June 1962 as CWO-4 and have been living in San Diego ever since.

The Phoenix Assoc. has put out a very nice T-shirt and it shows all the engagements it was in from Dec. 7, 1941 to July 10, 1945 at Balikpapan, Du Borneo. First three engagements listed occurred Pearl Harbor, Dec. 7, 1941, Guadalcanal, Aug. 30 - Sept. 1, 1942, and Cape Gloncester Landing Dec. 28, 1943 – (Cape Gloucester) you may recall that the USS Phoenix served as the harbor defense at Fremantle, Australia. If you are interested in purchasing the T-shirt as a memento contact Andy Wilson, Vader, Washington. I have one and the quality of the material is first rate.

This flier came this past month for the USS Phoenix bumper sticker and all the information is on it if you are interested in this. I have not yet got around to sending for one but plan on doing so.

I sincerely hope you locate someone who knew your brother.

Sincerely, M. J. Cagley

Mrs. Betty Young

:: :: ::

C. J. Horn   January 28, 1992
Long Beach, California

Dear Lew,

I haven't been able to come up with anyone who remembers your brother on the "Phoenix." Have you had any "feed-back" from Bill Rush? He might remember your brother if they were transferred together.

I put the "Phoenix" in commission in Philly in Oct. 1938. At that time the ship's organization consisted of 6 deck divisions.

1st Division	No. 1 turret	(battle station)
2nd "	No. 2 "	" "
3rd "	No. 3 "	" "
4th "	No. 4 "	" "
5th "	No. 5 "	" "
6th "	8 - 5-inch guns	- AA Battery

I was a boatswains mate and gun captain in the 6th Division at that time. I believe it was in 1943 while we were in the Navy Yard for overhaul, when the ship's organization was changed from 6 deck divisions to 4 deck divisions. I was Boatswain Mate first class at the time this change took place, and was put in charge of the 3rd Division. We then had the 5 inch battery and this "new" 3rd division was made up of men from the old 6th Division. It's all a little confusing. I know that your brother was never in my division – however considering the time frame that he was aboard the "Phoenix" he was probably in the "old" 3rd Division.

I have a "Master List" of the "USS Phoenix" Assoc. We have over 600 in the assoc. Not many have listed what division they were in aboard ship. We usually have over 300 at all our Reunions, which we have every year. The ship's Reunion in Hawaii was great. I have gone back to Pearl Harbor every 5 yrs. for the Pearl Harbor Survivors Assoc. conventions since 1966.

Sorry I couldn't be more help to you with info about your brother. If I should come up with anything, I will let you know.

Take care, "C. J."

:: :: ::

165

CONGRESS OF THE UNITED STATES
HOUSE OF REPRESENTATIVES
February 4, 1992
Mr. Lewis Holt
North Bend, Or 97459
Dear Mr. Holt:

I just now received your Pearl Harbor Commemorative Medal from Mr. John Pfeifer, Oregon Chairman of the Pearl Harbor Survivor Association. I am honored the Association gave me the opportunity to forward your medal to you.

Please accept it with my appreciation and respect.

Sincerely,
PETER DeFAZIO
Member of Congress

:: :: ::

Andrew J. Anderson   February 5, 1992
Lt. j.g. USN Retired
Palo Alto, California
Dear Lew:

Sorry to be so long in answering your letter. I am unable to tell you anything about your brother, but I am sure he did a great job on December 7, 1941.

At that time I was in "F" Division, responsible for the main battery directors in the control instruments in the five turrets. If your brother was in Division 3, he would have been in the gun crew in Turret 3. Since I would have been in and out of all of the turrets checking instruments, I would most likely have known your brother by sight.

I had somewhat the same experience as your brother. I was sent to the hospital in Boston in 1945 with tuberculosis. From there I went to Sampson, New York. I spent a year there. Discharged and moved to California. There I spent another year in and out of hospitals. Although I lost a lung in the process I have been in good health since and have had a good life.

I am curious how you got my name. I am sending you a history of the USS Phoenix (CL46). Hope you enjoy it.

Your friend,

Andrew J. Anderson

:: :: ::

Andy Anderson, Lt. (jg) Retired   March 13, 1992

Palo, Alto, California

Dear Lew:

I'm not much on writing. I scribble a note in long-hand and my wife does it on her Macintosh with her laser printer. She will be pleased with your nice comments. I have not written any history of my days at sea. My kids keep after me, but so far not much.

I am one of the few people that can really say they were aboard ship on December 7, 1941. I had shore patrol on Saturday night and Phoenix O.D. logged me aboard ship Sunday morning at 0320 hours. General quarters and the guns firing woke me about 0800 hours. I dashed for my battle station which was sky aft director. My regular station was plot because I was in the main battery. In port, if my section had the duty, I manned sky aft. Things were very busy, I was director operator and we took under fire any planes we could. The ship got under way and headed for the open sea. On the way out, we picked up about 50 Phoenix personnel from a motor launch that was picking up people swimming and people trying to get back to their ships. Among those that came aboard was the regular sky aft operator. He relieved me and I then went to my regular battle station in the plotting room. Down there we had the switchboards that control which guns were controlled by which director. My battle station was switchboard operator.

We were at sea for 3 days I believe. We came back into port, fueled up and then made two trips to San Francisco convoying ships. We ended up in San Francisco and it seems like we were tied up to a dock for several day while waiting for 3 ships we were to convoy to Australia. These ships were loaded with Army personnel, but I don't remember their names. We were underway for 29 days, at that time it was the longest non-stop convoy ever made.

We started out for Brisbane, the Japs came south, changed to Sydney, then to Melbourne. We stayed a few days and then to Fremantle. In and out for about a year. We made several trips north but didn't hit any ports in India. We were the allied fleet in the Indian Ocean for quite awhile.

We came back for overhaul and then were assigned to McArthur to guard his left flank. That's all I know.

Sounds as though you and your wife keep busy. I have great admiration for anyone who can play an instrument and entertain. I am tone deaf and can't carry a tune. My wife has a great voice and does the singing for both of us.

Sincerely, Andy Anderson

:: :: ::

M. J. Cagley   March 23, 1992
San Diego, California

Dear Mr. Holt:

Recently I found this picture that I believe would interest you as it is the sinking of the General Belgrano, this was formerly the USS Phoenix. I was the liaison Officer of the Argentine Navy in 1952 when their government purchased several U. S. Navy ships, among them was the USS Phoenix.

I still correspond to a friend who came to San Diego as an Ensign to help make the ship's transfer to Argentina. He is now a retired Captain and has promised to send a piece of the plank of the General Belgrano to me. Hopefully my son's supervisor will be bringing it back to the U. S. this coming week. If I do get it, I will try to send a piece of it to you. What the Japanese couldn't do in Dec. 1941 to the USS Phoenix, the British did to the Belgrano in May 1982. You can add this picture to your memories for your brother.

Sincerely, M. J. Cagley

:: :: ::

H. Fred Dietrich   7 December 1992 (51 yrs later!)
Chief Engineman
U.S. Navy, Retired
Redondo Beach, California

My dear Lew,

The ship I was on at Pearl harbor was the light cruiser, USS PHOENIX, the difference between a light cruiser and a heavy cruiser was the bore of the main battery, a heavy had eight inch diameter and a light six inches, however the light could carry more firepower, i.e., five gun mounts with three guns or barrels per turret – a salvo was fifteen shells at one time a heavy cruiser had three gun mounts with three barrels or nine per salvo.

The PHOENIX was one of three major ships that got out that morning practically unscathed. We bagged three planes with two shots from our five inch antiaircraft #3 gun when they attacked the ship – one plane flew into the explosion of another and was also destroyed. The other two received direct hits.

We met the ENTERPRISE task force off Diamond Head at 11 a. m. that morning – the ENTERPRISE was an aircraft carrier and had two heavy cruisers and three destroyers with her. With a total of 13 ships, as I recall we made a great circle sweep to find the Japs. We ran into two more of our heavy cruisers and a couple of more destroyers three days out – the Japs had gone the long way home and we missed them.

On our return to Pearl I remember the burned out hulks of the battleships and others that had perished. The stench was awful as dead bodies popped to the surface and were placed in wooden coffins stacked up at Aiea landing (dock).

We spent a couple of days in Pearl, getting ready for sea with provisioning and refueling. I remember getting a limited liberty to pick up some silk slips that I had made at a local Chinese shop for my sister and a current girlfriend. When I got to the shop it had a sign: JAPANESE OWNED – CLOSED, U. S. ARMY. So I lost the Christmas presents for them – I figure some Army Sergeant owes me yet!

We convoyed a shipload of dependents back to San Francisco, went to the Vallejo Navy Yard and had the barrel of #3 5 inch (that bagged the planes) replaced as the old one had swollen from the heavy firing.

I had the first part of this letter on my word processor with another paragraph or so which it refused to print from the disc, so you will note some typing errors as I switched to the typing mode.

Now, Lew, I was an engineer, a Second Class Machinist Mate at the time of the attack – in fact I had the top watch in the After Engine Room and paralleled generators in eight minutes instead of three and a half hours as the book called for – this enabled us to have the electricity required for training the guns which resulted in the planes being shot down. The Chief Engineer, Lt. Cmdr James C. Woelfel was duty command, however I had no official permission to do what I did. I learned four or five years ago that he got a General Court Martial for "gross violations of engineering procedures" at the attack – in any case he never made Admiral as a consequence and he died in 1982 the same year the BELGRANO or PHOENIX did at the Falkland Island dispute – anyway we troops didn't know when a senior officer got a court martial – so when I learned of it some forty years later, there was nothing I could do to mitigate the circumstances. C'est la guerre! as the French say.

Now as to your brother Bill, I probably knew him as in those days I knew every man on board by sight if not by name. There is some one who will recall him, I'm sure. C. J. Horn a Boatswains Mate on board had the Third Division and he is a personal friend of mine and I will hand carry your letter to him at the next meeting of the founding Chapter One of the Pearl Harbors Survivors Association in Gardena, California, Sunday, the 20th of December at our Christmas party meeting.

I left the ship in Brisbane, Australia in April 1943 – just three months after your brother did so I will continue with the saga of the "PHOO-Bird" as we affectionately nicknamed her.

After our short stay at the Navy Yard we returned to Pearl, convoying a shipload of munitions and then turned around and escorted another shipload of dependents to San Francisco; where we provisioned and fueled. I shipped over on the eighth of January 1942 while there and we left a couple of days later for Melbourne, Australia convoying six Matson Line and American Line cruise ships loaded down with American troops. The SEAWITCH (cargo ship – was or made the 7th ship of the convoy) with a cargo of P-40 fighter planes left us four or five days out of Melbourne and we learned later that the Japs sank her a couple of days later in route to Java. It took us 17 days to make the trip at a steady 18 knots. We steamed straight ahead and the merchant ships zig-zagged as they had plenty of fuel.

We were on our "cruising combination" which was our most economic speed as the steam went through the forward engine room turbines then exhausted through the after engine room turbines this making maximum use of the superheated steam.

We washed out our main fuel tanks with diesel from the emergency generator tanks and when we arrived in Melbourne we had three hours steaming left at full speed (32 knots), with three days left at the eighteen knots we were steaming. The eighteen knots were our maximum speed on "cruising."

We spent ten days in Melbourne refueling and provisioning, this time with Australian Navy rations, which caused a sudden change in menu. We had plenty of dried foods and canned goods on board but no fresh vegetables and meats. Along with 20 lb tea cans – instead of coffee – they had coffee too but it was horrible so we became strong tea drinkers in a hurry. There was plenty of "bully beef" and fresh mutton. The bully was either canned or dried and the mutton stank up the ship and was difficult to eat.

The American divisions were divided and some sent to Northern Australia for defense of Australia. The balance were placed aboard 5,000 ton British ships (small cargo vessels) about 20 of them as I recall. We proceeded around South Australia in the Great Australian Bight.

We traveled at the speed of the slowest ship, which was about 9 knots so it took us another ten days to reach Fremantle, Western Australia where we laid in another ten days refueling and provisioning.

During this period I met my future wife. We took the ships to within 200 miles of Indo-China and turned them over to a British cruiser – I understand since that these troops were on the Burma Road – building it and defending it.

Our return and the trip up were very (un)eventful. We engineers use to sunbathe and loaf on the fantail between watches as we stood four on and eight off around the clock while the deck force, such as your brother, stood four on and twelve off and maintained the ship between day watches. We maintained our spaces while on watch. Also we stood the same eight hours until we hit port then we "dogged" back a watch, i.e., an eight to twelve on reaching port became the four to eight, etc. On this trip I had the four to eight.

We were a week out of Fremantle, going north in the Indian Ocean when one of our two scout planes – both up every day scouting for the enemy – taxied up onto the trailing cargo net and cut the engine causing the net to engage the prong on the seaplane hull so that the ship's crew could pull it to the proper position to engage the hook from the crane located in the center of the stern. The pilot didn't wait to be hoisted on board in the plane as was the custom, but bailed out and ran up the stern's permanent welded ladder and on reaching the main deck ran forward on the starboard side (right side looking forward). We engineers surged after him as he ran up the ladder to bridge wing where Captain Fischer, our skipper stood. Panting and out of breath our senior pilot a Lieutenant gasped "the Sharnhorst is broad abeam just over the horizon Port side." There is an arm of the Jap fleet dead ahead – also over the horizon dead ahead I saw one heavy cruiser and two light cruisers with several destroyers between us and the Christmas Islands." The Skipper thought a second, "We can't beat the German – he's too much for us, we'll take our chances with the Japs."

The good Lord must have stepped in. This was ten a. m., at eleven it clouded up and rained for a week. We went right through the Japs and they never saw or found us, nor we them.

On the return we learned later that the Java Sea battle was in progress. Our Skipper, Fischer, broke radio silence and told the Dutch

Admiral on the DE CAMP that we could come through the Java Strait from the west and help. He radioed back, "PHOENIX, stay with your assignment, it is too late to help."

The next morning after the Java Sea messages we ran into a small ship which had a blocky silhouette like a British destroyer or a Jap. We engineers again had vantage points from our fantail. The ship was at 15,000 yards, an ideal range for our main battery with an average of six hits per salvo out of a broadside of 15 six inch main battery cannons. Again this was around ten a.m. and we went to Condition Two, one step down from Condition One or battle stations. At Condition Two the crew goes on watch, or four on and four off hours. I was in the off-watch so I stayed and watched our main battery train all six turrets on the starboard side target or ship. She was blinking straight Morse with no code. A signalman friend of mine standing by me read it, "Identify Australian Corvette BENDIGO on trial run no code book." It turned out some smart Japanese that was an USC graduate saved his destroyer as Captain Fischer let him go saying, "according to this there is a BENDIGO on the ways – she may be ahead of schedule – if we sink her – it's an International incident." Once again, such is war.

So far, this account has only accounted for action towards the enemy and not the attacks by the enemy on us on board PHOENIX. By this from attacks on us as a ship – we had dodged 38 torpedoes by the time I left the ship in Brisbane in April 1943.

When we sailed out of Pearl Harbor the day of the attack we went to Condition Two. I was in the off-watch and struggled at the end of the promontory on the port side going to sea. A Japanese plane was crashed into the spit where the Army had a large shore battery set up on the previous Friday when the Fleet came in from sea. The Army had started a two week maneuver the previous Sunday on the 1st of December. The maneuver was called off on Saturday the day before the attack! Collusion?

Looking aft out back I could see dense black smoke rising from the wounded ships in Pearl Harbor. We had just broken the mouth of the harbor when an old Chief (CPO) yelled, "Belly down sailors! torpedo attack Port side!" My face was in the scupper, a metal foot wide trench about an inch deep which ran down each side of the ship with overboard flows every few feet to empty overboard any seas that came aboard. I was looking over the side and saw the wakes of two of the four torpedoes fired. We had turned into them and our bow pressure forced them away and alongside the ship. This was done with visual sightings, as we had no sonar as it had been removed the last Yard period in 1940 and was to be modernized and installed on the next schedule period some eighteen months later. The ship was returned to the East Coast and finally got her sonar in the summer of 1943, after I had left her.

PHOENIX was in the Indian Ocean from February to the middle of July 1942 when she left and around the East Coast of Australia sailed into the Pacific and joined in the Defense of Guadalcanal sea battle. I was on the starboard lookout station using the lookout's spare binoculars sighting and identifying the battleship NORTH CAROLINA which was brand new and two new pocket cruisers, one of which had the Sullivan brothers aboard and GOT SUNK LATER. We sounded Condition Two and "torpedo attack starboard side." On the J. V. (sound powered) phone, again using the spare or backup set I heard, "We are trying to pick up a span of four torpedoes aimed at the SARATOGA. I watched the wakes boil up under our shallow fantail – they missed us and one hit the SARA on the Starboard bow – she reared like a bronco with water cascading over her flight deck from the explosion. A heavy cruiser, the Northampton I believe, put her in tow within a half hour after she lay dead in the water. They towed her in a huge circle at about ten knots. By dusk she was on her own power and left in the dark to Hawaii for repairs.

We visited Cairns, Australia and Townsville, Australia during those months of Summer and Fall, 1943 (Summer and Fall to us but Winter and Spring down under!) We put into Sydney, Australia around the first of December if my memory serves me correctly and entered Cockatoo shipyard in Sydney for emergency; for repairs to the brickwork in #3 boiler (strained at Pearl Harbor attack) and other engineering and deck problems that had developed since then. By hook and crook, my buddy Roy Weber and I got our wives to travel from Perth to Sydney by rail and we had a Christmas with our wives for the first time. I was threatened with a court martial as I told my wife in a letter that passed the censor, "... it would be a good idea if you visited your Aunt and Uncle Tom and Jess at Christmas take Vicky with you." The Executive Officer said I had circumvented the intent of the regulations as the Japs could have found out that her relatives lived in Sydney.

We left again for the war in the Pacific early January 1943 – that must have been the time your brother left the ship. I left her in April 1943 and got duty on the submarine base at New Farm Wharf, Australia – Weber and I connived again and got our wives to Brisbane (then in the war zone) and mine and I had a happy eleven months there. I made CPO the first of March 1944 and our eldest daughter was born there the 5th. We celebrated our 50th wedding anniversary on 30th of June 1992 here in Redondo Beach with lots of relatives including four great-grandchildren with many friends in attendance.

Well, Lew, that about tells the story of the PHOENIX while your brother and I were aboard.

Sincerely, H. FRED DIETRICH Chief Engineman U.S. Navy, Retired

P. S. VICKY AND ROY WERE OUR MATRON OF HONOR AND BEST MAN ON OUR RE-CELEBRATION OF VOWS, JUNE PAST. (THEY LIVE IN LONG BEACH, CA – 12 MI AWAY).

PPS, I am also a veteran of Korea and Viet Nam – some of us lucked on out !!!!

:: :: ::

December 14, 1992   I called the Dietrich residence and talked to Mrs. Dietrich (Jean). Fred was at a meeting.

December 15, 1992   I called this evening and talked to Fred. He was talkative and had stories to tell – recalling names, facts, and figures. He asked me if he had written that the PHOENIX had escorted the Queen Mary on two occasions and the Queen Elizabeth on one occasion in the Indian Ocean. The Queen Mary from East to West and the Queen Elizabeth from the East to the West. The Phoenix was the best gunnery ship in the Navy he told me. He joined the Navy in

Tampa, Florida in 1937 but was not called to serve until January 1938. Although his father signed for him to take the "kiddy" tour (he was 17 years old), Florida had a quota, so he did not go in right out of high school. Another fellow who was a place behind him had just recently lost his father and he and his mother could not make a go of it on a five-acre farm so the recruiter asked Fred if he would go later. That is why he was not called up until January.

:: :: ::

December 24, 1992   We had gone to Salem the day before to be with our daughter, Patty for Christmas. On Thursday, the 24th, Patty needed to take Mavia, her babysitter for the week to Oregon City, she asked me if I would go along. The night before I called Dick Hans and asked him if he would be home and could I drop by to see him. Patty and I took Mavia to her parents and then drove to Oregon City. I called Dick. He said that he would drive out to the main road where he would meet me in a yellow Suburban. We drove 2.5 miles as he directed and there he was. We followed him several blocks back to his house. He directed us to his dining room where we sat down at the table. His wife came in and he introduced Patty and me to "Alice." Dick went into the other room to bring in his papers about Pearl Harbor. He shared his clippings, newspapers articles, picture albums, and certificates with us. I was complimented when he gave me the opportunity to bring home a number of things to copy. We left in an hour so we could get back to Patty's for Christmas Eve and so Dick could go to his daughter's. I shared with Patty, as we drove down I-5, that she should always remember what she heard this day, that she had been listening to a veteran of the attack on Pearl Harbor. Many years from now when all of the veterans are gone, she can say that she knew one – that she had met him 51 years after the attack. The attack on Pearl Harbor will go down in history along with such great battles as the battle at Gettysburg.

:: :: ::

January 23, 1993   At Christmas time my son, Tim, checked two books out of the O.S.U. library about Pearl Harbor. *AIR RAID: PEARL*

HARBOR! Edited by Paul Stillwell. Naval Institute Press Annapolis, Maryland. There is an interesting chapter: "Like Swatting Bees in a Telephone Booth" By commander Ted Hechler, Jr., U. S. Navy (Retired) 1981.

I called information and was able to get Commander Hechler's telephone number. I called his residence. Mrs. Hechler answered the telephone. I told her my name, where I was calling from and why I was calling. I asked if I might speak to Mr. Hechler. She answered, "He died ten years ago." Before I called I was concerned that this might be the case, although he was born in 1916, so I knew that I still had a chance.

Quoting from his book: "Theodore Hechler, Jr., (1916 -   ) graduated from the Naval Academy in 1940 and reported to the Phoenix in August of that year as assistant control officer of the forward antiaircraft director (sky forward). In 1942, he reported to flight training..."

I had a nice visit with Mrs. Hechler. She told me that she receives calls often asking for him. She is hesitant to say too much since she is a widow and feels threatened by people who might take advantage when they found out that Mr. Hechler is dead. She talked freely to me. She said that it didn't seem like ten years since he died and that she missed him. She reported that he liked to write and wrote articles when asked. I explained why I had called. She was a little confused and asked me if I knew her husband personally. I again told her that my brother had died in the war. She asked if he was a battle casualty. I again told her that he died of tuberculosis. She told me that they had attended several reunions of the Pearl Harbor Survivor's Association and of the Phoenix. We discussed the weather. She was surprised when I told her that we basically did not have snow here in the part of Oregon where I lived. She said that she thought that Oregon had a lot of snow. (She lived in the Washington, D.C. area.) She has letters that she had written to (or received from) "boy friends" during the war but thought that she would throw them away since she had no heirs. I wanted to ask her for her address but since she said that she was threatened by calls from unknown people, I chose not ask her for it. I thanked her for allowing me to talk with her. She seemed thrilled and was very pleasant. I had grasp at a straw that did not produce anymore than the pleasure of talking to the widow of a WWII officer who had been at Pearl Harbor when it was attacked.

:: :: ::

<u>March 27, 1993</u>   This afternoon I called Mrs. Richard (Florence) Trent in Salem and asked if I might visit with her about her husband who was a sailor aboard the Phoenix for six years. I drove to southeast Salem to her place. She brought out different memorabilia that belonged to her and her husband. She showed me a picture of them when they were first married. She was a nurse or in nurse's training in Philadelphia when they met after the war. I believe the Phoenix was in the area to be decommissioned. They moved to Salem in 1946. Mr. Trent died in 1989 at the age of 67. We visited for almost two hours. She looked at many of the names of those that I had written to. She could relate to several. She and her husband had attended several reunions. Flo gave me information about the two words Torrance and Creviston that I had in my notes after I talked to her when she called a year ago. I have written to John Creviston in Torrance, Ca. – a friend of her husband and her.

:: :: ::

ANOTHER SIX-HUNDRED by J. Daniel Mullin
CHAPTER SEVEN "Simmering Down"

Quote: "0800 March 5, '42: The men on the four destroyers had been assembled at quarters: The following information was dispensed:

1. The PHOENIX, that beautiful new treaty cruiser, had been laying in port for several days. When WHIPPLE landed the survivors from LANGLEY and PECOS, it triggered the BLACK HAWK liberty party into a brawl with PHOENIX's liberty party. The men had been kept fairly well aware of the incidents in the Java area and the resentment arose by the sight of this many gunned cruiser sitting by the dock while their friends and shipmates up north were being slaughtered, had finally

exploded. Liberty for PHOENIX had been canceled for this day, if any were met ashore, leave them alone.

2. There would be port and starboard section liberty and it would commence at 1500 and expire at 0730 on March 6 (42). Stay away from PHOENIX."

:: :: ::

U.S. ASIATIC FLEET 4-STACKER DESTROYERS, INC.
North Bend, Oregon
June 6, 1993

J. Daniel Mullin
Mt. Pleasant, South Carolina

Dear Mr. Mullin,
Recently my wife bought me your book *ANOTHER SIX-HUNDRED* at a library sale. I quote from it, "Aloha Frank. It was a hectic 85 days. (Signed) J. Daniel Mullin." She bought it for me because it had a short article about the USS PHOENIX. My older brother was on the Phoenix at and after Pearl Harbor until he became ill in January of 43. He died of tuberculosis in 1945. I have been researching the Phoenix by writing to many sailors who were on the Phoenix the same time as he was on it and by reading articles that mention the Phoenix.

Fortunately I have found three sailors that remember my brother after 50+ years. Time is against me for finding others who knew him. Hopefully I will find you in good health and willing to answer my letter. I found your story of the conflict between the Phoenix crew and the Black Hawk crew very interesting. One sailor remembers it and another denies it, so it has been interesting. Thank you.
  I remain,
  Lew Holt

:: :: ::

From: J. Daniel Mullin   10 June, '93
To: Lew Holt
      North Bend, Oregon

Hi ! Your letter Re: PHOENIX

The situation between BLACK HAWK AND PHOENIX was as stated in the book. Black Hawk tho not a combatant ship was continually exposed in the forward areas as a sitting duck. With our guns and torpedoes our emotions had a release in the battles, while she had no release, except to repair the Destroyers, and supply us when she could. She was very close to the 13 DDs. Again, she gave us her last torpedoes at Christmas Island and left for Fremantle a couple of days before the Japanese South Java battle fleet arrived in the Indian Ocean, possibly missing being caught by the carrier planes by one day. Our grapevine was excellent and she knew of our doings. The Black Hawk and DDs had a strong bonding, in fact most personnel had good friends and had served on both. We all had a personal feeling about our ships in this isolated duty and felt differently than the nice new Stateside Fleet. FORD arrived after the fiasco, as the book states.

Later I became an officer and could separate my fo'c's'le thinking for the whole picture. We all knew first hand that Java was lost. It was pure luck that we successfully ran the gauntlet, even heard the finishing salvos and M.Gs over the horizon, for those ships caught. Couldn't think of helping for we were out of torpedoes. With this background, I can remember the bitterness of seeing this beautiful, clean, sleek Cruiser (Phoenix) with her sailors in spotless whites, tied up to the dock. To send her up North, she would have been bombed and shelled to death in 15 minutes, to become another statistic. Resentful yes, but understanding.

I'm enclosing the name and address of the Sec'y of the Black Hawk Organization who was there: Mr. G. H. MASON, 2212-122nd Ave. E, PULYALLUP, WA 98372-1614.

I'm also enclosing a book report on *ANOTHER SIX-HUNDRED* as published in the Naval Academy magazine *SHIPMATE.*

J. Daniel Mullin   C/C/ G. H. Mason

:: :: ::

PHOENIX REUNION IN PORTLAND

<u>August 23, 1993</u>   Alice and I stayed at Patty's Sunday night in Salem and on Monday morning I drove into Portland to the Jantzen Beach Red Lion. I walked into the Red Lion and went to the main desk to inquire about the Phoenix reunion. A lady walked up wearing a Red Lion Jacket so I asked her about the reunion. She told me that it did not start until Thursday and showed me the schedule of the breakfast Thursday morning.

I walked outside, definitely disappointed. I sat down in the car to think about what I might do... Then for some reason I had the idea to go back into the desk and ask if Andy Anderson had checked in yet. A girl at the desk told me that he had. She wasn't allowed to give me his room number but she did dial his room and handed me the phone. Nobody answered. Then she said that he and others were probably down in room 414 – the hospitality room.

I went down to the room and sure enough, there was the Phoenix group. I recognized Andy and went directly to him. He introduced me to C. J. Horn. I knew C. J. from several letters and telephone calls. Already the day was successful.

Later Andy offered me the opportunity to look through the box of pictures that the widow of Ronald J. Erwin, Ship's Photographer, had sent him. I looked at what I estimated to be 500 photos and negatives. I did not locate any that indicated they were taken during Bill's time aboard or any that might have had Bill in them. Although I did not locate any exciting pictures, I felt very fortunate to have had the opportunity to go through all of them. Had I heard about them and not have had the opportunity, I would have always wondered what I was missing. I took several pictures of the Phoenix to the motel desk to have copies made.

I had the opportunity to talk to all of those who came in early. My notes said to write to Louie Dukich asking him for his Pearl Harbor story and the Black Hawk story, to Gerald Wheaton to ask about the Catholic launch and the bulge in the barrel. He also remembered the Black Hawk incident. Also I am to send him the picture that I have of a sailor taken in Chile. Gerald was on that cruise. I had a very nice chat with Harry Rogucki from New Jersey. I had written to him several years ago and received a nice letter back from him at the time.

The box of pictures turned out to be more important than I thought. About 4:30 I went to the main desk to have a letter and a picture copied. When I was returning them to the box Jack Struthers from Aloha, Oregon walked up and asked me about the picture. I introduced myself to him. He immediately started apologizing for not answering the letter he had received from me. He said that he had received my letter, that he knew Bill but had just not gotten around to answering my letter. What had been a very good day now turned into a "super day." I had not thought much about meeting somebody who knew Bill. I thought that I had exhausted all opportunities through the many letters I had written. I just wanted to meet some of the men who were on the Phoenix and perhaps get some new first hand accounts, but to have someone walk up and say that he knew Bill made the trip even more worthwhile.

This was to have been the culminating activity of my research but, rather, I feel that it has opened new doors. I will write more letters, ask Andy for addresses of Argentine officers that he met two years ago, and go through the updated roster which lists all of the Pearl Harbor survivors.

:: :: ::

Louie Dukich   March 11, 1994
Spokane, Washington

Hi, Lew,

It was very nice to meet you at our reunion. Trying to think back almost 53 years about Pearl Harbor is going to test my memory.

I was sixteen years old. I joined the Navy in Dec 40 but they wouldn't take me until I got my mother to sign the papers or closer to my next birthday. Then and during those days, there weren't too many jobs. I had a year to finish high school. Which I finished during my hitch in the Navy.

We did our training at San Diego, Calif for three months. After that I was assigned to the USS Phoenix. I went aboard the USS Platte which was an oil tanker at San Diego. Then to Pearl Harbor.

We went to sea for almost eight months for training. We went to the Philippines Islands and Cebu and did target practice at sea.

We came back Dec. 4 to Pearl Harbor.

Dec. 7 at 7:55 I was getting ready to go on liberty cause I had duty on Saturday. I was down below getting ready to go on liberty. When I heard a loud boom, boom.

I went topside. I saw the Arizona blow up and saw the other battle wagons going up and burning and smoking. We went to our guns. I was a pointer on a 5 inch getting settings from our range finder.

We had to wait till we got our crew back from liberty. We had to take down awnings around our guns and turrets.

We got out of Pearl Harbor around 11:45 and met the St. Louis and DE Blue. We also met the Enterprise carrier and two more destroyers out at sea. We looked for three days but couldn't find any ships at sea. So went back to Pearl and escorted Marimpose back to U. S. – San Francisco. We took a convoy to Dutch Harbor, Alaska. Came back to San Francisco. Then took a convoy to Pearl and back to San Francisco. Then we took a big convoy to Australia to Melbourne in the middle part of Jan. 42.

Then we went to Perth, Aust. Picked up carrier Langley and tanker Pasco and Seawitch to Java. We were half way to Java when we got orders to return to Perth. Three days later we got word they were sunk at Java.

The Black Hawk was in port at Perth. They figured it was our fault they were sunk. They figured we should stay and fight. So Sat. night about 20 got into a fight in Perth. They finally found out that we were not at fault. I think we put quite a few in the hosp. They put us and them on martial law and couldn't go ashore. Our stay at Perth was short. We left Perth for Melbourne and then to Darwin and Port Darwin where we stopped the Japs.

I hope some of this will come in handy with your book. If you need more, please write. Thank you.

Louie Dukich

:: :: ::

Jack D. Struthers   May 4, 1994
Beaverton, OR 97006

Dear Lew:

I'm truly sorry for not writing to you earlier than this but I was looking for a picture of Bill and me and 4 other sailors that were on the PHOENIX but I can't find it. I know I have it some place in a trunk with a lot of other pictures of guys off the PHOENIX.

As I told you at the reunion at the Red Lion here in Portland that I knew Bill. We went ashore several times together.

The first time I went ashore with Bill Holt was in Honolulu in October 1941. He and 4 other guys off the PHOENIX decided that we would rent a car and drive around the island of Oahu. So the six of us pooled our money as that is the only way we could afford a car rental. (REMEMBER WE WERE ONLY GETTING $21.00 PER MONTH.) We needed a sedan and as I remember the car cost us $8.25 for 24 hours. We started out about 11:00 A. M., on a Sunday morning and we did drive around to Likelike highway and then decided that we had better get back to the rental place before dark as we figured that we would never find it in the night time. When we got back to Honolulu the other guys left for a bar. (I BELIEVE IT WAS THE BLACK CAT ACROSS THE STREET FROM THE OLD YMCA.) Bill and I thought that dinner would be great which we did have and then headed back to the ship.

I was in the second division deck force at that time so Bill and I would see each other during the day and we tried to get in the chow line at the same time so we could get to the same table (WE ATE FAMILY STYLE THEN.)

Bill and I got along real well as we both liked the same things and besides we were about the same height. He was always concerned about how his cloths looked and always had a good shine on his shoes. I was the same way and maybe a little more particular about the way my uniform looked and especially my shoes. We seemed to hit it off the first time we met because we liked the same things.

After Pearl Harbor Bill & I didn't see much of each other because I got transferred into the yeoman gang and left the deck force. I was assigned to the gunnery office and I would see Bill once in a while when pay day came as the pay office was next to the gunnery office and Bill would always stick his head in the door and say hi.

After the bombing on that Sunday we finally got underway about 10:00 A.M., and went out to sea.

When we returned we took on a few sailors off some the battleships that got sunk. One of the guys off the Nevada and I seemed to like each other right off and he was in the same division as I was. We started going ashore together. When we arrived in Melbourne, Australia my friend off the Nevada, Bill & I went ashore together and we ended up at a pub called MacIneries. The guy that owned the place made us feel real welcome and kept on chatting with the three of us and kept saying WE ARE GLAD YOU'RE HERE YANKS. We drank some beer and ate oysters on the half shell. As I remember Bill did not go for the oysters. I had to laugh.

Lew, I believe that was the last time I went ashore with Bill Holt. I do remember typing out the transfer papers when the ships doctor said this man has to go to a hospital. Of course I lost track of him once he left the ship and was really surprised to hear that he had passed away in Walla Walla.

Also, Lew, you should be commended for all the effort that you have done over the years to gather information about your brother.

Once again, sorry for the delay in getting this info to you.

Sincerely, Your brother's shipmate,

Jack D. Struthers

:: :: ::

I wrote earlier about Elsie Harber and included several of her letters to Bill. Elsie married Mr. Teerman and had two sons. Elsie died suddenly one night after a short illness, leaving her husband with two little boys. He later remarried. The following is from my journal.

November 1, 1994   I have delayed contacting Mrs. Teerman – not

185

quite knowing how she might take my intrusion. Today as I took my car for a lube and oil change I stopped at her place. (I chose not to call ahead because people get strange calls and are sometimes threatened by them.) The curtains were closed. I rang the doorbell but did not get an answer. I rang again and no answer. I walked to the car and returned to check with the neighbor in the duplex. The curtains were drawn there, too, so I turned back to my car. A voice asked if he might help me. A neighbor of Mrs. Teerman from across the alley walked over and asked what I wanted. I explained to him why I was looking for Mrs. Teerman. After he listened to my story and knew where I was coming from, he volunteered that she was in New Zealand and Australia visiting a stepson. He said that she would be back in a week or two. We talked for sometime about my project. I asked him to mention to Mrs. Teerman that I would be calling her. I will check back later in November.

November 17, 1994   I called Mrs. Teerman today (Mr. Teerman's second wife) to see about stopping by her place for a visit. We ended up talking on the phone for almost thirty minutes. She was very friendly and willing to talk about Elsie. She was intrigued by my call and thanked me several times for the interesting call. She had just returned from visiting her stepson (Elsie's son) in Australia. She told me that the boys were one and three when their mother, Elsie, died. She spoke tenderly of Elsie saying how she had involved the boys in memory of their mother – although she had adopted them after her marriage to Mr. Teerman. They put flowers on their mother's grave. Mrs. Teerman said that her husband, Howard, never spoke of Elsie writing to a sailor but that she had a pen pal in England. She went through all of Howard's stuff after he died. There were no letters from Bill tucked away as I had hoped. It was always my hope that Bill's letters to Elsie might still exist.

Elsie and Howard Teerman had been married 8 years before the first boy was born. When the oldest boy was 3 and the youngest 1 year old, she complained of being tired. The doctor thought perhaps she was tired from having the young family to take care of. One evening when her husband came home Elsie was particularly tired so he took her to the doctor. A neighbor took care of the little boys. They waved good-bye to their mother, never to see her alive again. This time the doctor immediately recognized the symptoms of leukemia and sent her to the hospital.

Howard stayed with her, but left later saying that he would be in to see her in the morning. During the early hours of the morning she had a cerebral hemorrhage and died immediately. Howard called her parents in Dallas during the evening to say that she was in the hospital. He had to call them the next morning to say that she had died during the night. Mrs. Teerman said that Elsie's death was a terrible shock to Howard and Elsie's parents.

One of Howard's brothers in Wisconsin volunteered to take one of the boys but he could not take both. Howard declined. He hired a housekeeper and was able to keep the family together. He married Mrs. Teerman two years later. She said that she had lost her husband through death – there was no divorce involved in either previous marriage, so everybody was open and shared their previous associations.

Naturally, the one-year-old did not remember his mother. The three year old did remember her. He now lives in Nevada and the younger one in Australia. The Nevada son will visit here at Christmas time and she will tell him about his mother's letters to Bill and ask him if wants to read them. The son in Australia will be home for a visit next summer.

:: :: ::

Dallas Itemizer Observer Dallas, Oregon November, 1995

Bill Holt, Dallas High School Class of 1941, joined the Navy and was inducted just a few weeks after graduation. He took his basic training in San Diego and shipped out for Pearl Harbor without the typical leave to come home. He was assigned to the light cruiser, USS Phoenix at Pearl Harbor. After surviving the attack by the Japanese on Dec. 7th the Phoenix later ended up in Australia. Bill contacted tuberculosis in 1943 and was sent back to naval hospitals in California and then died in 1945 in the veteran's hospital in Walla Walla, Washington. Bill did not share any of his wartime experiences with his family. His mother saw him for a few hours just a month before he died. In later years his brother, Lew, began a search to find out about Bill and his ship. Through many books, letters, telephone calls, visits, naval archives and other channels he has compiled over 350 pages of letters, pictures and information and was able to locate men who remembered Bill on the Phoenix. Lew Holt will explain the process and the outcome of his several years of research at the general membership meeting of the Polk County Historical Society and Museum at 1:30 on November 11.

:: :: ::

Chapter Eleven

Rita Barron – Another Serendipity

On November 5, 1995 Alice and I attended a birthday party for an old time fiddler, 89-year-old Jack Smith, in Gresham, Oregon. When Jack introduced his daughter-in-law, Kathy, he mentioned that she would soon be visiting Perth, Australia. Later that afternoon I went to her and introduced myself. I told her about trying to locate people who knew my brother Bill during the war. I told her about my brother having a girlfriend during the war in Perth in 1942. She told me that she was leaving for Perth the next day. I asked her if she might bring back addresses or sources where I might request information and if she could check out the address of Rita Barron. I called her that evening with information that I had from 1942 when Rita wrote to my mother.

:: :: ::

It seemed forever but finally after five weeks, I received the following letter from Kathy when she got back from her trip to Australia.

West Linn, Oregon
Dec. 12th, 1995
Dear Mr. Holt,
Just got back from Perth and had a wonderful time. King St. has now been totally re-modeled so North 40 is not the same.
I am enclosing addresses of the Australian Red Cross which was suggested to me as a good place to trace people. Also, have included clipping from local newspaper that comes out daily. Do hope these 2 can be of help to you with your family history.
Merry Xmas – Happy New Year
Kathy Smith

:: :: ::

Salem, Oregon U.S.A.
December 18, 1995

Letters to the Editor
West Australian Newspapers
Private Bag 54 GPO
Perth, 6001,
Western Australia, Australia

Please publish in the CAN YOU HELP?

Wish to contact: Miss Rita Barron who lived at 40 King St. Perth, West Australia (1942 address). I have letters and pictures from her to my mother, Vintie Holt, who was the mother of S/C 1 Bill Holt who was aboard the USS Phoenix. Bill died later on in the war from tuberculosis. I am trying to locate Miss Barron or any one who knew her and other friends who knew my brother when he was in the U.S. Navy in Australia during 1941 - 1943. Please contact: Lew Holt 1625 19th St. N. E., Salem, Oregon 97303 U. S. A.

Thank you very much.
Sincerely,
Lew Holt

:: :: ::

I did not know when my letter would be printed or if I would get an answer so I had almost of put it out of my mind. One day when I opened the mailbox and saw the stamps from a foreign country, I wondered who I was getting a letter from and then I remembered writing to the newspaper. I opened the letter with great anxiety hoping for an answer from Rita but then I read the too often phrase "unfortunately I can't help you." It is an interesting letter.

:: :: ::

Alexander Heights 6064   January 16, 1996
Perth, Western Australia
Hi Dear Mr. Lew Holt,

I read with great interest your advertise article in our local morning paper about the USS PHOENIX.

I am very sorry to hear about your brother Bill as many young men died in the war, unfortunately I can not help you in your request regarding the friends of your brother Bill in Western Australia.

But you may be able to help me in my quest for many years, regarding a young sailor called Ray Earlin Sutherland or (Sullivan) who was on the USS PHOENIX.

He was approximately 5'9" tall, slightly built and would be now age 71 or 72 years old. He was at Pearl Harbour on another ship, (I'm afraid I can't remember name of ship) which was sunk in the Japanese attack. He came to Port Fremantle and was on leave in Perth.

In Perth we had what you would call a stage door canteen for servicemen and all servicemen in allied service. I have three sisters who did volunteer work there and they invited Roy to our home in a town called Bassendean, it was approximately 10 miles on the Railway from Perth Station, which is also famous for the home of Roy Harris, the world famous entertainer. Roy use to come to our home every weekend for meals and some times stay the whole weekend.

My late Mother & Father looked after Ray like a son. When he went back to leave with the Phoenix we lost all contact with him, but I hope you just may know of him and hopefully he survived the war.

We have followed with interest the USS PHOENIX whenever able and saw where it was sold to Argentina and renamed the Belgrano, and was sunk by a British submarine during the Falklands War.

I am 67 years old, was too young to go the war; also have 2 younger brothers.

If you and your family ever come to Australia, you are most welcome to visit us anytime. We have a saying here in Australia, the kettle is always boiling for a nice chat and a nice cup of tea. Hoping you can throw some light on the matter and let us know if Roy did survive and is still well.

My wife and I were sorry to hear of the death of your brother. My wife will write this letter for me as my hand is a bit shaky. Happy New Year to you and family.
I remain
Yours sincerely,
Kath & Campbell Craig

:: :: ::

January 17, 1996
Alexander Heights
Perth, Western Australia
Dear Kath & Campbell Craig,
What a thrill it was to receive your letter. Now, hopefully, I will receive others with information or seeking information as you are doing.

Checking the muster roll of the USS Phoenix for March 31st, 1942 I find Roy E. Sutherland listed. He was assigned to the Phoenix on December 10th, which gives validity to your statement that his ship was damaged during the attack and that he was then assigned a few days later to the Phoenix. And then I again find his name listed for March 31, 1945 which indicates that he served aboard the Phoenix for the duration of the war. This hopefully indicates that he survived the war. The Phoenix lost only one man because of war injuries when a bomb exploded in the water near the Phoenix. Shrapnel from this bomb killed him. I have no way of knowing how many died from disease and other causes.

I have written to Andy Wilson, President of the Phoenix Association, asking him if he has any information regarding Roy (not Ray). The Phoenix Association Roster does not list Roy Sutherland as a member. Either he chooses not to join, does not know about the association, or is deceased. Perhaps Andy can answer our questions. I have visited Andy who lives about 3 hours from me. We go to Seattle (220 miles) to visit our son. Andy lives in a little town (Vader) just a few miles off the interstate highway. When he answers my letter, I will notify you immediately of his answers. I find this a great challenge.

I will, also, write to the Pearl Harbor Survivors Association asking if they have any record of Roy or if they have any suggestions for locating him. There are several other sources that I will seek if need be. (Military records, census, etc.)

I don't suppose you remember his home town or home state. Let me know if you do.

Both of our interests of course go back over 50 years – certainly a difficult situation. Time is a factor. We cannot put off seeking our answers too long. In a few years it will be too late. I have already lost sources of information by "father time."

Campbell, I will be 67 in April so we are close in age. I, too, was too young to serve in the war but I was very involved – my brother Bill was at Pearl Harbor, took ill in January of 43 in the Coral Sea, transferred to Townsville, to USA and then died in February of 45. I had another older brother serving in the infantry in Europe and was wounded two times. My mother was widowed in 1939 leaving her with four young sons. Our father was killed in a logging accident.

I have been researching my brother Bill for several years... I received many letters in return – eventually hearing from 4 men who remembered Bill. I read every book that I could find that mentioned the Phoenix and if sailors were mentioned I wrote to them...

I have entered all of Bill's letters written to us at home into the computer as I have the letters to him that he had saved, the many letters from Phoenix veterans, history of the Phoenix, newspaper articles, sections from books and many other bits of information. I have about 350 pages and almost 2/3rds of a million words. It has been a time consuming project which I have enjoyed very much. Your letter is now one of those important letters because you knew of the Phoenix. Perhaps you can relate other stories of the Phoenix to me.

Now I am seeking a "girl friend" in Perth...

I have written to Argentine sailors...

My wife, Alice, and I appreciate your invitation. How tempting. I told my daughter about it and she said, "Let's go, Dad." It isn't that simple so don't put the water on, yet...

I look forward to more letters from you. I will share some of my material with you in my future letters.

Thanks again for your letter.

I remain,

Lew Holt

:: :: ::

February 20, 1996   (From my journal) December 18, 1995 I
wrote to the newspaper in Perth, Western Australia asking for Rita
Barron, a girlfriend of Bill's, or wanting to hear from anybody who
might have known her. Today was probably the peak of my dreams in
my search for information. My wife and I have been receiving many
letters for fiddle membership so I wasn't too impressed by a stack
of letters in the mailbox. But when I sorted through them, I was
pleased to see two letters with Australian stamps. One did not have a
return address but when I turned the second one over, there was the
return address for Rita (Barron) Warrilow – the very person I had been
hoping to find someday. When I wrote my letter to the newspaper in
Perth, I hoped of course to find Rita but I have had so many failures in
my searching, I was not too optimistic. After I had received the letter
from Kathy and Campbell Craig from Perth asking me to help them
find Roy Sutherland who served aboard the Phoenix, I knew that my
request for information had been printed. I carefully checked the mail
every day for several days. As time passed I became less optimistic so
receiving the letter from Rita was a thrill.

When we dropped Bill off at the Guthrie School that June day 1941
and turned towards Monmouth to pick berries, we did not realize that
Arlie and I would never see him alive again. After the attack on Pearl
Harbor his letters became very generic with no details of what he was
doing or where he was. This did not concern us too much at the time
but after he died and as I grew older and more curious about his life,
this left a tremendous void.

Rita Barron wrote to Mom in March 1942, telling her that she knew
Bill and that he was happy and safe. She also sent pictures of Bill
and her. Kathy Smith from West Linn, Oregon, upon her return in
November from a visit to Perth, Western Australia gave me an address

of a newspaper in Perth.

After writing to the newspaper in Perth I went on with my life – really not anticipating a letter from Australia. Fifty four years after receiving the letters and pictures from Rita Barron in Australia, I had an answer to my request in the Perth newspaper. A dream had come true. The following letters are the results of that request for information.

:: :: ::

Rita (Barron) Warrilow
Rivervale
Western Australia
11 - 2 - 96   (February 2, 1996)
Dear Lew,
Sorry to take so long in responding to your information request in our newspaper. I am the Rita Barron who worked at the clothing factory at 40 King Street Perth back in 1942. I was about 20 at the time. I recall Bill became part of our social group for about 6 months. It was such a long time ago and my memory is a bit vague but I certainly recall he was a fine looking lad and a lovely natured fellow as well. Bill had given me photos which I thought his mother would like so I forwarded them on to her. I don't know the where abouts of the rest of the group. Was sorry to hear Bill died so young.

Kind regards,
Rita

:: :: ::

(The other letter that I received the same day on February 20, 1996)

10-2-1996   (February 2, 1996)
Western Australia
Dear Mr. Holt,
I am writing this on behalf of my sister-in-law, Rita Barron, who now is Mrs. Rita Warrilow. In answer to your request in our Western

Australia newspaper.

Rita would have answered, her eye sight is not the best, has had a lot of trouble with them for some time.

She remembered Bill, in 1943 Rita had her 21st birthday they, with some others celebrated it. (Bill was in the Coral Sea in January of 43 when he became ill and was transferred from the Phoenix to the Army Hospital in Townsville, Australia so would not have attended Rita's 21st birthday celebration.)

Rita knew Bill for about six months, they went around together. She didn't live in King St – that was where she worked doing sewing for service men.

She remembers writing one letter to Vintie Holt and sending some photos she thinks. Doesn't remember getting a letter – a letter back.

It was my daughter, who saw the request in the paper, rang me, and told me. I in turn told Rita, as she doesn't get a paper. She was very sorry to hear what happened to Bill. She calls him Billy.

Rita can't remember much else about that time. She will be 74 this year. Is now a widow.

If you wish to write to Rita, someone here can read the letter to her and even answer it for her.

Sorry for the delay in writing. I don't see Rita often. When I did, she was worried because she hadn't answered so I said I would for her. Rivervale is a suburb of Perth, Western Australia. Mandurah is south of Perth about 52 miles.

Yours sincerely,
Rita's sister-in-law
Mrs. Joy Barron
Western Australia

:: :: ::

Rita & Mervyn 1966　　　　　　*Rita and Grandchild 1996*

Rita and Bill　　*Australia – 1942*　　*Rita*

:: :: ::

The same afternoon when Alice and I returned from playing fiddle music in a church in downtown Salem, there was a message on the answering machine. It said: "My name is Linda Vaughn. I lived in Perth, Western Australia. I received a letter from my sister-in-law saying that you were looking for information."

I called Linda Vaughn immediately but her line was busy. Alice and I had to leave in a few minutes, so I wasn't able to return her call until that evening. I called her home and a child answered the phone. I asked for Linda. I heard the child calling "Grandma" to the phone. Linda came to the phone and was very anxious to talk to me and to share her story.

Linda told me that she had lived in Perth but that she didn't know my brother. She was a war bride from Perth but maybe her husband had known Bill. He was in Perth for 5 years and was on the submarine Kingfisher. She had lost her husband in 1989 from cancer. He would have been 72 this April. She had also lost her brother in Australia just last Saturday. He and his wife had been here in Salem a year and a half ago. Her sister-in-law in Perth had seen my request in the paper and had sent it to Linda because her sister-in-law read that I, also, lived in Salem, Linda lived in Salem and they had visited in Salem.

Linda said that she would be 70 in 1997 and that she had planned to go back to Australia to celebrate – that her birthday was also in April as was her husband's. I commented that mine was also in April. We compared dates and were pleased to find that both of our birthdays are on April 11. We enjoyed the coincidence.

Linda now lives with her son, Mike, daughter-in-law, Mariana and granddaughter, Rebecca in south Salem. Her daughter Candice and son-in-law, Carl, live in Phoenix Arizona.

Linda and her husband were married when Linda was 18 and he was 21. They came to the U.S. when she was 19. He was originally from Texas but they lived in Salinas, CA for many years. After he died she felt insecure living in a neighborhood of violence and drugs so she moved to Salem – building a place for her to live above her son's house – to get around building codes.

She typically returns to Australia every other year. At first she and her husband went to Australia at Christmas time but it was too hot so they changed to later in the fall in Australia. (May - July in U.S.)

The last time she went she took her grand daughter Rebecca. What an adventure for a little girl.

I asked her if I might have the print from the paper or at least a copy of it. We will get together in the future for a "cup of tea" and a chance to share our stories about WWII and American service boys in her area in Australia.

Truly a day I will always remember and cherish.

:: :: ::

Salem, Oregon   Rita (Barron) Warrilow
February 22, 1996   Rivervale 6103
                       Western Australia

Dear Rita,

You can't imagine what a thrill it was to me to receive your letter. You have been a part of our family conversations over the many years since the USS Phoenix was stationed at Fremantle. My mother, Vintie Holt, was a great saver of letters and pictures. Tucked in among Bill's things were the letter and pictures from you. My mother has had a picture of you and Bill on display for many years in her home. We knew that you were just friends but it represented a period of time in Bill's life that we knew nothing about.

My mother passed away in 1988 at 89. About that time I became curious about the time after Bill left home to join the Navy. I started writing many letters to research Bill's life in the Navy. Bill joined the Navy in June of 1941 just before he turned 18. The morning he left for the Navy we rode with a neighbor 4 miles towards town. We dropped him off and left the main highway and went to a berry field to work. He hitch hiked on into town to the Naval recruiter. We did not realized that morning that our mother would only see him for a few hours during her visit in January before he died on Feb. 6, 1945 and that my brother and I would never see him alive again. We were 11 and 12 years old when he joined the Navy.

On Dec. 7, 1941 a neighbor came to our house to tell us that Pearl Harbor had been attacked. In our rural home we did not have electricity or a radio at that time. Several weeks later we received a short note from Bill saying that he was OK. From then on his letters were very few and short and when we did receive one, it didn't say anything about what he was doing.

Your letter to us was written on 8th of March, 1942. It was the first we knew where Bill was so it was very much appreciated. You can't imagine the excitement it caused in our home. I remember it very well. This is why 54 years later I am writing to you. I never, ever, thought that we would have an opportunity to express our appreciation to you personally for writing to us.

Bill was in the Coral Sea in January of 43 when he became ill. I have a letter from the sailor who diagnosed his illness, who put him on a destroyer, took him to Townsville and checked him into an Army Hospital. Out of the hundreds of letters that I have written, I have found 4 men that remembered Bill. Their letters, too, have allowed me to know more about the war years when we did not know where Bill was or what he was doing.

In March of 1943 Bill was sent to the U.S. and was at two Naval Hospitals in California until November of 1944 when he was discharged and sent to a veteran's hospital in Walla Walla, Washington. When we received a telegram that he was seriously ill, our mother went to see him. She was only allowed to see him for a few hours. Less than a month later he died.

I have typed into my computer all of Bill's letters that he wrote home, my mother's letters to him that he saved, other letters to him and many letters from men who were on the Phoenix. Many of their letters told about the Phoenix during those early war years but most men did not remember Bill which was not unexpected when a ship had a 1000 men all dressed in white. The sailors for the most part were confined to their part of the ship and only knew those who they were in contact with. When I finish my research I will have an interesting account of Bill's Navy life for my family.

The same day that I received your letter I received a telephone call from a lady, Linda Vaughn, who now lives in Salem but who grew up in Perth and married a sailor from the submarine, Kingfisher. She did not know Bill. She had received my request from the newspaper in Perth from her sister-in-law who lives near Perth. The sister-in-law had visited here in Salem a year and a half ago. I thought it was interesting that I would receive your letter and her call the same day. Her husband died 5 years ago and she moved here to be with her son and his family. We discovered that we both have the same birthday, April 11. She is two years older than I am. My wife, Alice, and I want to visit with her one of these afternoons for tea.

My wife and I both play the fiddle. Last November we attended a birthday party for an 89-year-old fiddler. During the celebration he introduced his family and mentioned that his daughter-in-law was from Perth. I introduced myself to her and told her of my interest in the area and my desire to try to locate you. She told me that she was going to Perth the next day and that when she returned a month later, she would bring me addresses of places to write. She brought me the address of the Perth newspaper and one of the columns out of the paper. I wrote December 18th. Later I received a letter from Perth, I thought it might be a letter from you. It was from a man whose family had a young sailor from the Phoenix come to their place on week-ends. When the Phoenix left, they never heard from him again and often wondered about him. He asked if I might know of the sailor's whereabouts. Since then I have tried to locate him but no luck yet. I have information about many Phoenix sailors but nothing about him. I am still trying to locate him. I know that he, Roy Sutherland, went aboard the Phoenix on Dec. 10 and that he was still on the Phoenix in 1945. It indicated that he made it through the war ok but that is all I know about him.

I am enclosing pictures that you may have forgotten about. I feel that I must apologize to you for being so personal as to ask you to share with me stories from so many years ago. I hope that I do not offend you but rather that I will give you an opportunity to remember those days of 54 years ago. If you would, please, I would like to hear from you again and would appreciate any memories that you would care to share with me. It adds so much to my story of Bill and those years that we did not see him. I might suggest the following questions – Do you remember when you first saw the Phoenix? (If you did.) How did the war affect your life? Did you have brothers in the service? Did you fear that the Japanese might bomb Perth?

Again I want to express my appreciation for you writing to me. It means so much to my family and me. I want to express that I hope that I have not become too personal and that I am not treading in an area where I shouldn't be. I found more pictures than I had remembered so I am sharing them with you. You have lived your life for the last 54 years. I hope that you don't mind me reminding you of the time when my brother was in your social circle. Thank you for your patience.

I remain you friend,

Lew Holt

:: :: ::

February 24, 1996   This was very interesting day. I stopped by the LDS Church this morning and made an appointment to use its computer Monday to search the Social Security records for Roy E. Sutherland. This afternoon I went to the Salem City Library and used the CD-rom telephone directory. I found 20 or so Roy Sutherlands and specifically found 4 Roy E. Sutherlands. I made notes of addresses and telephone numbers. (In 1996 telephone numbers were on CDs at libraries. Just a few years later the information was made available on my computer.)

When I got back home, rather than writing letters and waiting for answers, I decided to make telephone calls. I called the first Roy E. Sutherland, who lives in Cassville, Missouri. Mrs. Sutherland answered the phone. I hesitated asking to speak to a Phoenix veteran. On several occasions I was talking to the widow. I asked her if Mr. Sutherland was in the Navy during World War II. She said that he was and asked if I wanted to talk to him. When he came to the phone I asked him if he was on the USS Phoenix. He said that he had been on the Phoenix so I knew I had the right person. One telephone call and I was talking to the man I had been trying to locate for the Campbell Craig family in Perth, Australia.

I told him my name and why I was calling. He did not remember Bill. He asked me the name of the people in Australia who were asking about him. I hurried upstairs to get the letter and then I read it to him. He didn't remember their name or exactly remember the family. After we had talked for some time, I asked him if I might give his name to the Craigs in Australia and he said that it would be fine. He thanked me for calling and genuinely appreciated my call.

Bill had a book (*My Record of Friends in Service*) which was a log of service friends. Many men and nurses had written in it when he was in the hospital in Corona, California. I chose one name of a veteran who had been on the Phoenix and was in the same ward as Bill. I found his name in New York State and his address in the memory book was also New York State. I called the Jos. E. Thyroff residence in Pittsford, N.Y. A lady answered the phone. I asked her if Mr. Thyroff had been in the Navy during World War II. She said that her husband's father had been but that he was dead. She asked if I wanted to talk to his son. The son, Joe, came to the phone. I explained to him that his father had served on the USS Phoenix with my brother and was in the same ward at the Oak Knoll Naval Hospital as Bill. I asked if his father had tuberculosis, too. He did have and was afflicted by it all of his life. He died when he was 67. He must have been older than Bill because the records indicate that he first went aboard the Phoenix in 1938. Joe was very pleasant to talk to. He was very pleased to talk to me about his father and encouraged me to write to him. I told him that I would send him a copy of his father's note to Bill.

"Joseph E. Thyroff G.M. 2/c 23-10 Jackson Ave. Long Island City, N. Y. September 30, 1943 USS Phoenix We sure came a long way together & we've got plenty of miles ahead. Best of luck always."

Muster Roll of Crew USS Phoenix for the quarter March 31, 1942

	Name	Service Nr	Rate	Date of Enlistment	Rcvd on Phoenix
861	THYROFF, Joseph E.	223 43 17	G.M.2c.	21 Mar 42	10/3/38
833	SUTHERLAND, Roy E.	356 46 97	Sea.1c.	15 Jan 41	12/10/41

:: :: ::

February 24, 1996
Perth, Western Australia

Dear Kath & Campbell Craig,

I have had an exciting week. Last Tuesday I received a letter from Rita (Barron) Warrilow who lives in Rivervale and also one from her sister-in-law who lives in Mandurah. (It was her daughter who found my request in the paper.) The letter from Rita was a fulfillment of a dream. And then that same afternoon I had a telephone call from a lady here in Salem who had grown up in Perth, married an American sailor and has lived in the U.S. since she was 19. She did not know my brother but had received the article from the Perth newspaper from her sister-in-law. We had a very pleasant chat.

I wrote to the Phoenix Association and my request for information regarding Roy E. Sutherland was published in their last newsletter but no results. I wrote to the PEARL HARBOR SURVIVORS ASSOCIATION and they knew nothing about him. This morning I stopped at the LDS church which has many records and knowledge of how to find information about people. I made an appointment to use their computer Monday to check social security records.

This afternoon I went to our city library and used a CD and a computer. The CD has all of the telephone numbers in the U.S. I looked up Roy in all four regions of the U.S. I found perhaps 20 or more and 4 Roy E., so when I came home I called the first one. (Missouri in the central part of the U. S.) I asked the lady who answered if her husband had been in the navy in WWII. She said that he had been. When her husband came to the phone I asked him if he had served aboard the U.S. Phoenix and he said that he had. I had found the Roy E. Sutherland that you wanted. I explained why I was calling.

We had a very pleasant conversation. I read your letter to him. He couldn't remember your name and was a little vague about the events. I asked him if I might give you his name and address and he said that he didn't mind. He was pleased to get my call and pleased that you should ask about him. I would encourage you to remind him of what you did on the weekends, the members of your family, about your house, the area around your house, where you lived and any experiences that might re-kindle his memory about 54 years ago.

Lots of luck. I hope to hear from you again.   Roy E. Sutherland
Your friend,   Cassville, MO.

Lew

:: :: ::

February 27, 1996   The last several days have added a new dimension to my research. In Bill's material there was a memory book with names, addresses, comments of men and women he met while in the hospital. The material was old and perhaps not applicable but with the excitement of finding Rita in Australia and Roy E. Sutherland in Missouri, I figured it was time to search out these names. I went to the Salem Library to use the CD-rom and computer to find names and telephone numbers of men who were in the hospital with Bill both at Oak Knoll and at Corona, California.

I knew that locating some would be very difficult. I went to the library on Saturday, the 24th and spent more than an hour searching.

Monday I went back to search further. I searched the Central, Midwest, Northeast and Southern regions but was unable to get access to the Western region. That evening I called Bruce Copper in Charles City, Iowa. I had the name of B. Copper in Charles City so I thought I had my person but it was not. He suggested his Uncle Bob who lived in Marion, Iowa. This evening I called him but he was not the B. Copper I was looking for. We had a nice visit. He took my telephone number and was going to do some searching. I called several others but they were not home. Others were not worth the try in that there might be many, many names all the same. Some there were no listings under the name I was searching for. I was surprised that a name as common as "Clarence Smith" was successful. If I were desperate, I would write or call the 10 "Jack M. Davis's but none of the names are listed near the home address in the memory book.

Today I went to the library to look up the names in the Western region. This evening I called a Russell Gass but he was not the one I was looking for. I called Clarence Smith in Salt Lake City and talked to his widow. I had found the right name but he had died at 66 of a heart attack. I called a Glen L Flock but again the wrong person. I called R.M. Hill in Kirkland, WA, the wrong person. Finally I called Ralph Brown in South Bend, IN. I was optimistic about this one, since the name and the town were the same as in the memory book. I found the correct man. He had been at the same hospital as Bill and had signed the book. He was not a patient at the hospital – rather a corpsman who was on duty there. He was not too involved with the patients and did not remember Bill. I am to write to him and will send pictures of Bill.

:: :: ::

February 29, 1996   The West Australian Newspaper Limited
Salem, Oregon 97303   Box D162 GPO
                                       Perth 6001, West Australia

Dear Mr. Holt,

We are happy to advise that your request for the Can you Help? column was published on Jan. 8.

We are interested to hear whether your inquiry met with success.

Yours sincerely,

(Mrs) JENNY KOHLEN

Compiler

CAN YOU HELP? COLUMN

:: :: ::

Mrs. Joy Barron
Western Australia
21 - 3 - 1996   (March 21, 1996)
Dear Lew and Alice,

I was very pleased to receive your letter, glad Rita decided to write to you. I must have changed her mind. She did ring and tell me that she had heard from you. She was very excited, gave her quite a lift. Also, brought back the memories of that time for her, which was great.

I must try and see Rita soon. We don't have a car so to see Rita, it is to catch three busses to get to her place and three to get back home – all day traveling.

A bit about myself. Mervyn is my husband's name. He is retired after 34 years in the same job. Has been retired for 11 years. Was in the army. Joined up at the age of 16 years. Was in Darwin, North Australia when the Japs bombed Australia. Was also at Rottnest – an island out from Fremantle. He didn't go overseas. He does get a service pension as Darwin and Rottnest were classed as War Zones.

We have lived in Mandurah for 45 years in May. Before that I was born Fremantle. Lived at a place called Bibra Lake. I met Merv there, as there was a search-light camp at the bottom of our farm (poultry and vegetables). I was quite young then. Later we married. Have our fifty anniversary on the 28th of June, 1996. Have one son then two daughters Lynn and Margaret, 9 grand, two great grand sons.

I have one sister, Mary. Two brothers all younger than me. Bill I haven't seen since our father died in 1991. Bob the other brother is 16 years younger than me. They all live in Mandurah except Bill and my daughter Margaret. Bob is a crayfisherman so is my son Ken. They are not happy unless they are wave walking. They are both skippers of boats.

My mother died in 1967 at the age of 60 years.

Wartime we didn't have electricity at first. Later Dad got a generator which allowed us two lights. We did have a radio which everyone in the neighborhood would come and listen to the BBC News and the cricket.

I lived with my grandmother, Dad's mother after grandfather died in 1938. After five years gran got sick. We went back home to Mum's and Dad, gran died Xmas 1943.

Your birthday is in April. Mine is the 19th and Margaret is the 28th. Mandurah use to be a lovely place to live in a seaside town. Not anymore. Was only a small lot of people and about 800 cars. Now buildings everywhere, houses, all our lovely bush has gone. In its place is concrete. They have gone mad with shops and the crime rate is shocking not safe any more. I use to write to several people in the USA. They have passed on.

I am very interested in doing up our family tree. Found a few surprises there. My maiden name was Stone. The great G grand father came out to Western Australia in 1829 from Lunbridge Wells, England. He was the Registrar Clerk and Master of the Supreme Court. He also was an attorney, a solicitor in England.

He was also the keeper of records such as births, marriage and death in Western Australia in the very early days.

I am a fourth generation born in WA on my father's side. Dad's grandfather's wife goes back to a First Fleeter who came out with the first ship to land in 1788 where Sydney now is. He was a marine on the ship "Friendship." He later went over to Norfolk Island. Married there to a convict lady had two children. 1796 they came back to Sydney. Their daughter Elizabeth married a James Kelly. They went to Tasmania where their daughter Sophia married a Henry Ashton from England. Henry and Sophia came to WA. Their daughter married Dad's grandfather, a William Alfred Stone. I might add, first born in the Stone family were boys until I turned up. I might add, I upset the apple cart. I broke the tradition, not very popular.

My mother's father came out to the Eastern part of Australia on a sailing ship which he was a seaman. He came from Brazil about 1888-9. Nothing is known of him. We are not sure of the spelling of the sir name. I have tried through the shipping discharges. No luck. All it says is South America. Even his naturalization papers have South America. Rio Grande. Not North, not South, has been said he came from a place called Oporto, others say Olindo. I guess I (will) never know.

Have one Irish great-grand parent on Mother's side. One G.G. Grand from Scotland, father's side.

I have been to Norfolk Island, went with my sister last year seven nights, eight days. We both enjoyed it. Rita's and Merv's ancestors came out in 1829 to WA. Edward Barron was a Color sergeant of 63rd Regiment. Later he was a policeman. His son Edward Georgie Barron was Rita and Merv's grandfather. Their father was Robert James Barron who was married twice. First wife died. Married again Merv and Rita are from the second family. Edward Barron and his wife came from England.

I think Edward was born in Ireland haven't been able to find out. It would be (in) a church record. I don't know what Parish. Hope I haven't bored you to tears about my ancestors. I could write a book on them.

My sister has been to America. Her daughter was over there last year on a holiday.

I am a very keen gardener. Have lots of hanging baskets and pot plants, also have Paws-Paws, Bananas, two kinds, many shrubs, roses, love growing unusual plants.

Photo enclosed of Merv and me. Taken in 1994 at Lynn's place. We are the first two. The others are my son-in-law's father and step-mother.

A couple of post cards. One of King's Park, Perth, our Christmas tree. The other is Fremantle.

I could have seen the Phoenix when I lived with gran. We were on a hill, which was about four miles from Fremantle. Could see Gages Roads. I use to go have a look nearly every day. I remember the "Queen Mary" being there as a troop ship. Merv was on Rottnest when the "Sydney" sailed. Was never seen again.

Sorry the letter is a bit messy. I have arthritis in my hands. I tend to scribble.

Hope all is well with you and Alice.

With best regards,

Joy Barron

Thanks for the stamps on letter.

:: :: ::

4 - 14 - 96   (April 14, 1996)   (Post card)
Dear Lew and Alice,

I was delighted to get your letter and photos. It brought back many wonderful memories. Will be writing a longer letter shortly. I will be telling you of my last 54 years in my letter and hope to be able to send some pictures of Fremantle and Perth in the war years and as it is now. Always thinking of you.

Rita (Barron) Warrilow

:: :: ::

Many interesting letters have been exchanged with Joy Barron, Rita's sister-in-law over the years that followed but because of space, I will not include them all.

:: :: ::

Rita Barron Warrilow   Received May 28, 1996
Riverdale
West Australia
Dear Lew and Alice,

Was very good to hear from you both & your grandson. What flowers are in the back ground? It looks so lovely. I don't mind you asking about my life 54 years ago. I still remember the memories when Bill was with me & my friends. I feel proud to know your brother still has the photo on display. When I show my friends the photos of Bill and me, they say you weren't too bad then. You can't stay youthful all the years of your life. I must tell you my mother met Bill. I didn't live at home as it was so far out of Perth to get to work. I used to stay with friends. A place called East Perth, could walk into Perth so Bill was always with me, so he didn't have to go back to his ship every night, that's why we could go so many places during his stay.

I can't remember seeing the Phoenix during the war time. It would have been anchored just outside the harbour in what was called Gage Rd but today the ships do come in & some are opened to the public & of course there's always lots of girls waiting to pick-up sailors.

I had several brothers, one was killed in Crete, World War 2. Some of my other brothers were in the armed forces but didn't go to the war zones. I had several friends & relations that went to the island. My nephew went to Vietnam twice. He had his 21st birthday there & he's still in the Army for another 3 years.

Lew you must know all that happens in Australia as we do get the news from America & London so we know what goes on. Australia was a very good place. Hundreds of tourist & migrants settled here now one isn't safe to go places at night & during the day at times. There are so many people without a job & drugs are always plenty things so of course it comes down to robbing people.

I was married for 47 yrs & had 5 children. Own my own home & live alone which I don't like. My home is secured, it has to be like that.

My eldest son is a proffalish fisherman. Has his own boat. He is down the south of Perth so he doesn't get to Perth too often. He & his partner have built their own house a beautiful place. My son is what they called is a greenie. He doesn't like trees being cut down & forests getting cleared. My eldest daughter lives in the country. She doesn't come to Perth often. She had 3 adult children, but she looks after 2 little boys which are both retarded & need a lot of attention. My 2 other sons went on a working holiday & stayed 13 yrs. I lost one son 3 yrs ago (with aids) & the youngest one had a job with British Actors Equity for 12 years. Now he's got a job in Sydney. Got recommended by his London job. He has people under him. He also does voluntary work helping with aids suffers, he has been trained to help people that need advice. My youngest daughter 41 in August has 3 beautiful children & is expecting her 4th next month. One is 7, 5, & 3. She also works 3 days a week. She's a dental receptionist, her husband works in the main roads office but he doesn't think home duties are his affairs.

I live about 4 KM from the city and I'm close to the Domestic & International Airport, gets a bit noisy at time, always know when there's a ship in – the helicopters fly continuously to the airport to pick up mail, etc.

I have 2 nieces that live in America, one in San Diego & the other one is on a farm in California. I used to get a call from a lass in Seattle,

Washington. She was a friend of my sons. She married a doctor doing physics work but she has come back to Australia to live, she rings me at times. My son that is in Sydney went to America & other countries. When he was in England he (went) to Disneyland & other places.

We have had some rain which was needed. (It's winter here.) I used to do all my gardening but am unable to do it now so all my bulbs & pansies are in pots so I can just watch them grow.

My health isn't that good. I am a diabetic & my eyes aren't that good & I have to have a walking stick when I walk. Last year I had a bad fall pulling up a few weeds & fell & struck my left elbow on the concrete floor & dislocated my elbow. I got over that and 2 weeks ago I had another fall but didn't do any damage to any limbs just shocked me. I don't want to give my home up & go into any hospital for the old folks. I can get all the help I need. I have a cleaning lady once a fortnight & a person comes twice see me when I shower. My eldest son took out my bath & put a shower recess in which I can shower myself as I have bars to hold on to.

I must tell you about my 3 yr old grandson. My friend knitted him a sailor boy. We named him Bill & when he sees a boat he says that's my Bill's boat.

I do hope you can read my writing. Regarding the mistakes I have new glasses that do help. I wished I could do more things that I used to do. I can crochet rugs. I used to teach crafts & have classes. I even used to teach some men in a local hospital near where I live to do macramé & they used to try knitting & crotchet. Better than just sitting doing nothing.

In 1942 Jap subs were spotted just outside Fremantle 16 miles at a place called Rottenest but they didn't do any damage. When they left there was a war ship sunk. Some say it was the Japs & some say Germans. The Japs did attack Darwin & Broome that's up the north from here. We had air raid shelters in Perth & did have black outs and used to have to go into the shelter till the all clear went.

I do hope you both don't think my letter is so hickly pickly but I will send you some photos later on and hope you will write again and that I haven't bored you both. Kind of you both to go down to

Alice's mothers. Does she look after herself? I have never driven a car only rode my bike everywhere. I used to keep fit and have done Tai Chi. I taught keep fit for 8 weeks while our teacher took a holiday to Belgium. I used to belong to several clubs but it's funny once you drop out nobody comes to see you. Never mind I did all I could to help people. I lost my husband 9 years ago. Well I will close now hope I'll hear from you in the future.

I remain your friend,

Rita

I forgot to tell you when Bill left Australia when he left I went to Fremantle with him at night. I didn't hear from him again but as he went to the Coral Sea where he took ill he was taken to Townsville which is another Eastern State where the Army was stationed. If he was brought back to West Australia, I perhaps would have found out, no use thinking what could have been. Tell me where is he laid to rest. Take care.

Love to hear from you both.

Rita

Chapter Twelve

The Numbers are Becoming Smaller

Late in March, 1996, I wrote to several men who were on the Phoenix that remembered Bill requesting their pictures. I thought that their pictures would make the men and their letters more meaningful. I received my first reply on August 8, 1996.

July 14, 1996   (Mrs. Sam Bailey)
                       (Cary, NC)

Dear Lew,

I just reread your letter to Sam written on April 3, 1996. Sorry I haven't answered sooner. Sam passed away on Father's Day June 18, 1995. He was ready to go. All our children were there from Wash. State, Boston, Mass & Atlanta, Ga and Roger from local – Knightdale, N.C. I miss him so much but accepting it. He died of kidney cancer – refused chemo or radiation. He bowled with his team 2nd week in May and died on June 18. Happy and is in the arms of Jesus who cared for him thru the war and all his life. Sam was 77 yrs old when he died.

I've got to find it but I made a copy of Sam as a chief & also the Phoenix steaming out of the bay, received the picture from the Australian newspaper. I'm going to enclose them before I mail this hope I can find it. Thank you for your letters. I'm so glad you've heard from the people.

May God bless you & yours. I'm going thru letters, etc., that we hadn't looked at for years – it's just a little tough.

God's blessing.

Sam's wife

Carmelita S. Bailey

:: :: ::

September 29, 1996 Sunday

I am entering this little story of today because an experience brought meaning to a June day 1941 and centered in on what I believe to be only a little incident in the story of Bill but to me has some of the greatest impact and perhaps a feeling of guilt 56 years after Bill left to go to the Navy. Today Alice and I went to Guthrie which was the little old gymnasium of the Guthrie School four miles south of Dallas, Oregon. The one room country school house is long gone and the gym has been converted to a community center. It now serves many people – especially in folk music. Today we played music and celebrated the 50th anniversary for our friends, Lew and Jean Standiford.

Early in the afternoon I went to my car to get my fiddle and stopped to talk to Jean. I told her that 56 years ago that we drove down the highway with Mrs. Harvey in her Model A Ford and turned on to the Guthrie Road "right over there." It was an emotional moment for me but I was able to finish my story. I continued – We dropped Bill off, waved "good-bye" and drove on to the berry patch to work. Bill hitchhiked into Dallas and Salem where he went to the Navy recruiting office, on to Portland and then by train to San Diego and basic training. I wondered what Mama thought about that day as she picked berries and that evening when we sat down to "supper." She must have thought of the separation but, of course not about Pearl Harbor, Australia, tuberculosis and still later his death in Walla Walla. I don't know how we could have said good-bye any differently. Those were the times and our lives and the way we lived.

As Jean and I talked she, told me that yesterday she and Lew visited the grave of their son who had died last winter. It was his birthday. It was an especially sad day for them. We stood there in silence, each with our own sorrow.

I told my story to several people that afternoon. It weighed heavily on my mind. I have driven around that curve in the road and the Guthrie Road that leads off it many times but it never had the meaning that it did today as I stood there looking back to June 16, 1941, over 56 years ago.

:: :: ::

Salem, Oregon
Oct. 24, 1996
Dear Joy,

Thank you for writing to tell us about Rita, but we were saddened to read that she had the stroke. We hope she can make a come back and again become active. I will drop her a note, too.

I am sending some copies of postcards to you (and the same copies to Rita). The person at the copy machine put them on in the wrong order. I should have checked them before they were printed.

Alice and I enjoyed the story of your trip. It sounded like a good chance to get away for a while and to see an interesting part of your area. I noticed on the map that many of your roads run north and south along the coast. The Oregon Coast has one highway along the coast with roads every 60 miles or so leading to the east over the coastal mountains to the valley.

We will drive one of them tomorrow when we go to Coos Bay to check on Alice's mother. We were to have gone last weekend. We asked a neighbor to check on her and maybe buy a few groceries. We played at a banquet for the Oregon Council of the Blind on Sunday and for a wagon train that had just traveled a thousand miles along the old trail. My brother was in charge of the festivities and he wanted our fiddle music as part of the program.

The leaves are turning color and falling and the weather is wet and cool. Fall is definitely here.

Please write again — especially letting us know how Rita is doing.

Our best regards,
Lew and Alice

:: :: ::

November 16, 1996 Today I visited Linda Vaughn. She had called me yesterday to invite me by to pick up the article out of the Perth newspaper. Her sister in Perth had seen my request in the paper and because the two of us lived in Salem and because she had visited Salem a couple of years ago, she sent Linda the article. Linda called me on February 20, 1996 when she received the article but we never had gotten together. Today her daughter served us coffee cake and tea. As we visited, we discussed wartime Australia and other related items. She asked me to tell them the story of Bill. I enjoyed the family and was pleased with our visit. Linda and I share the same birthday, April 11.

The article in the newspaper that Linda gave me reads:

> **WARTIME FRIENDS:** S/C 1 Bill Holt was aboard the USS Phoenix but was to die later on in World War II from tuberculosis. His brother in America would like to find anyone from Perth and WA who remembers Bill. He was stationed with the US Navy in Australia from 1941-43. The whereabouts of Miss Rita Barron, who lived at 40 King Street, Perth in 1942 and who corresponded with their mother, Vintie Holt, is also sought. Contact: Lew Holt, 1625 19th St. N.E., Salem, Oregon 97303 USA.

There can be many surprises as I research – literally the whole world – looking for people and information about Bill and the Phoenix. An article that I asked to have published in Perth, Australia ends up just a few miles away from me here in Salem, Oregon. (Little did I know when I wrote the above thought that I would experience contacts in three more continents.)

:: :: ::

Chapter Thirteen

ARGENTINA – COCO

By Directive dated March 1946, the USS PHOENIX (CL-46) was to be deposed; and by Directive dated January 1951 was transferred to a South American government and stricken from the Navy list.

The Argentine Government took possession of the USS PHOENIX at Philadelphia on April 12, 1951, and was given the name 'GENERAL BELGRANO.' She was quickly made ready at Philadelphia Navy Yard and on December 5, 1951, put into Puerto Belgrano Naval Base (Argentina) and joined the Sea Fleet.

Argentine Cruiser Commissioned

General view of the Argentine cruiser "17 De Octubre," formerly the U. S. light cruiser Phoenix (left) being commissioned at Philadelphia. Capt. W. J. Suits, USN, speaking. (AP)

'GENERAL BELGRANO' is the sixth ship of this name in the Argentina Navy, named for Manuel Belgrano, forefather of the May (1810) Revolution, creator of the national flag and victor of Salta and Tuouman (battles against colonial Spain). 'GENERAL BELGRANO' is the first Argentine vessel armed with "Sea Cat" surface-to-air missiles

:: :: ::

Again my story might have ended here. But a series of chance happenings created opportunities to extend the story about Bill and his ship, the Phoenix – to Argentina, to England and ultimately back to Japan. When World War Two ended, the story of the Phoenix did not end. It had another chapter in its life, yet to be experienced. My story might have easily ended with Bill's death. Or after finding the four sailors and his girl friend in Australia who remembered him. My story might have ended with the tragic sinking of the Phoenix/Belgrano during the Falkland Island War between Argentina and England.

During the Falkland Island war in 1982 between Argentina and England it was in the news that a light cruiser, General Belgrano, had been sunk by the British. Before I read the full story I told Alice that it must have been the Phoenix. I had remembered the Phoenix had been sold to Argentina in 1951.

To carry my research farther I wrote several letters to sources Washington, D.C. and in Argentina trying to locate an Argentine veteran who was on the Belgrano when it was sunk. None of my letters were answered. I was about to give up until one day, early in May of 1999, those of us who belong to the Phoenix Association and who have e-mail, received a letter from Andy Wilson saying that C.J. Horn, a Phoenix veteran, had died. Several days later we all received the letter below. It was signed "Nestor Cenci (Republica Argentina)"

:: :: ::

May 12, 1999
Dear Andy:
Thank you for letting me know about C.J. Horn. I'm so sorry to hear this.

Please, I want you to give my condolences to his family.

Nestor Cenci (Republica Argentina)

:: :: ::

I saw this as an opportunity to contact someone who perhaps was on the Belgrano when it was sunk. The signature indicated that the writer was probably a veteran of the Belgrano. Andy had written earlier of the joint meetings and visits of the Phoenix – Belgrano veterans.

I wrote to Nestor Cenci that evening explaining to him that I wanted to write to someone who had been on the Belgrano when it was sunk. The following series of letters will show our friendship and the information I wanted. I have many more letters from "Coco" as I call him now. Our friendship has continued to grow as will be shown in future letters – leading to giving him a hug and shaking his hand near San Francisco in March, 2003.

:: :: ::

May 13, 1999
Dear Lew:
Thank so much for your letter, and I will try to explain you something in relation with the ARA General BELGRANO, but I have to apologize to you because of my poor English. I hope you can understand me. I am Captain, retired since 1988, but I was Commander (Chief of Accountant) when I was assigned for two years, to duty on the ship, in early 1982. After 3 months, the sinking happened, and I was one of the survivors. The ship was on duty for the Argentine Navy since 1951, is to say 31 years. (About 20,000 Argentinean sailors learned on the ship during those years.)

In 1988, I was at the Phoenix Reunion in Las Vegas. I gave a short speech about the experience as a survivor in that reunion. I am 60 years at the present, and four children: a daughter, (38), 3 grandchildren, a married son 35, who lives in Virginia, USA, and two more single sons, 33 and 23 years.

We travel once a year with my wife, Martha, to the US, to visit my son, Guillermo, and this year we are thinking to be in Oakton, Virginia, and Los Angeles, California in early September. Maybe we can talk by phone at that time.

I've read your brother was William Harrison, from Oregon. Are you from OR too? I appreciate your interest, and I am glad to write to you, and I wish you to write to me again.

Keep in touch.

Nestor Cenci (Argentina)

:: :: ::

May 21, 1999

Dear Lew and Alice:

It has been very grateful to receive your news, and to know you, Lew through the photo that, YES, I could open, in which you are with your "fiddle". A Pleasure! It was a very emotional letter, I was reading and translating it to Martha, and we enjoyed too much each paragraph that we were reading.

You must have to know that it is not easy for me to read in English (and is worse for me to speak), even though I understood totally your letter, and after I read it, I take the work of translating it in the "Power Translator," to be certain that I was reading the letter totally right. Thank you very very much for your letter. It seems to me that we both are friends of many years. I also will send you a photograph, but through the mail, because I don't know how to send it by Electronic mail. I have to ask to my son, Martin, how to do that. In a next E-mail, I will send you the small speech that I gave in Las Vegas, and I would like to have the book that you have written, that you mentioned in your letter.

Since I retired, I have made several trips to USA, to visit my son that lives there since 1985. I believe that there have been maybe 20 trips, and I had the opportunity of knowing some places, as New Orleans, Anchorage and Fairbanks, Louisville, New York, San Francisco, Seattle, Los Angeles (where one of my best friends lives), Phoenix, etc., and in spite of this, I have not learned to speak well your language, but I can write a little bit, because writing allows to me to amend what I have written before sending the letter. Now we travel a little less, for money reasons, and only to visit Laura and Willie, in Virginia, and to enjoy their company once a year at least. They don't have children yet.

My daughter-in-law, Laura Webner, is American, and an excellent girl. Now she is learning Spanish.

I try to imagine the emotion that you have had to feel when you got news from Australia, from Rita Baron, and how many things there were to ask her about your brother.

Tell me something on this topic, and tell me too about your brother, in connection to his stay aboard the USS Phoenix. Also, tell me more about your friend in Norway.

About my family: Martha is 60 years old as I, and it is an excellent wife. She doesn't speak nothing at all of English. (we are 39 years married)

My daughter, Beatriz, and her husband, Gerardo, live in Mar del Plata city, 250 miles from here, they have given us 3 grandsons, German (13) and Ana Ines (12) and Maria Belen (8). Regrettably, the youngest has cerebral paralysis. My daughter speaks very well English, and studies too much that language. My son-in-law is an electronic engineer.

The second son, who lives in Oakton, is called Guillermo (Willie), married 2 years ago with Laura. He works for a company called Insignia, and he is director of information technology, Laura is property manager of a company in MD.

The third son, single, Fernando Luis, works as Director of Advertising in a local company, and the fourth son, Martin Angel, who lives with us, is specialist in MacIntosh computers, and works in that brand representative in Argentina. In fact, I have a Macintosh Powerbook1400cs.

OK, Lew, Alice, I think I am boring you. I apologize again for my English, I try to make the best, don't laugh. Tell me how many things you don't understand from me. I will try to explain it again. By the way, my nickname is Coco. I look forward to your next letter.

Nestor Cenci
Coco and Martha

Cocoa & Martha

:: :: ::

May 23, 1999
Dear Lew:
This is the speech I gave in Las Vegas in May 1986. Keep in touch.
Coco.

I am Commander Nestor Cenci, from the Argentine Navy. First of all, I would like to apologize for not expressing myself correctly in your language. You may find mistakes in my pronunciation, but I think we all know, that the essence of our meeting here today, is to honor a ship who was loved by you, as well as my Navy. I am sincerely grateful to your Association for your kind invitation.

This allows me to share with my comrades-in-arms, the commemoration of a heroic combat unit, who participated in innumerable campaigns, and who served your country as well as mine, for more than 30 years. She was used during those years in the preparation and training of Officers, Enlisted Personnel and Cadets.

She was par excellence, a school of Artillery men, Flag Ship of the Navy; finally, I would say that about 20,000 Argentine sailed on her decks.

There they learned to be technicians and professionals, and above of all, they learned to love her, just as I know you have loved her.

Her last Commanding Officer, Captain Hector Bonzo, kindly asked me, to bring a letter of his, addressed to Mr. Andrew Wilson, but which is meant for all of you. In it he appoints me, to be the bearer of a piece of wood from our cruisers deck. That same deck, which you have walked on sometimes between 1938 and 1946.

I also bring to you some ribbons from the caps which were worn by the ship's personnel, and a note with the captain's Bonzo signature, rather emotional perhaps, since it was written after the sinking of our ship. Because, as you know, 4 years ago, on Sunday, May 2nd, 1982, the Veteran Cruiser from Pearl Harbor was fatally damaged by two Tigerfish torpedoes in the waters of the South Atlantic.

The first of the torpedoes penetrated frame 106, aft of the machine room. The second, within a few seconds, entered between frames 12 and 15, close to the keel, causing the loss of about 60 feet of her bow.

We, and I say we because I was on her at the moment, immediately proceeded to try to prevent the flooding and control the fire, but partly because many of the men assigned to damage control, had been either hurt or killed, and partly because our cruiser had not been designed to bear such severe damage, after 25 minutes, the Captain gave the order to abandon ship.

Half an hour after the attack, the ship had a 30 degrees portside list. By the time, the damage caused by the impacts determined the end of our glorious ship. One hour later, approximately at 5 PM, she had disappeared from the surface. And some explosions from the boilers interrupted the silence of the immensity of the ocean.

I have that awful sound engraved in my mind; it was as if those were her last words while she sank, to rest forever in the cold waters,

6000 feet below the South Atlantic. A total of 321 men died, 272 in the catastrophe and its immediate consequences, and another 49 either while abandoning the ship, or during the tough voyage on the rafts, or as a result of burns and serious traumatism.

Probably, the account of this incident might seem a little dismal and perhaps its retelling is not in accordance with the spirit of our meeting, but I find it impossible to refer to it, without being moved by my feeling for such a brave ship and for so many lives that went with her.

This beloved ship, Veteran of World War II, and for over 30 years at the service of the Argentine Navy, perished during the Malvinas conflict. As a survivor of this catastrophe, I have the privilege of telling you, men of the sea, men of the USS Phoenix, men of the Navy, that our ship was sunk, in the line of duty.

I hope that the flame that keeps your Association united by the spirit of this Ship, is never extinguished, and that the USS Phoenix might always be in your hearts, as the ARA General Belgrano Cruiser is in the hearts of all the Argentine people.

.:: :: ::

I found this information on a website. The Belgrano, a light cruiser which was formerly the USS Phoenix and survived Pearl Harbor, lies at a depth of 13,780 ft in international waters, about 115 miles off the coast of Argentina. An exposition by the National Geographic Magazine failed to locate the Belgrano. (Coco had been invited to go on the exposition but just before it left, he was bumped in favor of somebody else.)

:: :: ::

May 23, 1999
Re: Speech copy
Dear Coco,
You can't imagine how pleased I was to receive a copy of your speech today. It is exactly what I have been looking for, for several years – a first person account of the sinking. I didn't want it from a

newspaper or from a book but rather from a person who was there.

Please send me your mailing address and I will send you a copy of the book. It is rather detailed with many family letters to my brother Bill, letters from him home, letters from a girl that wrote to him, get well cards, etc., as well as 40 or 50 letters from sailors who were on the Phoenix with Bill during the attack on Pearl Harbor. I found 4 men that remembered him – after 50 years. One was the man who checked Bill in to the sick bay, diagnosed tuberculosis, put him on a destroyer and took him to an army hospital in Australia.

In 1940 my mother and her 4 boys ranging from 9 to 19 years old moved to a little farm – just 25 miles from where I now live. Today Alice and I went to the same place where my younger brother still lives to celebrate my mother's 100th birthday. She died at 89. My brother had many birthday parties for her over the years. Today many of her grandchildren and friends gathered to remember her.

Tuesday a friend and I are driving to Seattle (220 miles) to take up a load of violins/fiddles which we will put in an auction. Next Friday Alice and I will go back up for a large Folk Festival and the auction. We will stay with our son, Steve and his wife, Karen, in Seattle. It will be a busy week so I will not be home to write very often. Please be patient with me.

More later. Lew

:: :: ::

June 9, 1999
Hola!
Dear Lew:

I got a shock when I was reading your brother's narrative. I felt a sharp cold in my spine. Reading so amazing true-story. It is a shame I can't tell you (because of my poor vocabulary), how I felt after finish the reading. I don't need the dictionary to understand your brother's story at all, and I enjoyed so much this letter. Thank you Lew.

Where is Walla Walla ? Where is Bridgeport?

Well, Lew, I have to tell you that I am still waiting for your book, I think it will come on this Friday, but I'm anxious to see and to read it.

Could you open the photos I sent you last week?

I see you are a very enthusiastic of violins. Is it only a hobby? When do you start with this? Is it a way of life? These are some things I ask to you, to know you better.

I am retired from the Navy since 1988. The first years I made some trips, but now I have not enough money to make the same now. My retirement pay is small, and I can't work in any activity, because the employment is very very difficult in Argentina, and is worst for a man over 40 years. Actually, non-employment is one of the most important problems in my country. If you wish, I will tell you something about my country.

I use to live in this neighborhood since 1980. Before that year, I was in several places, in duty of my professional activity as member of the Navy, but in 1980, I moved with my family to a house in Martinez. I was Commander at that time. After this I intended to get a small house, because my children were gone from our house. Only Martin left with us. He is now 23 years old.

In April 1998, I bought a sandlot, and built a new house. We live in it since December 1998, is not enough small, but comfortable and practical. It has a small garden, and I waste my time doing the gardening, and take care of the grass.

I use to read much of the time, and now, I'm trying to improve my English, making letters to my friend Lew

I look forward to your next letter. Please write.

Coco

:: :: ::

June 10, 1999
Re: Hola

In a message dated 6/9/99 12:15:34 PM, Cenci writes:

> I got a shock when I was reading your brother's narrative. I felt a sharp cold in my spine.

>reading so amazing true-story.

Dear Coco,

Friends of mine who read your speech, said exactly the same thing about your writing. If you don't mind, I will quote what my friend in Norway wrote about your speech, "... a speech about what I would anticipate was the most emotional moment of his life. A speech with undertones of sorrow, comradeship, pride and love for a weapon as a national symbol of national heroism."

>Where is Walla Walla? Where is Bridgeport?

Walla Walla is a town/city in Southeastern Washington – several hundred miles from Seattle.

Bridgeport is just a little community. It is 25 miles west of where I live in Salem. We moved there in May 1940. My father had been killed in a logging accident in November and my mother wanted a small place to raise her 4 boys. My younger brother was 10, I was 11, Bill would have been 16 I think and Charles about 19. Bill joined the navy a year later when he graduated from high school. Charles went to a nearby college and did not go into the service until several years later. You will read about Charles in the book.

My brother, Arlie, still lives on the old home place. A little river with an Indian name of "Luckiamute" runs just a few feet from the house. A small country school is across the river. I went to the 6th, 7th and 8th grades in the little one-room school. There was one room with all 8 grades and 1 teacher. Dolores was the other student in my class. She died earlier this month.

After I graduated from the 8th grade, I rode a school bus 8 miles into Dallas for 4 years to go to high school. After high school (1947) I went to a small college just 9 miles away. In January 1948, I was in a bad automobile accident and missed the rest of the school year. I was in bed 3 1/2 months with a broken leg, broken jaw and other injuries. That fall rather than going to the college to live, I lived at home and drove to school every day for the next 4 years.

In January of 1952 I was in my last term of college. I received a telephone call from the school district in Coos Bay – 175 miles down on the Southern Oregon Coast. I quit college and taught a 6th grade class until school was out in June. I met Alice while I was living there and became very fond of her. In June, 1952, I moved back home and went to college that summer to graduate. That fall I went to another college to do graduate work. Alice and I were married in February 1953, on St. Valentine's Day – 46 years ago.

After I graduated in June of 1953 I didn't look for a teaching job because I thought I was going to be drafted (although I could not have passed the physical exam with my bad leg). In July Alice told me that we were going to be parents so I started looking for a job. I went to North Bend (next to Coos Bay) and planned to stay one year but ended up working there for 31 years – until I retired. I taught the 5th and 6th grade 12 years and was an elementary principal for 28 years – 9 years I was doing both.

Five years ago our daughter called and said, "Mom and Dad, there is a house for sale across the street, why don't you come and look at it." We did. That was in August. We went back to North Bend, sold our place, announced to our friends that we were moving and by December we were moved to Salem. It was one of the greatest things we have done. We enjoy the climate; we enjoy the people and enjoy being near our daughter and her son. This afternoon I will pick him up at school and take him to swimming lessons. I'll probably stay there until he finishes and then bring him home. Neither his mother nor father can work it into their schedule today. There – you have my life – a little bit of it anyway.

>Well, Lew, I have to tell you that I am still waiting for your book, I think it will come on this Friday, but I'm anxious to see and to read it.

I hope it arrives soon, Coco. I am anxious for you to see it. It is not a great book but rather just a collection of my brother's letters, other letters and the history of his ship/your ship.

>I see you are a very enthusiastic of violins. Is it only a hobby?

Yes, it is a hobby. I play and Alice plays. I also buy and sell violins as well as repairing them. I have maybe 25 or 30 of them.

>When did you start with this?

I started when I was 50 years old – 20 years ago.

>Is it a way of life? These are some things I ask to you, to know you better.

Yes, it is just about my whole life. Almost everything I do is built around fiddles/violins. Today I am copying audio tapes for a friend. It will take me many days to finish. I have violins to work on for people.

Monday we played at a senior retirement home. Yesterday we played at a nursing home for old people. Saturday we drive 60 miles to the coast to play for campers at a campground.

>because the employment is very very difficult in Argentina, and is worst for a man over 40 years. If you wish, I will tell you something about my country.

Yes, Coco, I would enjoy reading about your country. I taught 6th grade students about Argentina many years ago. I am sure that I was not accurate about what I taught – gauchos, mate´ from a gourd, the Pampa, Patagonia, (it has been a long time ago). Someday we can write about Peron.

Please tell me where you live in Argentina so I can find it on a map. I live just a few miles from the 45th parallel – so I am half way between the equator and the North Pole.

>I use to live in this neighborhood since 1980.

I enjoyed reading about where you have lived.

>I use to read much of the time, and now, I'm trying to improve my English, making letters to my friend Lew.

I hope that it is not a too big of a challenge. I just write in English – you are doing all the work. I feel very fortunate to have met you and am enjoying your letters very much.

>I look forward to your next letter. Please write.

Yes, and I enjoy writing, too.

It is a beautiful day today. It will get about 75 degrees. Alice and I worked out side this morning.

:: :: ::

June 15, 1999

Dear friend Lew:

You have to forgive me not to answer quickly, but I need enough time to read carefully this wonderful book. I read completely the preface, and, let me tell you that it thrilled me, and I need to congratulate you to write this book. It's fascinating

COCO

:: :: ::

Later I wrote to Coco asking information about his life. Here is his answer:

Dear Friend:

I started answering you some of your questions:

My family from my father, surname Cenci, came to Argentina aprox. in 1875 from Italy. About from my mother, surname Vaquero, maybe was at the same time, but from Spain...This is all the information I have...

I was born in Bahia Blanca, a city in the Province of Buenos Aires, a little more than 400 miles from the Capital. Bahia Blanca is one of the important cities in Argentina. It is near Puerto Belgrano, the most important naval base from our Navy.

I went to school in Bahia Blanca, to : Escuela No. 4, from 1st to 6th grade (primary education) (1945 to 1950)

After that I went to: Escuela Nacional Superior de Comercio, from 1st to 5th year (secondary School) (1951 to 1955)

After that I went to the University, (1956-1957) to Universidad Nacional del Sur, also in Bahia Blanca, I began Civil Engineer, I went 2 years there, and after that, I decided to join the Navy.

In 1958 I joined the Navy, starting the Naval School, in Naval Base of Rio Santiago, 30 miles from Buenos Aires.

I will follow answering you later, but tell me if you need some more information about this I am sending now...

A hug for you Luis, excuse me to be so short.

Coco

:: :: ::

This exchange of letters between Coco and me show both the advantage of email over my many previous letters to others and the letters show how our friendship has developed. Over the years we are still writing, talking on the phone, exchanging gifts and enjoying our friendship. Out of necessity for space, I am forced to leave out many interesting letters between Coco and me. (And several years after writing this paragraph, I had the opportunity to visit with Coco when he was visiting in San Francisco. (March, 2003) The story of the visit will follow.

:: :: ::

Chapter Fourteen

MEETING "N" (NARENDRA SETHIA)

After locating Coco, a veteran of the Belgrano sinking, I had the inspiration to locate a British sailor/veteran who was on the H.M.S. Conqueror, the submarine that sank the Belgrano. I checked many web sites with no success. Finally I located British Submarine Bulletin board where I posted the following letter.

:: :: ::

January 6, 2000

Dear Sir,

I have been checking out your wonderful web site researching the HMS Conqueror. Let me explain. My brother joined the U. S. Navy in 1941 and was aboard the USS Phoenix during the Japanese attack on Pearl Harbor. While still aboard the Phoenix in 1943 in the South Pacific, he contracted tuberculosis, returned to the United States and died in 1945 at the age of 21.

My life became involved through high school,...

...I thought my book was completed but recently I located a sailor from Argentina who has written to me describing the sinking. Now I would like to add to the final chapter of the book, a letter from a British sailor who was on the HMS Conqueror during the sinking...

Would it be possible, please, for you to put me in touch with a sailor or officer who was aboard the HMS Conqueror during the sinking of the Belgrano? I would like to correspond with him regarding the sinking.

I thank you very much.

Lew Holt

:: :: ::

Nine days later I received this letter.

January 15, 2000

Dear Lew

I was the Attack Stations Ship Control Officer of the Watch on board HMS CONQUEROR when she sank the Belgrano. What can I do for you?

Best wishes

"N" (Narendra Sethia)

:: :: ::

This simple letter added a whole new element to my story with many implications. It was the first letter that would give me much information and become an important part of my story. It, also, changed the lives of two men, one from England and one from Argentina. And eventually leading to them becoming "Brothers of War."

:: :: ::

January 15, 2000

Dear "N,"

What a pleasant surprise to receive your letter this morning. I will explain my reason for wanting to contact someone who was on the HMS Conqueror. My next older brother, Bill, joined the U.S. Navy in June of 1941 and was aboard the U. S. Phoenix at Pearl Harbor on December 7th during the Japanese attack. Bill contracted tuberculosis in 1943 in the South Pacific, returned to the U. S. and died in 1945. I was fifteen years old at the time of his death.

Fifty years later I became curious about my brother and his ship. I wrote hundreds of letters and located four sailors who remembered my brother. One had put him on a destroyer, took him to Australia and checked him into an Army hospital. After 54 years I was able to locate my brother's girl friend in Australia and have had many interesting letters from her.

I have compiled all of the information for my family – all of my brother's letters, letters to him and the letters from the sailors, girlfriend, etc., and the basic history of his ship.

Because I have "first person accounts" dealing with my brother and his ship, I am now asking you for a "first person account" from the

HMS Conqueror of the sinking of the Belgrano. It must have been a tense and exciting time for those of you on the Conqueror. I have read about the sinking in books but a letter from you describing the action on the Conqueror, the crew and you personally would add much to what I have collected. Would you do that for me, please?

The best to you.

Lew Holt

Salem, Oregon USA

:: :: ::

(From my journal) I received the first letter from N at 9:00 A.M. on January 15, 2000. I immediately wrote the above letter. At 4:00 that afternoon I received the following letter. I was very fortunate to have contacted N. He writes very well, expresses his feelings and is willing to write and share his story.

:: :: ::

Saturday, January 15, 2000

Dear Lew

Thanks for your e-mail. I'm sorry to hear about your brother – it must bring back painful memories. By way of background, I joined HMS CONQUEROR in May 1980 and my duties were Ship Control and Attack Stations Officer of the Watch, Trimming Officer (responsible for trim or buoyancy of the submarine), Supplies & Secretariat Officer (in charge of all accounting, stores, correspondence, welfare, catering, etc) and Bridge Watch keeping.

We had been away from harbor for the first 3 months of 1982 and in late March I was enjoying a few days of hard-earned leave before being recalled to the boat.

We set sail on 2nd April 1982 on a fast passage south, heading for South Georgia. We were excited but relaxed and we never thought that we would end up going to war, although as a professionally trained submarine crew of 124 men, we were ready to do whatever we were instructed.

We arrived on station off South Georgia around 16th April. We heard the Fortuna Glacier from about 80 miles away on our sonar equipment, and in the early hours of the following morning whilst on periscope watch, I was treated to a dramatic view of the island with its glaciers and a pod of grey seals playing in the water ahead of us.

We stayed in the area of South Georgia for around a week, disappointed that we had not taken part in the attack on the submarine Santa Fe which was sunk by a helicopter, but were then called to the Falkland Islands where we were to enforce the 200 mile exclusion zone that had been established around the islands.

We arrived on station in the last week of April and settled into a rather boring routine of patrolling the southern perimeter of the zone. The highlights of our day were meals and movies after dinner. We still felt that we would never go to war and we believed that the politicians would sort it all out and call it a day.

On 29th April our intelligence informed us that an Argentinean Task Group (called TG 79.2), consisting of 2 destroyers, 1 light cruiser (the Belgrano) and an oil tanker were heading in our direction, and on 30th April we picked them up on sonar and started trailing them from around 20 miles astern.

On 1st May, whilst on afternoon periscope watch, I was the first to sight the masts of the ships which were engaged in a RAS (replenishment at sea). The four ships were steaming abreast of one another and I had them in my sights – and noted in my diary that evening that they would have made a superb target – four in one, so to speak. But we were not authorized to attack the ships since they remained around 30 miles outside the exclusion zone.

Throughout the night of 1st May, the ships appeared to be paralleling the exclusion zone – in other words they were evidently at pains not to enter the zone. They were not carrying out any anti-submarine maneuvers such as zigging or transmitting actively on sonar.

My usual sleeping hours were from 0830 to 1230 and the following day I was woken up around 1220 by the Action Stations Alarm sounding. I threw my clothes on and rushed into the Control Room, as my duty was Attack Stations Officer of the Watch, in what is called "the bandstand," behind the 2 crew members who operated the planes, and adjacent to the engineer who operated the ballast, trim, hydraulic and high pressure air systems.

I discovered that twice during the morning, the submarine had received a signal instructing that the Argentinean Task Group was to be attacked. Whether because of poor reception or because the Commanding Officer of the submarine could not believe what he was being told as the Task Group presented no threat and was OUTSIDE the exclusion zone (the Official Secrets Act prevents me from telling you which), I do not know. But the instruction was questioned on a third occasion and at around 1400 a very serious looking Commanding Officer, Chris Wreford-Brown, gave the order to "shut off for Attack."

We closed in to around 5,000 yards and started to make the various preparations through which we had been schooled so often. The Captain decided to use vintage Mark 8 torpedoes which contain 810 pounds of high explosive torpex. His reason for doing so, rather than using the wire-guided Mark 24's (which can be fired from a range in excess of 20,000 yards) was that, knowing that the Belgrano had been the Phoenix, we also knew that she had thick armour plating beneath the waterline and therefore we needed to use weapons with a high explosive content (the Mark 24's have only 240 pounds of explosives). So we decided on a visual attack rather than a "blind attack" and this meant directing the attack via the periscope at close range.

The Captain manned the periscope and the various fire control solutions were fed to the attack computers which were manned by the Weapon Engineering Officer, Lieutenant Commander Mike Garland.

The forward torpedo tubes were loaded, flooded and equalized. And at that point, I think that we felt as if we (were a) part of a surrealistic circumstance – still not really believing that we were going to fire weapons at a ship which had human beings on board, yet so well trained that there was barely time to think, at least not to rationalize on the moral issues. We simply got on with our jobs, and the adrenaline started to flow. When adrenaline flows like that, it's an amazing feeling.

At 1500, the Captain moved away from the ships and asked me to "catch a trim" which involved slowing the boat down to around 2 knots and then pumping water between various tanks in order to achieve, as nearly as we could, a state of neutral buoyancy. This took me about 15 minutes and when I was satisfied that we were in trim, the Captain ordered us to close the Task group which was still steaming on quite unconcernedly and completely oblivious to our presence.

By 1545 we had closed to around 1600 yards from the ships, ahead of the Belgrano's port beam. The Captain described everything that he could see – all 4 ships were visible. We prepared for the attack.

The Captain had decided to fire the traditional salvo of three weapons. The Belgrano was the main target, followed by the two destroyers.

At 1558 the Captain ordered "Fire!" and the first torpedo left its tube, traveling at around 45 miles per hour. The submarine rocked, and we had to clear our ears. Then the second weapon left the tube, then the third.

The seconds passed by and seemed like an eternity. There was complete silence throughout the boat, and you could have heard a pin drop. I don't know about others, but my palms were sweating and my heart was racing.

After what seemed like hours but was in fact less than a minute, the Captain raised the periscope, stopwatch in one hand, and immediately there was a massive explosion that rocked the boat. The Captain started shouting that he could see a ball of orange flame. Then there was another massive explosion and the boat lurched to one side, whilst the Captain continued with a running commentary, saying that he could see flames and smoke. The submarine Control Room erupted with cheers.

At that point the Captain decided that we should go deep and leave the immediate area, as we expected the destroyers to come after us. We were very surprised that they had not started transmitting on sonar which would have been the obvious immediate response from a destroyer after a submarine attack.

As we headed away, fast and deep, we could hear muffled explosions (fuel tanks and ammunition stores on the Belgrano) and then the Sonar Room reported that they could hear the sounds of the ship breaking up – the crunching and grinding of twisted metal. I put my earphones on and listened and could hear it, but had no time to think about it.

After a few moments, we were depth-charged by what turned out later to be the destroyer Piedra Buena. Two of our torpedoes had hit the Belgrano – the first one had blown her bow clean off and the second one had gone through her machinery and accommodation spaces. Amazingly, the third torpedo had run past the Belgrano and had hit the other destroyer, the Hippolito Bouchard, but had failed to detonate – though the damage was sufficient for her to have to return to her home port of Ushvaia in Argentina for "storm damage".

After the depth-charge attack, during which most of us thought that we were about to die, we ran at high speed for an hour. We then slowed down and the First Lieutenant said we could have a cigarette before we came back up to periscope depth. As I was reaching for a cigarette, a depth charge landed almost on top of us. We had not heard the Piedra Buena but somehow her Captain had worked out the most likely place for us to run, and had started heaving Hedgehog anti-submarine charges over the stern of ship. They were way too close for comfort.

A young mechanic who was in charge of our laundry, started a washing machine in one of the machinery spaces. A Medical Attendant, standing near him, knocked him unconscious. The act of radiating a new frequency could easily have led to our being discovered.

We ran fast for another hour, and shortly after 1800 we came to periscope depth, cleared our stern arcs and found that there were no vessels in the area. At that time, we raised a mast and transmitted a report back to UK headquarters.

The Captain had not seen the Belgrano actually sinking, although we had heard the breaking-up noises, and at dawn on 3rd May we returned to the datum but found only debris and a hospital ship searching for survivors. So we pulled away and left them to it.

Two days later, HMS SHEFFIELD was sunk by Exocet missiles, and on 6th May we were torpedoed by an air-launched heat-seeking Mark 46 torpedo but, through a remarkable and rather unnerving series of evolutions, we were able to escape it.

When I emerged from the "bandstand" around 7:30 p.m. on the evening of 2nd May 1982, I felt mentally and physically drained. I was two weeks shy of my 26th birthday. I went to the Wardroom and sat down with a few of the other off-watch Officers. I drank a glass of wine. We were all very subdued, and Lieutenant Commander Garland said that he felt that we had been "the instruments of the politicians' incompetence." I have never forgotten that phrase.

We talked about the rights and wrongs, and we wondered how many sailors had been killed – young conscripts, most no more than 18 or 19 years old. It turned out in fact that 334 men died in those first two massive explosions, and an additional 34 in the life rafts overnight. Many died from oil burns.

That night, I could barely sleep and when I did, I dreamed of bombs and explosions. When someone dropped a spanner on the floor, I jumped out of bed. For more than a week afterwards, most crew members felt the same. There was little sleep and our dreams were only of torpedoes and bombs.

It took me a while to get over it all, and the truth is that I'm not sure I ever will. I still have nightmares about it, and, having read first-hand accounts written by Argentinean survivors, I still feel disturbed when I think of what happened. The only regret I have in my life, apart from smoking cigarettes, is that I was a party to the sinking of the Belgrano, an act which I genuinely believe was perpetrated for purely political reasons and not because the ship posed any serious threat to the British Fleet. I resigned from the Navy immediately afterwards and came to live in the Caribbean. I am still haunted by what we did.

Lew, this is the first time in nearly 18 years that I have ever written about this to someone. I did keep a detailed diary parts of which were, without my permission, leaked to the UK Press in 1984 as a result of which the British Government investigated me and threatened me for exposing "official secrets". The British Police tried to obtain that diary but they never did and I still have it. It was written every evening, throughout that patrol, sitting at the Wardroom table, and it is a very detailed description of everything that happened. I am thinking of publishing it one day but will probably have to do so outside the UK as the British secrecy laws are draconian.

Much of what I have written has been reported in the book The Sinking of the Belgrano written by Arthur Gavshon and Desmond Rice, and if you are researching the Belgrano, this will give you very interesting information as to why the sinking should never have happened.

What I've written to you in this e-mail is completely off the top of my head – which shows you how clear it all is even after so many years. I will never forget a moment of it.

For your information, our Wardroom was as follows: Commanding Officer – Commander (now Captain, DSO, retired) Chris Wreford-Brown; First Lieutenant – Lieutenant Commander (now Commodore, OBE) Tim McClement; Marine Engineer Officer – Lieutenant Commander (now Captain, Retired) Dave Hall;

Weapon Engineering Officer – Lieutenant Commander (now Commander, Retired) Mike Garland. Supply Officer – myself, Lieutenant Narendra Sethia, now Retired; Sonar Officer – Lieutenant (now Retired) Robin l'Oste-Brown; Navigating Officer – Lieutenant (now Commander) Jonty Powis;

Torpedo Officer – Sub-Lieutenant (now Lieutenant Commander) Peter Carroll; Deputy Marine Officer – Lieutenant (now Commander) - Tim Hutchinson; Deputy Weapon Engineer Officer – Lieutenant (now Commander) Paul Brockwell; Officer under training – Sub Lieutenant Gordon Lester; Medical officer, carried especially for this trip – Surgeon Lieutenant Commander MacDonald. I hope this helps. Let me know if you need anything further. Thanks for the walk down memory lane.

Best wishes

N

:: :: ::

Saturday, January 15, 2000

Dear N,

What a fabulous story. You can't imagine what it means to me. I also appreciate your writing it from your heart as well as writing it as a historical event. Both aspects are important. The books don't bring out the emotions of the story.

Yes, writing about my brother did bring back painful memories. As a 15 year old, I didn't fully realize the consequences and the full ramification of my brother's death. Naturally I was sad at the time. The last time I saw my brother was in June of 1941 when we dropped him off 4 miles from town and turned down a side road to work in the fields. Of course I didn't realize that I wouldn't see him again until his funeral in February of 1945.

On December 7, 1941 a neighbor came down to tell us that Pearl Harbor had been attacked by the Japanese. We lived in the country and did not have electricity or a radio. The neighbors did have a radio – so they had heard the news of the attack. Several weeks later we received a mimeographed letter that Bill was safe.

And then there was the telegram in 1943 that he was ill. My brother and I were called out of our high school class in January of 1945 to deliver a telegram to our mother that Bill was seriously ill. A step-cousin took us 8 miles out to our home so we could tell our mother. (My mother was widowed in 1939 when my father was killed in a logging accident.) And then a month later we were again called out of class and took the telegram to our mother that Bill had died. My oldest brother was in the army in Europe. Later that spring we received two telegrams from the war department – each time saying that he had been wounded. Those were not pleasant times.

Then it was two more years in high school for me followed by college, work, marriage, children, and a busy life. As the years went by, I wished I knew more about Bill and his ship. I was able to contact the president of the Phoenix Association and then it becomes a long story of many letters, phone calls and luck. I spent many, many hours typing all of my collected material. It was only then that I fully felt the tragedy of my brother's death. I feel fortunate for having the experience of getting to better know and understand my brother over 50 years after his death.

I have become a good friend of an Argentine Sailor who was on the Belgrano. He was in the U.S. in September and we talked four times on the phone. We have not written of the politics of the Falkland Island War – just friendly letters about the weather or families and those things. He did send me a copy of a speech that he gave in Las Vegas in May 1986 at a reunion of the Phoenix Association. It told about the sinking from his viewpoint. I must share with you my friendship with him so you will better understand why I appreciate your letter so much. Your letter and his letter will probably be the last pages of my collection of material. (Little did I know.)

I am 70 years old so I have many memories of times – Dec. 7, 1941, Pres. Roosevelt's death, when I heard the mill whistles blowing in town because the war was over, the assassination of Pres. Kennedy, etc. In 1982 when I heard that an Argentinean light cruiser had been sunk, I told my wife that I knew the Phoenix had been sold to Argentina and that I bet that the Belgrano was the Phoenix. I later read that it was.

But it wasn't until almost ten years later that I started searching for a sailor from the Belgrano to finish my story. I wrote several letters to Argentina but never received any answers. One day the president of the Phoenix Association sent an e-mail letter to those of us who are members who have e-mail that a member had died. Several days later a letter came by e-mail and it was signed "Nestor" (Argentina). That was the clue that I wanted and I wrote to him and he answered. We have exchanged many letters.

One day, the impulse came to me to locate a British sailor from the Conqueror. Last fall I looked at web sites and wrote several letters to submarine museums in England telling of my desire to contact a British sailor. I never heard anything back. Then earlier this month, I checked web sites again and sent several letters telling of my desire. I had hoped that I would hear from someone but when I checked the mail this morning and found your letter, I was ecstatic. I was gone for the rest of the day and when I got home, my wife said, "Wait till you see what you got in the mail today!!" I knew it had to be a letter from you.

I have kind of rambled. I hope that I have not bored you but rather I have given you a better understanding of what I have been doing.

Again, I must say that I appreciated the depth with which you wrote. But your diary shows your appreciation for recording events. So many of the veterans of Pearl Harbor have literally forgotten the attack – age is a factor with some, others blotted it from their minds and others just got busy with life and let the event slip by.

I hope that you saved what you wrote to me and have filed it away for others to read many years from now. I read recently "If it isn't written down, it never happened." I wrote to my mother every week for 35 years. She saved my letters which I thought was "silly." Later I got them back and have typed 25 years (850) pages. (I since have typed the last 10 years.) They read almost like a journal and I am proud of them – even though they are poorly written – usually written in haste late Thursday night.

Your life in the West Indies must be pleasant. I have never been there.

I hope to hear from you again N.

Lew Holt

Salem, Oregon

:: :: ::

My letter to N

Sunday, January 16, 2000

In a message dated 1/16/00 4:58:08 AM, barebum...

>By the way Lew, a thought occurs to me: please feel free to pass my e-mail to your Argentinean friend if you think it would be appropriate.

Good morning N,

I will get back to you later but wanted to specifically comment on this. I am toying with the idea how I might present your letter to him. I think your comment above and the rest of your short note will set the stage for me. It will demonstrate your sensitivity and the lack of glorification.

I will send you his speech and several of our introductory letters. I think you might enjoy them.

My wife and I are both "fiddlers." Yes, "folk fiddlers" you might say. Today we go to a near by town for a potluck and a jam for 3 hours this afternoon.

More later.

Lew

:: :: ::

Sunday, January 16, 2000

Dear Lew

Well I have to say that your tale is quite remarkable. You must have had a tough adolescence – but the human spirit is extraordinary.

I do understand what you are doing and what it means to you. I think that writing what I wrote – and what I will write when I eventually get around to the full book – is somewhat like "dealing with unfinished emotional business" – putting something to rest – perhaps the same as you. It's funny how writing from the heart can bring a sense of relief, sort of like crying on a shoulder.

I'm not surprised you never heard from the British – like I said, their secrecy laws are so ridiculous. Technically, you can go to prison for disclosing the colour of the carpet in the office where you work. Their Official Secrets Act was written in 1911, yet it's never been amended, and so there's a certain amount of paranoia amongst serving and retired personnel about discussing matters which took place during their service.

I definitely have not been bored by what you've written. On the contrary, it's reminded me of an aspect of human nature that one sometimes overlooks. I had 30 business e-mails waiting for me when I came to the office this morning – but yours was the first that I read and the first to which I have responded.

Thanks for writing. Stay in touch ... and should you ever feel the urge to come to a warmer climate, come and say hello.

Best wishes,

"N"

:: :: ::

January 16, 2000

Hi Lew

Thanks for your e-mail. I would very much enjoy reading the speech and letters – thanks for taking the time to send them on. And, yes, I'd be really interested in getting in touch with any former crew members from the Belgrano.

Have a great fiddle!

Best wishes,

N

:: :: ::

Sunday, January 16, 2000

By the way Lew, a thought occurs to me: please feel free to pass my e-mail to your Argentinean friend if you think it would be appropriate. For many years, I have wanted to go to Argentina to place flowers at the Belgrano memorial and to stand there in silence for a few moments. I think that's part of the "unfinished business" that I need to deal with. One day I'll do it.

Best wishes

N

:: :: ::

Monday, January 17, 2000

Dear N,

I wrote to Coco (Nester Cenci) this morning introducing you. I explained to him that I was writing to you and quoted a couple of paragraphs from your letters. Hopefully I will have laid the ground work for an exchange of letters among the three of us. Translating English is difficult for him. I will type out a long letter in a few minutes but when I do, I then encumber him with a long letter to translate. I talked to him four times on the phone last September. I could understand him very well and it would appear that he was speaking easily but I really don't know. I asked him several questions and he always answered them so from that, I have to presume he was getting most of it. His favorite was "How are you Luis?" He could say that very well and asked me numerous times. It makes me feel guilty in that I make no attempt to speak/translate Spanish – as if I could.

I basically wrote a short letter so that I wouldn't overwhelm him with too much. Based upon his response to my letter, I will give him more information. But I want to know how he feels. I don't suspect any negative feelings but I cherish our friendship and don't want to jeopardize it in anyway.

You can't imagine what your letter has meant to me. It has added to that "last little bit" to the history of the Phoenix. The Phoenix Association is holding its 2000 reunion in Washington State this August. It will only be about 100 miles from here so I hope to get to it for at least one day. It is at a poor time for me but maybe I can "squeeze it in." I have attended one other reunion for one day.

Thanks for your invitation "to stop by" sometime. Yes, that would be interesting. That would really be "frosting on the cake."

Lew

:: :: ::

January 18, 2000
Dear friend Luis:
Good to hear from you, my friend. Nice and very interesting letter.....
I am astonished with your story about the British sailor.......and from the HMS Conqueror ! ! ! I can't believe that, you have to tell me how did you contacted that guy.......Who is he ?.....I can't believe that....

You surprised me with the transcription of parts of letters from N, and I am satisfied you write to me about this guy, please tell me more about this matter. I am excited.....

>>I have written a lot of English for you to translate today. Does Martin help you? >>
No, Luis, he doesn't help me fortunately, because it means I am forced to improve my English......
Your friend,
COCO

:: :: ::

Tuesday, January 18, 2000

Dear Lew

I cannot tell you how much your e-mails have meant to me, in the same way that mine have helped you. Thank you so very much.

In an extraordinary way, we seem to have helped each other – by chance I saw your message on a bulletin board and replied to it and have managed to provide you with the final link in the story of the Phoenix, and you have now started to fill in some missing gaps in my life, important issues that have really bothered me for many years.

Thanks for getting in touch with Coco – I definitely do not want to be cause for any problems and I think that your sensitivity of approach is laudable. For nearly 18 years I've hoped that one day I would be able to correspond with or meet someone who was on board the Belgrano and the opportunity to do so would, in an odd way, enable me to find some peace and lay something to rest. It might sound strange, but whilst, on the one hand, I "did my duty" as those on the Belgrano did theirs, on the other I felt a need to say to someone "I'm sorry" – somewhat lame perhaps, but nonetheless a genuine expression.

Does the Phoenix Association have a web site?

Thanks again Lew. Look forward to hearing from you

Best wishes

N

:: :: ::

My letter to N

Tuesday, January 18, 2000

In a message dated 1/18/00 5:11:50 AM, barebum@caribsurf.com writes:

>In an extraordinary way, we seem to have helped each other – by chance I saw your message on a bulletin board and replied to it and have managed to provide you with the final link in the story of the Phoenix, and you have now started to fill in some missing gaps in my life, important issues that have really bothered me for many years.

Good morning N,

The first thing I do when I get up every morning is to check my e-mail. This morning I received the letters from you and from Coco. A great way to start my day.

I had wondered and was going to ask you how you happened to know about my request for someone from the Conqueror. Now I know. I especially appreciate your willingness to share and your sensitivity about the matter. You are certainly no "ordinary" person.

>Thanks for getting in touch with Coco – I definitely do not want to be cause for any problems and I think that your sensitivity of approach is laudable.

Coco's letter will demonstrate, I feel, his interest and no doubt willingness to write to you. I will write to him again and ask him if I may give his address to you. I sense that he will be honored. You can tell by reading his letter that he is literally translating some of the English and it comes out in a way that we might not write but it communicates very well. He and I have written many letters to each other since last May.

Lew

:: :: ::

Tuesday, January 18, 2000

By the way Lew, one interesting detail in Coco's speech: Many people incorrectly reported that the ship was sunk by wire-guided Tigerfish torpedoes which are the Mark 24's, but as I explained to you in a previous e-mail, this is incorrect – the weapons were Mark 8's which were originally designed after World War One and were upgraded after World War 2, but they were vintage weapons of an old design and chosen specifically because of their high explosive content. Had we used Mark 24's, we would have been able to fire from 20,00 to 30,000 yards. Because we used Mark 8's, we had to carry out a visual attack at close range.

There is, funnily, another reason that we did not use the Mark 24's. This is because, during trials of these modern wonders of technology, they had a habit of turning around and heading back towards the submarine which fired them ... a little disconcerting.

Best wishes

N

:: :: ::

[Because of space limitations, I will leave out a series of interesting exchanges over the last several years between N and me. I cannot imagine how I could have met two such men, one from the Belgrano and one fro the Conqueror. Two men who are so willing to write and to share their individual stories. And their willingness to meet each other – two men who truly are "Brothers of War." LH]

:: :: ::

Chapter Fifteen

Coco and N

January 18, 2000
Good morning N,
Yesterday I wrote to Coco asking his permission to give you his e-mail address. This morning I received the following two letters:

:: :: ::

January 18, 2000
My dear Luis:
PLEASE, yes, give him my E-mail.
Coco

:: :: ::

Wednesday, January 19, 2000
Dear Lew
What can I say? Do I mind? How could I? To say that I was interested in what you have written would be totally inadequate. It's extraordinary, and I thank modern technology for enabling us to communicate in this way. Thank you, too, for sharing these things with me.

Have you written, or are you writing, a book? I wondered because for many years I've wanted to write a book from the Conqueror's perspective, but firstly I encountered the problems of Britain's secrecy laws, and secondly I wondered if anyone would really be interested. Perhaps that was a little naive.

If you haven't written a book, you definitely should. Your insight and perspective is remarkable.

Communicating with yourself and Coco is giving me renewed energy in this matter and makes me think that I should pull my old diary out and sharpen my pencil and get writing.

I am going to compose a letter to Coco and I will copy it to you.

I will have to think long and hard what to say and how to write it, although it's something that I've been preparing myself for, for many years.

Thanks again

N

:: :: ::

Wednesday, January 19, 2000

Dear "Coco"

I have been given your name by Lew Holt. What a hard letter this is for me to write.

I am going to try to keep this first one short and simple, to introduce myself – and to thank you for letting me write to you.

In 1982 I served on board HMS CONQUEROR during the Malvinas conflict and I was the Control Room Watch Officer on board the submarine when the ARA GENERALE BELGRANO was torpedoed and sunk.

Nearly 18 years later, I have not forgotten one moment of the events of the afternoon of 2nd May 1982 and whenever I think of that time, it is with profound sorrow and regret for what you and your crew experienced, and for those that died and for their families. I have been haunted by it ever since. To say that I am "sorry" would seem inadequate, but I cannot change the past, I can only help to improve the future.

For all these years, I have wanted to contact someone who was on board the BELGRANO and now I have your name and address and I am writing to you with my hand stretched out in friendship, and asking you and your family and the people of Argentina to forgive us for what we did. Although what we did was our "duty", in the same way that you performed your duty, nevertheless it was a needless act and one which should never have taken place.

I hope that we will be able to write to each other, and I hope also that one day I will be able to fulfill my wish of visiting Argentina and standing at the Belgrano Memorial to stand humbly in silence and remember those who did not return home.

Yours Sincerely,
Narendra Sethia ("N")
Lieutenant, Royal Navy (Retired)
Ship Control Officer of the watch, HMS CONQUEROR, 1980 - 1982

:: :: ::

January 19, 2000
Dear N,

I indicated to you that I would send a picture of Coco to you. I found one this afternoon and copied it and I will attach it.

I was very, very touched by your letters. I stood there with a "big lump" in my throat as I read your letter to Coco. It was so well written and so sensitive. Truly a piece of literature. I compliment on your writing.

Let me quote a sentence from my brother's letter – "Well, I found myself crying it was so moving. One could not dredge this out of one's creative imagination if one tried. Great stuff."

N – I am sending this to you as a compliment.

Now, I hope that if you choose, that you would share Coco's reply with me. But if you choose not to, that would be fine, too.

I can only imagine how interesting your diary must be. Perhaps you will get it in book form someday.

You mentioned that I should write a book. I will send you the material I have put together about my brother. It is 450 pages long – his letters home, letters to him, letters from veterans of the USS Phoenix, the history of his ship, pictures and other items of interest. Some of it, I have been told, shouldn't be in it – I kept a journal of letters that I sent and received and such material but I wrote it for my family and I included the "process." I need to get a copy bound – perhaps tomorrow. The last pages will be the speech from Coco and your account of the sinking... but maybe I won't have them, yet, for your copy.

I look forward to your next letter.

Lew

:: :: ::

Thursday, January 20, 2000
Dear Lew
Thank you, thank you, thank you.
I am attaching a reply I received from Coco, and my response to him.

N

:: :: ::

January 20, 2000
Dear Narendra Sethia:
Your letter made me tremble.   I am very pleased to meet you. I have to thank Mr. Lewis Holt, a very good friend, to make it possible that you and I can be in touch.

You will see, I speak a little English, and for this reason, my vocabulary is poor, and on occasions like this, I am sorry for can not to express all I feel.

But the first thing I want to express to you, is I am joyful to have your letter, and to know you want to write to me. Believe me, I'm very glad for this.

It is not easy for me remembering the sinking. I prefer to talk about this unhurried in the future. I was commander at that time, and the third officer from the Captain, and 44 years old. Now I'm 61, and retired since 1988, after 30 years on duty.

I live in Martinez, a city near Buenos Aires, the capital of Argentina. My wife is Martha, also 61, and I have 4 children. One girl and three boys: Beatriz (39), married and 3 children.   Willie, 36, married with Laura. They live in Oakton, Virginia, USA. Fernando, 33, almost ready to be married, and Martin, 24, single.

I know your Country in 1968, during the sixth trip from Frigate Liberty. I was Lieutenant at that time, and we were in Portsmouth, and we visited London, also.

I congratulate you for your letter, and I am glad you to think like me about Malvinas conflict. I wish you will be able to come to Argentina some day, and is for sure I will be your humble host.

I liked "my hand stretched out in friendship" I accepted it !

Good to hear from you! More next time.
Nestor Cenci (Captain retired)

:: :: ::

January 20, 2000
Dear Nestor (Coco)

What a tremendous pleasure to receive your e-mail today – and, like you, I thank Lew for enabling us to "meet". E-mail is a wonderful thing, to enable people to communicate like this.

Your written English is very good – and I apologize that I am unable to write to you in Spanish, though I have a friend here from Venezuela and I might ask her to translate some of my letters into Spanish. So if you prefer to write in Spanish, it should not be a problem.

I understand everything you have written. It's hard for me also to think about the sinking.

I am 44 years old and I was born in Scotland. My father was Indian and my mother English. I went to school in England and France, and as a child I was lucky enough to travel to many places in the world – North America, the Caribbean, the Middle East, the Far East, Africa.

When I was 16, I obtained a scholarship to enter the Royal Naval College at Dartmouth in England, and at the age of 18 I went to the College as a Midshipman to start my Naval training. After one year at the College, my best friend, Captain Paul Robinson, was awarded the Argentinean Gold Medal by an Argentinean Admiral.

After I completed my Naval training, I qualified as a submariner and served in three submarines – one diesel electric submarine, and two nuclear-powered submarines.

Although I was a "full career officer" which meant that I was supposed to stay in the Navy until I was 55 years old, I resigned in 1982 and sailed a 9.5 metre sailing yacht from England to the Caribbean, via France, Spain, Portugal, Morocco and the Canary Islands.

I arrived in Barbados after a 29-day crossing of the Atlantic – and without money! I found work as a yacht Captain in the island of St Lucia and I spent 8 years there – first as a yacht Captain, then as an Officer Manager & Accountant, then finally as Managing Director of a yacht chartering company.

In 1989 I sailed away again on my own yacht – but I was caught in a big hurricane and my yacht was destroyed. I managed to repair the yacht and I sailed down to Venezuela where I spent 1 year driving a jeep up to the Andes and down to the Orinoco. It was a wonderful time, and I am only sorry that I was not able to visit other countries in South America.

I sold my yacht in Venezuela in 1992 and flew to India where I spent a few months, visiting Indonesia, Thailand and Malaysia. But then I had no money so had to work again, and I went to Virginia, USA, to run the reservations office of an American yacht chartering company. I see that your son Willie lives in Virginia – I lived in a place called Gloucester which is close to Williamsburg and Yorktown. It is a beautiful, part of the country, but as a single man I found it very quiet.

In 1996 I came back down to the Caribbean where I live in a beautiful island called St Vincent and the Grenadines. Here I also manage a yacht charter company and you can see all the information on our web site at http://www.barefootyachts.com

The Grenadines are small islands with white sand beaches and wonderful diving and sailing.

I was married for a few years but I got divorced and do not have children which I regret, although in another way it does mean that I have the freedom to travel.

Apart from sailing and running my business, I like to write and I am working on 3 books at the moment.

I have had some of my short stories published in magazines and newspapers.

This tells you something about me.

I have been thinking of going to South America next year and what an honour it would be for me to come to Argentina and meet you.

Before then, it's my hope that we can exchange correspondence – and I thank you from the bottom of my heart for writing to me.

Best wishes

"N"

:: :: ::

January 20, 2000

Good morning N,

Thank you so much for sharing your letters. It is a little presumptuous of me to ask you to share your "personal letters" with me but I am thankful. It is a compliment that you would share your letters. I especially enjoyed the story of your life.

I might take a moment and write you about my background. I was born in Oregon in 1929. By the time I was 11, we had lived in 15 different houses. My father was a logger, it was depression times, so we moved often. He was killed in a logging accident when I was 10 years old. My mother with her 4 sons moved to a small farm near where I live now.

The war came in a year after we had moved to the farm and our lives changed. Two older brothers were in service, Bill in the Navy and Charles in the Army. My younger brother and I worked hard during the war, as we were needed by the farmers.

I graduated from high school in 1947 and enrolled in a nearby teacher's college. In January of 1948 I was in a bad auto accident and was in bed 3.5 months. I went back to college in 1948. In January of 1952 I lacked just 7 hours of electives to graduate. I was offered a teaching position on the Southern Oregon Coast. So I loaded up the car and moved. It was here that I met my future wife.

I left in June, went back to college and graduated. That fall I enrolled in the University of Oregon to do graduate work. Alice and I were married in February. I graduated in June with an M.S. in Education. I did not look for work because I thought I was going to be drafted. In July Alice told me that she thought we were going to be parents. So I wasn't drafted. (Although injuries from the automobile accident would have prevented me from being in the Army.)

I went back to the coast and started teaching in North Bend (on Coos Bay) where I worked for 31 years as a teacher and as an elementary principal. I took early retirement at 55 and have enjoyed doing what I have done – centered around fiddle music. Alice and I both play.

One day our daughter called from Salem and said, "Mom and Dad, there is a house for sale across the street. Why don't you come up and look at it." So we did. After 41 years we told our friends "good-bye" and moved. It was a shock to all of them but it has been a very nice experience. We see our grandson almost every day. And we have many and varied experiences.

Our daughter works for a large department store here in Salem. Our oldest son is an engineer for Boeing in Seattle (220 miles) and our youngest son is a computer programmer in Corvallis – which is 40 miles from Salem.

Your description of the sandy beaches sounds intriguing. Our beaches are sandy and sometimes rocky and rugged but the water is cold. They are very picturesque but you don't lie around sun bathing very much – just too chilly. We have our share of rain and fog – and wind. Very beautiful but I like the warm summers much better here in the Willamette Valley where we live now.

Lew

:: :: ::

January 20, 2000
Good morning Coco,

I am very glad that you and N are writing to each other. Both of you are to be complimented for "extending your hand to each other." I wish everybody in the world could do that. Wouldn't it be a better place to live!!

Your friend,
Lew

:: :: ::

Thursday, January 20, 2000
Dear Lew

Thanks so much for the lovely picture of Coco and his wife. What a great looking couple. I sense something sad about him – I wonder if you do too? The expression is of a man who has an unhappy memory, which, naturally, he does.

I'm glad you liked my letters – if you are interested, I will keep you copied on any future correspondence between Coco and myself. I am really serious about getting down there one day, to shake his hand. How soon, I do not know, because I think it would be a very emotional experience for both of us and, as he wrote to me, this is something to be approached in his own, unhurried time. I feel the same – but I do think it's something necessary (for me at least) a sort of "cleansing," if you know what I mean ..... putting ghosts to rest.

I thank you also for the compliment of sending me your brother's writing. And anything you send me about your brother's story would be greatly cherished. I'd also be very happy to cover any expenses incurred in sending it.

I definitely want to get my diary into book form and plan on starting work on it very soon. In fact the contact I have had with you has re-energized me and given me the impetus that I needed. If I ever get it published, you will certainly be one of the first to receive a copy. I am asking my brother to send it to me from England where it has been laying in a box in his attic for the past 17.5 years. I am going to brush the dust off its cover and put it all on computer.

I have never been to Oregon but I hear it's the most beautiful place. One day, I hope I will have the pleasure of visiting, and meeting you, and shaking your hand too, and thanking you in person. One more question, if I may. Can you tell me something about the Phoenix Association? Are there a lot of members? And how did they feel about the ship's final fate?

Thanks again Lew

N

:: :: ::

Friday, January 21, 2000
RE: Coco/Argentina
Dear Lew
Thanks for this one.

It's not presumptuous to ask me to share my letters. On the contrary, you have been very kind in sharing yours with me and in any case I do not think that the nature of the letters is such that I have any problem revealing the contents. In the same way that I have been fascinated to read what you have sent me, I guess that this unexpected new correspondence that you have generated is of interest to you.

What a tough youth you must have had. How sad to lose your father at such a young age, and how difficult to see your two brothers leave for war.

I'll bet you were a great teacher. It comes across in your writing.

I am sure you must be happy to have a great family, some living close by. "Family" is so important. I don't have much, but what I do have, I cherish. My Mum lived in Barbados for many years after my father died when I was 18 but she moved back to the U.K. 5 years ago. I have two brothers in the UK. They're both surgeons. The oldest one is assistant Professor of Cardiac Surgery at the Brompton Hospital in London – he's the assistant to Professor Sir Magdi Yacoub, the Egyptian heart transplant specialist. My brother's specialty is pediatric cardiac surgery – he does heart operations on tiny, premature babies, some weighing less than one pound. My other brother is a Urologist and specializes in impotency and the prostate. They both have 4 children each, so although I do not have any of my own, I have great nieces and nephews and some of them even came out here last summer and I took them sailing through the islands for a week.

I love to hear the fiddle played and it's a regret that I never learned to play a musical instrument. But music is an important part of my life and I listen to music on a daily basis. I love classical, jazz and blues. Can't say I'm crazy about pop or Country & Western though. I also like music from other countries, especially Flamenco.

Although I live in the tropics, I do sometimes miss the seasons. Here there are only two seasons – the winter, which is warm and dry, and the summer which is warmer and wet. I remember, with nostalgia, English Autumns, crisp winters with snow on the ground, and the beauty of Spring when the first daffodils appear. When I lived in Virginia, the Autumns (Fall) were spectacular.

More later

N

:: :: ::

Friday, January 21, 2000

Dear Lew

Gosh, we probably have the makings of a book based on this correspondence alone!

I feel sad that Coco has no job opportunities. It must be hard for him. I wonder how he makes out. What a tragedy to have held high position in the Services and then to find oneself unemployed. I would imagine that he has a Naval pension but in Argentina it is probably a lot less than he would have received in the USA or UK.

When we returned from the Falklands, we were all given medals. "The South Atlantic Medal" with a rosette. I know that it has always been a tradition to hand out medals, but I did not feel terribly happy about being rewarded for taking part in an event that caused loss of life. So I sold my medal and have no regrets. I spent the money on paint for the hull of my yacht when in Venezuela. Much more useful. My brothers were upset with me and said that they would have bought it if they had known I was selling it. But I did not really want to have it in the family.

HMS Conqueror approaches her base at Faslane, Scotland on her return from the South Atlantic, and sinking of the Belgrano.

I suppose that I sound somewhat naive. After all, when one voluntarily joins the Armed Forces, as I did, one must know that one is being trained for war and that one day there is a very real likelihood that that training will have to be put to use. But when I joined, Britain's Navy had not really been to war since Korea in the 50's. I was young and exuberant and eager to get away from home and to see more of the world and stand on my own feet. I think that all of us who joined felt like that and, perhaps foolishly, we never really imagined that one day we would do what we had been trained to do. When we returned from the Falklands, many of our crew felt like that, and resigned. The reality of being in "action" had shown some of us that we were not cut out for the Navy and, today, the majority of HMS CONQUEROR's crew are out of the Navy, pursuing other careers.

You definitely have been a source of motivation Lew. Isn't it strange how paths cross and lives change? And all because of a chance encounter on something called "Internet".

I am really looking forward to receiving your package and will be reading every word eagerly.

Stay in touch
Best wishes
N

:: :: ::

Friday, January 21, 2000
Dear Friend Luis:
I am excited with the news about Mr. (N), I have received two E-mails from him, and everybody who knows this matter, feels like me with this.

I'll never forget you were the searcher of this special man (could be our son......?) and I am very pleased with his position about the sinking. Do you?

I don't know if you have this information, but I am sending you his second E-mail, for your knowledge.

More later.
COCO

:: :: ::

Tuesday January 25, 2000

Dear friend (N):

I'll try to write to you in English, because it makes me practice the language, I count on you, to understand me, with a quota of indulgence.

Your letter was written thinking of people like me, with easy words, and I thank you for that.

I'll tell you that my name is Néstor Antonio, but my nickname is Coco forever, and all my friends call me that. Narendra means something? It is a curious name for me.

I am impressive with your background, it is a story, and I will like to write longer with you, with enough time, to know details about things like the crossing of Atlantic, years in St. Lucia, driving in Venezuela, etc, etc. I hope some day this will be possible.

Besides that, I envy you living in such a nice place like the Caribbean.

I was seeing www.barefootyachts, and I can imagine how nice is that place. After I read that, I went to a lottery shop, and bought a ticket. I promise you if I win, I'll visit you at least for a week. I haven't seen in travel magazines in Argentina, ad about St. Vincent's and the Grenadines. Is it a very very expensive place or unknown yet?

I can imagine how many different people you will know through your work, and I suppose you write about this matter.....Please, tell me about.

If is true you wish to visit Argentina, be sure I will give you the most heartfelt and warmest reception. My home is yours.

Thank you for writing to me. I hope we will be true friends. I look forward to your next letter.

Yours Truly,

COCO

(Attached to N's letter to Coco.)

Dear Coco

Thank you for your e-mail.

Do not worry, I will understand, and I will also understand that you are writing in a language which is not your own and so I know that it is not always possible to express yourself in the way that you wish. I have lived in many countries and spent much of my life with people from other countries so this is something that I am familiar with. It is only my regret that I cannot write to you in Spanish – but one day perhaps I will learn.

My name has no special meaning – but it is a name from India so I do not think that many people in the West have heard of it. That is the reason that many people call me "N" as they find it easier.

Yes, I have had a very interesting life and have been lucky in this respect. Since I was a small child, I wanted to travel and see the world. When I joined the Navy, I thought that this would be one way to travel. But, as a submariner, I found that I did not see many places – although at the same time I grew to love my job and I was happy to be in the Navy.

When I left the Navy, the only way I could travel around the world was by yacht, so this is what I tried to do. But, as I wrote to you, when I reached the Caribbean, I had no money – so I stayed.

St Vincent is a beautiful island with an active volcano, rain forest, waterfalls. And the Grenadines are small islands with white beaches, coral reefs and lovely sailing. I will send you a magazine tomorrow, with plenty of pictures of the islands. It is fairly expensive here, but this area is not so well known – it is not so full of tourists, rather unspoiled. I hope you win that lottery ticket!!

In my work, I do meet people from all over the world. Many from America, Canada and Europe – but also sometimes from Brazil, Venezuela, etc.

For some years, I used to work with yachts which were built in Argentina – beautiful yachts, designed by German Frers and Arturo Cibils in Buenos Aires – these yachts were called "F & C 44" (Frers y

Cibils) and they were lovely, high quality – we had 10 of them in our fleet, but this was many years ago and now we have different boats.

The question of my visit to Argentina is not a question of "IF I come" it is "WHEN I come". I know that I will come, but the only thing I cannot say right now is "when". You are very kind to offer your hospitality. We have only just "met" but, like you, I hope that our correspondence now is the start of a long and fruitful friendship. I hope you know that it means a lot to me to have the opportunity to correspond with you, and it will mean even more when I finally get to shake your hand.

Warmest wishes

"N"

:: :: ::

February 14, 2000

Dear Lew

Your extraordinary book is sitting on my office desk. I have not had a chance to go through it in detail yet, but I wanted to drop you a short line not only to say that I have received it, but also to tell you that, having thumbed through it quickly, I have to say that it is a remarkable document and you should be really proud of what you have put together. When I've had a chance to go through it, I will write back in further detail.

But for now I'd like to thank you very much for sharing this with me. I am truly complimented.

Thanks

N

:: :: ::

February 19, 2000

Dear Lew

I do not think you have given me your mailing address but if you will do so, I will send you some things that may be of interest. I have just received my "war diary" which my brother Fedexed out from the UK. In the diary are some documents that I've copied for you and which you may find interesting. So let me have your address and I will mail them to you on Monday (note that mail from here to the USA can take 2 weeks or so).

I thought you may be interested in the following extracts which are verbatim from my diary which I used to write up each evening at the wardroom table. The original is much more detailed and hopefully you will see it in print in a year or so.

Best wishes

N

:: :: ::

2nd MAY 1982

This afternoon I knew what fear was. At 1400 we received a signal authorizing us to sink the cruiser BELGRANO, although she was outside the Total Exclusion Zone. We had been trailing her for more than 25 hours, and held her visually at Periscope Depth. After tracking her for a while, we went to Action Stations around 1500 and shut off for attack. The tension in the Control Room mounted steadily and around 1530 we went deep and opened from the cruiser's port side to around 4,000 yards. She was flanked by the two destroyers, HIPPOLITO BOUCHARD and PIEDRA BUENO. Shortly before 1600, we fired three Mark 8 torpedoes at the BELGRANO. The atmosphere was electric as the seconds ticked away and 43 seconds after discharge we heard the first explosion, followed closely by two more. Three hits from three weapons. The Control Room was in an uproar – 30 people shouting and cheering, and it became quiet only after two or three minutes. We went deep and then, after about five minutes, there was a loud explosion – a depth charge. Everyone froze, and the Skipper ordered shut-off for counter-attack and we took drastic evasive maneuvers, hurtling down to 600 feet.

There was silence throughout the boat. Suddenly, it was no longer "fun" to be doing what we were. We were on the receiving end. For an hour, we pressed on at full speed. Palms were sweating and you could have heard a pin drop. The tension was almost unbearable. Then we slowed down in preparation for coming to periscope depth,

18 miles from where we had attacked. After five minutes, another loud explosion, possibly another depth charge. We had just begun to relax, thinking that we were clear, and this brought us back to our senses again. More evasive maneuvers and complete silence throughout the boat. We were all very frightened. The destroyers were not transmitting on sonar, so how had they found us, 18 miles from the datum? Did they have a Neptune aircraft dropping Jezebel (listening) buoys? Suddenly, it was we who were the hunted. I felt scared, almost trembling, sweating and nauseated. I thought of what we had done, of the men we had killed. Although we may not have sunk the cruiser, the Skipper said he had seen flashes of orange flame as the weapons hit. My thoughts were numerous – my life, what I was doing here, my mother and brothers.

Scared, but determined, we kept going, praying that the destroyers weren't still on to us. We went on for another hour and finally slowed down some 26 miles from the datum. To our relief, we had no contacts and were then able to return to periscope depth to transmit and tell CTG (Commander of the Task Group) what we had done. After we did so, we received a signal stating that the CVA (the Argentinean aircraft carrier Veinticinco de Mayo) had escaped from the S-Boats (British S-Class nuclear submarines) and we thus became the first submarine to fire a weapon in anger since World War 2 and the first nuclear-powered submarine ever to fire a weapon in anger.

As I write, I am still overwhelmed by it all. I can hardly believe the enormity of what we have done. We can't go back and apologize now, it's too late. I wonder how many died. I wonder, even more, what the reaction will be.

The lads have all taken it very well – a couple were very frightened outwardly, and the rest of us made do with being frightened inwardly.

It was all over by 1915 local. I came out of the bandstand (watch keeping position of Ship Control Officer of the Watch) after more than 6 hours of concentration, mentally and physically drained.

We had a glass of wine in the Wardroom and spent the evening discussing what had happened. I don't think that most of them really realize it yet – they are still, as I am, a bit "high". They're smiling nervously, expounding on the rights and wrongs, recalling the tension and the feelings.

I went to bed at 2200, my heart pounding against my chest. Every little noise made me start. My ears have become sensitive to the slightest noise and we are all of us finding that we jump whenever anyone drops something.

A signal was received when we informed CTG of our attack, stating that "Her Majesty's Government has authorized the destruction of all Argentinean warships". Captain SM3 (The Captain of the 3rd Submarine Squadron based in Faslane, Scotland) signaled to us "Brandy is for heroes" from Oscar Wilde's "Port is for gentlemen, brandy is for heroes".

Our task now is still anti-shipping patrol and by 2100 we are heading back to the west at 12 knots. Twice, the two destroyers were heard searching and dropping the occasional charge. Perhaps they are looking for survivors?

It was, all in all, a very long day. I shall never forget it as long as I live. I think that most of us want to go home. We never really thought, on the way down, that we were actually going to do this. Now I think we are all stunned. The little things in life now seem relatively unimportant as the prospect of death becomes so real. The only consolation, I suppose, is that the end would be cold and quick. And we still don't know where their S209's (Argentinean Diesel Electric submarines) are ....

:: :: ::

3rd May 1982

The start of week 5 at sea. A funny day today .... There are an awful lot of very nervous people on board, including myself. I slept very badly, dreaming of bombs and explosions. I find myself starting at the slightest noise and my heart has been pounding away at an incredible pace. All the time we seem to be waiting for the next "bang" and are praying that it won't be a torpedo. I am constantly waiting for the Sound Room to scream "Torpedo! Torpedo! Torpedo!" or to say that they hold a destroyer at close range. But, today, at least, it never came.

Whilst at periscope depth, we were harassed by a Neptune aircraft which forced us deep on occasions. We headed west and, at 2000, started edging back towards the datum, the aim now being to have a go at the destroyers, BOUCHARD and BUENO.

We were told today that the BELGRANO is still floating (this was untrue) but drifting without steerage. Apparently, two of our weapons hit her and detonated, and the third ran on and hit the BOUCHARD but failed to explode. What a catch that would have been had we got two in one ......

Well, tonight we close in for another kill. I can't say that I'm looking forward to it. I'm very nervous, particularly as they will be more alert now. My eternal optimism tells me that we shall get home in one piece, but I still have a feeling of great fear.

:: :: ::

4th May 1982

Our main threat is now from Neptune and Tracker aircraft which carry Jezebel buoys and torpedoes. At 0400, we gained a 1 x 4 (1 propeller, 4 blades) surface contact at 112,000 yards on the "tail" (towed array sonar) and 78,000 yards on Sector (another type of sonar). She was doing 15.5 knots and steering 115 – a strange course and speed for a merchantman which is what she sounded like. We maneuvered and slotted in 800 yards astern of her at a depth of 300 feet. We could feel the pounding of her screw vibrating throughout the boat. At sunrise, we came up for a look and discovered that she was a hospital ship, supported by a destroyer. Shortly afterwards, we received a signal confirming that we HAD in fact sunk the BELGRANO. There were 1000 men on board, though we haven't been told if there were any survivors which seems unlikely.

We weren't authorized to attack the hospital ship, or the destroyer as she was assisting in the search for survivors, so we opened at high speed to the north.

Unfortunately, we were also informed that the Argentineans were, understandably, very angry and that eight MPA's (Maritime Patrol Aircraft) were searching for us. Although I slept well this morning, this piece of news once again made us all very nervous ... eight MPA's, all capable of dropping torpedoes. Some of the lads are getting very worried. I am trying to look at it philosophically and think to myself that if we are hit, at least the end would be quick. I hope it was so for the poor bastards on the BELGRANO....

There is much talk of "when we get back home", but we are all very subdued. The WEO (Weapon Engineering Officer) succinctly christened us the "instruments of the politicians' incompetence". It's interesting how now, we are effectively at war, it's no longer "exciting" or "fun" it's bloody frightening and nerve-wracking...

:: :: ::

5th May 1982

The first news of the day is not good – HMS SHEFFIELD was hit by Exocet missiles and is reported to be a floating hulk some 70 nautical miles south of the Falklands.

The BELGRANO, it seems, went down in one hour and gave most of her ship's company time to carry out a controlled abandon ship procedure. It's reported that they lost around 190 out of 1,040 men....

Christ, I hope the politicians see sense and call it a day. The ship's company remains nervous and subdued, though carrying out their duties admirably. This whole thing seems to have brought us all closer together than ever before, but one or two are noticeably showing the strain outwardly. The worst part is the waiting – not knowing what is about to happen, whether we are about to be depth-charged again. My moods seem to be "ups" and "downs" and they change rapidly. Others feel the same. One minute I am cheerful and optimistic, and the next I am a prophet of doom. My heart continues to pound away and there is a constant fear of ... the unknown? We have, all of us, started to think deeply about our motives and we are discovering a lot about ourselves. The First Lieutenant is gunning for war – he is, outwardly at least, remaining very cool about the whole thing. So, too, is the Skipper, although he is understandably pensive...

:: :: ::

6th May 1982

.... The latest news is that it has been confirmed that there were over 800 survivors from the BELGRANO, including their CO (Commanding Officer), so I suppose around 200 must have gone down with the ship. Does it make one feel any better knowing that we killed less than originally supposed? Can we believe that things are not so bad as only 200 died instead of 1,000? Do the numbers make the deed any less terrible? I think not.   (323 died)

:: :: ::

March 8, 2000

Hello Lew

Now that I have finished your vast tome – of which I read every single word – I wanted to write to you to say a few things. What a document it is. You must have had a very tough childhood. Looking at the photos of you as youngsters was, for me, like looking at a scene from an old black and white movie, of a poor rural family whose circumstances were made even harsher by the premature death of your father.

Your family, it seems, were very close-knit – a wonderful thing, and the many letters between you all testify to this. You must have been very proud of Bill, off to the Navy, and then overseas. I was touched by his continually remitting funds back home – I wonder how many youngsters today would have done such a thing – they would probably be more inclined to squander it on beer (or is that too cynical?).

Your mother's many references to what had been earned or spent suggests that money must have been very tight, and she must have had incredible strength to have kept going, with you youngsters still at home, and she struggling to provide a home and manage her affairs.

He seems to me to have been a young man who savored life to the full, loved his family dearly and showed extraordinary courage in playing down his illness and maintaining an upbeat tone throughout his correspondence, even when he must have known that the prognosis was not good.

You know, Lew, in a way you have brought Bill back to life. Here I am, thousands of miles away from you and we have not even met, and yet, in spite of the differences in our age, background and life story, having corresponded with you and read your work, I feel I know something profound of you and your family, and am honoured that you have shared such an important part of your life with me. Through your efforts, Bill will not be a faceless, forgotten victim of a long-ago war in a far-flung land. He is now as real to me as he is to your family, and as I write I can even see his face and imagine who and what he was.

Your hard work and research were worth every minute. I am not exaggerating when I say that it is probably the most touching biographical work that I have ever read. It reminded me that, regardless of our geographical origins or our place in time, we laugh for the same reasons, we cry for the same reasons, we are happy for the same reasons and we endure the same struggles in life.

There was Bill, more than half a century away, and here I am, reading his letters all these years later and looking at his photograph. Yet, there is no void, no gulf, just that singularity of human spirit which transcends time and makes us human.

Thank you.
Stay in touch
Best wishes
N

:: :: ::

March 8, 2000
>Now that I have finished your vast tome – of which I read every single word – I wanted to write to you to say a few things. What a document it is.

Dear N,
I can tell that you read it all. What a task... you are to be complimented. And I am complimented that you would read it all.

>You must have had a very tough childhood. Looking at the photos of you as youngsters was, for me, like looking at a scene from an old black and white movie, of a poor rural family whose circumstances were made even harsher by the premature death of your father.

N, you are very astute. Life was rough and life was simple but I didn't know any better so I never questioned it. Life was that way. I never went hungry. Life in the logging camps was simple, our houses were simple, no running water, no sinks, furniture made of boards. When I went to school, I knew that some other kids had more than we had but I knew my place and never questioned it. I dreamed about finding money – knowing, I guess, what I thought money could buy for me. Even in high school, I knew my country setting and obligations and never tried to compete for the things that I didn't have or couldn't have.

My mother did not want her boys to grow up in lumber camps and lead the life that our father did. We always talked about going to college and never thought there was any other choice. My mother knew that was the way out of our poverty. She had only a 3rd grade education and wanted the best for her four boys. She had chances to remarry but chose not to – her first responsibility was to her boys.

>Your family, it seems, were very close-knit – a wonderful thing, and the many letters between you all testify to this. You must have been very proud of Bill, off to the Navy, and then overseas.

Yes, we were. Bill often wrote telling us to write more often. When I was a teenager, writing a letter was difficult. I was unimaginative … couldn't think of anything to write. But as I read Bill's letters and think back, I feel guilty and regret not writing often. How simple it would have been and what enjoyment it would have brought to him.

>I was touched by his continually remitting funds back home – I wonder how many youngsters today would have done such a thing – they would probably be more inclined to squander it on beer (or is that too cynical?).

I was impressed by his loyalty to his "mama." He was 17 when he left home, turning 18 just a month later.

>Your mother's many references to what had been earned or spent suggests that money must have been very tight, and she must have had incredible strength to have kept going, with you youngsters still at home, and she struggling to provide a home and manage her affairs.

Every dollar was important, whether it was picking berries, picking hops, selling beans or chickens, working in the hop yards, etc.

>He seems to me to have been a young man who savored life to the full, loved his family dearly and showed extraordinary courage in playing down his illness and maintaining an upbeat tone throughout his correspondence, even when he must have known that the prognosis was not good.

This is exactly what I got out of his letters. He was protecting his mother. "He would be home for Christmas," "had good doctors." Just last night I reread the letters from the lady who visited him in the hospital, who wrote letters for him. It was sad – now as a father, grandfather and older, I can realize and feel what he must have been experiencing. No death, whether it is on a battlefield, on a beach or in a veteran's hospital is fair to a young man. Family would have been the most important thing to him but yet, he faced death alone. He never once reached out or cried out for us, he knew the reality of the times.

>

>You know, Lew, in a way you have brought Bill back to life. Here I am, thousands of miles away from you and we have not even met, and yet, in spite of the differences in our age, background and life story, having corresponded with you and read your work, I feel I know something profound of you and your family, and am honoured that you have shared such an important part of your life with me. Through your efforts, Bill will not be a faceless, forgotten victim of a long-ago war in a far-flung land. He is now as real to me as he is to your family, and as I write I can even see his face and imagine who and what he was.

N, what a beautiful, sensitive paragraph. Thank you for writing it. As I sit here alone at 11 p.m., it brings tears to my eyes. Yes, tears of sadness but also tears of appreciation. You may not realize but you have become a part of Bill's story. Several times I expressed in the story that my greatest regret was not having been able contact a sailor who was on the Belgrano. But it happened and Coco became very important. Now as the story continues – meeting you, sharing stories and eventually you and Coco meeting each other, will be closure for my story of Bill. I don't know if a fiction writer could have thought it through and made it believable but it is happening.

>Your hard work and research were worth every minute. I am not exaggerating when I say that it is probably the most touching biographical work that I have ever read. It reminded me that, regardless of our geographical origins or our place in time, we laugh for the same reasons, we cry for the same reasons, we are happy for the same reasons and we endure the same struggles in life.

Had I known who my readers might have been, I might have used a different approach – or at least changed my approach. I wrote it primarily for my family and as a record of my research. I included "dead end" letters, the journal of my letter writing and receiving letters – all so that I could have a time line and to show what I had done. Not the kind of thing for a "best seller" but maybe it will have value for future generations in my family.

>There was Bill, more than half a century away, and here I am, reading his letters all these years later and looking at his photograph. Yet, there is no void, no gulf, just that singularity of human spirit which transcends time and makes us human.

Beautiful, N. Thank you. Much of the value of the story for me is the people that I met along the way. We had the letter from Rita in Australia written in 1942. We had pictures of Bill and her and then 54 years later to be able to contact and write to her was powerful. To write to the 4 men that remembered Bill was what I started out to do. I especially liked the letter that told of admitting him to sick bay, testing him for tuberculosis and putting him on a destroyer and taking him to an Army Hospital in Australia – the very kind of information I was looking for. The only sad part probably, is that I didn't start 20 years sooner before memories had faded and before death took its toll of those who might have remembered him.

I erred when I sent out the 300 letters. I included Bill's story of the attack on Pearl Harbor and asked them to write me their account of the attack. Many wrote back "I can't add any more than what your brother wrote." If I hadn't tried to bait them, I might have received many stories about the attack. Oh, well.

I gave a talk several years ago to the Polk County Historical Society about my research and the book. One man, older than I, said that we all dream about doing a project but what actually caused me to sit down and do it? The answer was easy – I had thought about it often. I didn't want to always say that I was going to write Bill's story someday and then before I got started, have a stroke and then say "I wish I had written it when I could." I actually made myself do it when I could and before I couldn't.

I must have written you that I wrote to my mother almost every week for 35 years. She saved my letters. I have typed 25 years (850 pages) and have given them to my kids. The letters are a poorly written journal of the 35 years. Usually it is Thursday night, it is late, I am tired but I'll scratch out a note – so my mother would get a letter on Saturday. Knowing what I know now, I could have left a much better record. (Since I wrote the above, I have typed the last 10 years.)

I am helping an 82 year old man … I am writing the story of his family – from Norway. But that is another story for another night. (Marvin Helland)

Thanks for letting me chat with you this evening.

Lew

:: :: ::

March 9, 2000

Dear Lew

I'm glad that you were touched by my observations, in the same way that I have been touched by your work. You are absolutely right that a work of fiction could never have produced a story so extraordinary and so human. That, I feel, is its strength – had you written it to be a best-seller, I think it would have lost much of its human quality. It's REAL, and it's about real people, real events, real hardships, real joys, real tragedy – and it therefore appeals to the innate sensitivities of real people. What a wonderful legacy for your family, children, grandchildren and their grandchildren.

This week is a little hectic as we are in the throes of moving to our own new marina. Exciting, as we will no longer have to pay huge rent, and we will own our own little place. My problem has been figuring out how to move my 500-pound pig, Mr. Perkins, but we've solved that one by finding him a house in the country where he can retire peacefully (he will definitely not end up on a breakfast plate).

I very much hope that one day we will meet each other Lew. I have often wanted to visit Washington and Oregon, having heard of their beauty, especially on the coast. This year will be South America – but, who knows, perhaps next year I may be able to make that my next stop. E-mail is extraordinary and it's interesting how people open up to one another and are, perhaps, able to be more candid than they would have been had they met, for the first time, face to face. In a matter of weeks, a relationship is established, life stories are exchanged, and one feels that, despite having never met, one has a good friend in a distant place. The pinnacle of such a relationship would be to meet in the flesh.

Stay in touch

Warm breezes from the Caribbean

N

:: :: ::

April 11, 2000
Thank you
My friend Coco,

What a pleasure it was to receive your call just a minute ago!! Thank you very much. I am complimented that you would call me on my birthday. You are truly a great friend.

It was 9:30 here when you called so you must be 4 hours a head of my time.

I am looking forward to your navy pictures. I will copy them for more pages in my brother's book.

Your "old" friend,
Luis

:: :: ::

April 27, 2000
Dear Luis

I'm glad you have received the photos. How do you like the family Photo? We are now 14. (Thanks Veronica) I hope to have that photo in September with Narendra, but I'll tell you that I'm getting afraid, thinking if I'll be able to attend appropriately to N. I wish I knew more English.....

You will not believe: I have talked yesterday with Capt. Bonzo, and I felt disappointed after I talked him, because he thinks I'm wrong having our friendship with him. He thinks I have to be not so friendly...... I can't believe this man is so stupid and ignorant! He felt surprised when I told him I was invited N to come to my house, and it will be sure N will come here in September. Of course, I don't care what he thinks, and I promise not to call him again, unless he called me to let me know he has changed his opinion. Is not a big deal. Please, don't tell N about this. I feel shame, because N wants to meet Bonzo when he comes here.

Are you willing to go to the USS Phoenix Reunion in August? I wish I could go with you, but, if you are going, you'll be my agent...ha ha ha.

Well, my dear friend, this is all, and receive my warmest wishes.
COCO

:: :: ::

May 1, 2000
Fw: Translation of Captain Bonzo's letter
To: Members of the Phoenix Association
Subject: Translation of Captain Bonzo's letter

Dear friends:
According to a request from Andy, I'll try to send you a translation of Captain Bonzo's letter as accurate as I can:

"Dear friends
I'm writing in my own language, to greet you in the commemoration of the 18th anniversary of the sinking of the "ARA Gral. Belgrano "Cruiser, next May 2nd. Ships have a soul, and that soul is formed by their crews. That's why, on behalf of my crewmen we want to contact you, knowing that you share the same feelings for the ship and the same love for that noble unit.

We know about your annual reunions and congratulate you for them. We also hold comrades reunions once a year, in which the main subject is remembering our glorious ship. We still keep fresh in our hearts the visit of some of you to our country, five members of the Phoenix Assoc. with their distinguished wives.

The meeting of those of you, with the people of the "Asociacion Amigos del Crucero General Belgrano" (Gral. Belgrano Assoc.) is an indelible memory. I've read the book, and visited the web page of Mr. Bluemer and found them to be excellent. Our warmest feelings for you and your families all united under the memory of the Phoenix that presides in the shield of the Cruiser in both stages of its life.

With a big hug for all of you.

Hector Bonzo–Captain (retired).

Commanding Officer of the Cruiser ARA General Belgrano in 1982".

:: :: ::

May 31, 2000

Dear Lew

I thought you may be interested in a coincidence. I discovered, on another web site, a gentleman called Cristian Hendrickse who told me his brother was on board the Belgrano as a Midshipman.

So I told Coco this, and here was his response –

My dear N:

Unbelievable ! I was chief of accountant department in the Cruise in 1982, and my adjutants were 3: Lt. Ochoa, Lt. Montiquin, and.................Midshipman Hendrickse Guillermo.

At the moment of the first impact, I ran to the bridge, which was my combat position. The rest of the crew ran to the rafts. When Hendrickse saw I wasn't in our raft position, he ran inside the ship, to my cabin, to search for me, thinking I was still in my cabin. (He ran fighting against the rest of the crew, which ran to the deck to abandon the ship) It was an heroic act! Wasn't it?

I saw him 3 years ago, he is married now, and he was working at that time in Brazil, out of the Navy. It is not a coincidence? Please, tell me how do you contact his brother. I'll arrange a meeting with him, if you wish. I'll try to contact him tomorrow.

:: :: ::

Isn't that amazing? Again, the wonder of Internet

Hope this finds you both well

Best wishes

N.

:: :: ::

June 17, 2000

SORRY FOR NOT WRITING SOONER LEW.

Dear Lew

I have been inexcusably bad at responding to your last couple of e-mails – please forgive me.

Sounds like you've had an interesting few weeks. I particularly enjoyed your story about getting in touch with the fellow from Maine and the chap in Australia. Isn't Internet amazing? It has opened up a whole new world and, amongst other things, enabled you and Coco and me to meet each other.

I can tell that Coco is getting excited about our meeting in September, as I am. I actually have the air tickets sitting in front of me. It's an awful long way, but worth every bit of it for such a special meeting. I leave here around 5:00 p.m. on 15th September – and get to Buenos Aires at the uncivilized hour of 5:00 a.m. on 17th September, 36 hours later! The route takes me via Trinidad, Caracas in Venezuela, and Santa Cruz in Bolivia. It's further from here to Buenos Aires than it is from here to London!

He (or, should I say, Martha) seems anxious that I'm a vegetarian and so I've been trying to put his mind at rest and told him not to worry. I'm very easy about food. The wine is more important. Then he said that from 17th September they would all be vegetarians whilst I was there so I wrote back and told him definitely not to do that ... I know how Argentineans love their beef and I would feel terrible if they turned into veggies on my account!

I have been communicating with a lady in the USA who is going to help me get my book together. As you know, my original idea, years ago, was to get my diary published, but meeting you and Coco has added another dimension to the whole thing. I've been writing like mad for the past few weeks, trying to get everything together on computer. It's all rather disjointed at the moment, and I know nothing about formal writing (publishing, books, etc) so I felt I needed someone to point me in the right direction. She thinks that it has all the material for a documentary. We'll see.

I got myself a camera for my trip down South, and a bunch of film, so I will be snapping away when I get there. I'll definitely send you copies. I have to buy some clothes too – here in the Caribbean I live in a pair of shorts and a t-shirt. I rarely even wear a pair of shoes. But I know that Latin Americans tend to dress a little more formally, so I am now the proud owner of things like shoes, tie, jacket and long trousers!

We're into our hurricane season now. We rarely get seriously affected this far south, but we have to remain alert. In 1989 I sat out Hurricane Hugo on my yacht in the US Virgin Islands. We had sustained winds of 180 mph, gusting to 220 mph. It was an unbelievable experience but my crew and I survived. The boat didn't fare too well and my 45-foot Ketch was turned into a 36-foot sloop, but I managed to salvage her and get her afloat.

I hope this finds you both well and happy.

N

:: :: ::

June 29, 2000

Re: SORRY FOR NOT WRITING SOONER LEW.

Hi Lew

Thanks for your note. Sorry to hear you've been under the weather – and also that you can't take a spot of booze now and again because probably the best thing for you would be what my grandmother used to call a "hot toddy" – a finger of Scotch whisky, lime juice, honey and hot water. It works wonders.

Sounds like you had a nice trip. One of these days I've got to get myself up to your part of the world. From the pictures I've seen, it looks so very beautiful.

St Vincent, where I live, is about 90 miles west of Barbados, 60 miles north of Grenada and 23 miles south of St Lucia. Trinidad is about 140 miles south of us, and the Venezuela coast just a little further. St Vincent is more properly "St Vincent and the Grenadines" – the Grenadine Islands, which stretch immediately to the south of St Vincent, are real gems – lovely little islands with white sand beaches and great snorkeling, diving and sailing. There are about 32 small islands and rocky outcrops, but the principle ones are Bequia, Mustique, Canouan, Palm Island, Mayreau, Petit St Vincent and Union Island. In the middle of them all lie the Tobago Cays – 5 uninhabited coral islands set in the middle of the ocean and protected by one of the largest barrier reefs in the western hemisphere.

I'm attaching something at the bottom of this e-mail that I thought would interest you – it just appeared on today's internet news. The funny thing is that I actually agree with the Argentineans. In my humble opinion, they are 100% correct when they say that the ship was purposely attacked in order to scupper the Peruvian peace proposal. She was definitely steaming away from the Falklands and away from the British fleet, and she was 18 miles outside the exclusion zone ...

Have to rush now but will try and write a bit more over the weekend.

N

:: :: ::

August 16, 2000
Re: Story time
Hello Lew
Sorry I haven't been in touch for a while.

I really enjoy reading your stories – keep sending 'em!

I have been feeling very sad about the fate of the Russian submariners in the Barents Sea. Submariners are a close-knit community and, from whatever country they come, you feel that you're part of a club.

Anyway, I wrote this article, which was published yesterday in Britain's "Guardian" newspaper which is one of the big national dailies. Then the BBC called me for a live radio interview, so I had my 15 minutes of fame.

I am anxiously counting the days before I go to Argentina ... I leave here in 20 days. I am taking down a special bottle of Caribbean rum for Coco, and also a very nice, glossy, hard-backed book of photographs about St Vincent and the Grenadines.

I hope this finds you both well. Stay in touch!

Best wishes

N

:: :: ::

Iron coffin

A Russian vessel lies on the seabed with 107 men on board. It's every submariner's nightmare, says former Royal Navy officer Narendra Sethia

Special report: Stricken Russian submarine

Tuesday August 15, 2000
The Guardian

The accident that has befallen the Russian Oscar-class submarine Kursk, 480ft beneath the surface of the Barents Sea, is the ultimate nightmare upon which every submariner reflects at some stage during the course of his career – and, in many cases, long after he has retired.

Until the second half of this century, few submarines were fitted with escape equipment as it was believed that, given the operating circumstances of a submarine, such equipment would be superfluous. But in later years, the powers-that-be bowed to public pressure and fitted submarines with escape hatches, making a great show of conducting escape training exercises, though most submariners will tell you that they had little confidence of survival in the event of a serious accident at any appreciable depth. An escape tower might be handy when you're in a depth of 100ft in the North Sea, but when a submarine is more likely to be operating in the deeper waters

of the Atlantic, Pacific, or Arctic, it is more likely to be regarded as a useful storage compartment than as a viable means of escape.

I first read the book Das Boot, which chronicles the missions of a German U-boat during the second world war, while serving on a nuclear submarine about 20 years ago. I could not sleep for several nights, and had recurring dreams that our "boat" was on the bottom, 500ft down, and unable to surface. In my dreams, men lay perspiring in their bunks and their only sounds were whispered words and fear. In my dreams, all machinery had been shut down, and I could hear condensation dripping off the maze of pipework, and electrical wiring sparking in the darkness. Today, with the Kursk nearly 500ft down and reportedly seriously damaged after an unspecified collision, the 107 men on board must be feeling, awake, what I could only feel in my dreams.

In Das Boot, of course, the submarine in question was of 1940s design. The Kursk, by contrast, is a modern (launched 1995), 14,000-tonne nuclear-powered submarine which bears little resemblance to the "boats" of that era. Air-conditioning, movies and good food are all features of modern submarines, and, with water-making equipment on board, submariners are even able to enjoy regular showers – something unheard of 40 years ago (or even 20 years ago on a diesel-powered submarine).

Nevertheless, despite the

amenities, life on board any submarine is still cramped by most people's standards. There may not be sufficient bunks for every crew member and, on one long patrol, I remember we carried so much food that we had to use every inch of deck space and effectively raise the level of the deck by two feet. We were able to stand upright only after we had eaten our way through the food.

The cramped conditions and the fact that a submariner's only "view" of the outside world is by means of electronic listening devices, intensifies one's feeling of isolation. There are no windows through which to peer, no sun or sky at which to look. All that the men on the Kursk can see are the instruments, machinery and pipework which surround them, and the anxious looks on the faces of their colleagues.

The fact that the Kursk has not apparently attempted to surface reinforces the fears that her damage must be serious. The possibilities include damaged propulsion systems; ruptured ballast tanks, which would prevent her from achieving positive buoyancy; and flooding, as the result of collision or other mishap. With her nuclear reactor shut down, Kursk may not be able to operate air purification equipment such as electrolysers, which produce oxygen, or scrubbers, which eliminate carbon dioxide. The air will grow stale. As carbon monoxide and carbon dioxide levels rise, the crew will develop severe headaches. I have experienced that,

and even remember being unable to light a match on account of low oxygen levels. But I, at least, was not sitting at the bottom of the Barents Sea.

At 480ft, the submarine is subjected to extreme pressure. Without the assistance of a DSRV (deep submergence rescue vehicle) or a diving bell which could withstand the stresses encountered at that depth, escape will be all but impossible. The US Navy's DSRVs are incompatible with non-US submarines and it is unlikely that the Russians have similar technology. The tragic reality is that the Kursk is likely to become an iron coffin, the name by which submarines have been known for nearly a century.

Twenty years ago the cold war was alive and well, and Russia was "the enemy". As I think of the Kursk now, I do not see her crew as Russians but as fellow submariners.

The close-knit community of submariners signifies a profession in which, even in war, there is no gulf of nationality or language, but a singularity of human spirit which transcends such borders. My heart goes out to every member of the Kursk's crew, and to every one of their relatives. I feel sure that all other submariners, the world over, will feel the same as I do.

• Narendra Sethia served on HMS Conqueror

Chapter Sixteen

"Brothers of War"
N's Visit to Argentina

September 12, 2000
Bon Voyage
Dear N,
. . . . . .Again, have a good trip. Give Coco hug from me. Thanks.
Lew

:: :: ::

September 12, 2000
Re: Bon Voyage
Hello Lew

Sorry I didn't answer your other e-mails yet – polishing through mountains of work before I leave here. I enjoyed seeing the photos and reading your articles.

I actually leave here on the morning of Friday 15th – I fly to Trinidad and spend that day and night there with friends. Then Saturday morning I fly from Trinidad to Caracas, Venezuela, spend the whole day there, and then travel that night from Caracas to Buenos Aires, via Santa Cruz in Bolivia, arriving at BA around 5:00 a.m. on the morning of the 17th. An ungodly arrival time, for sure, but Coco insisted that he would be at the airport to meet me, which is really kind of him.

So, my extraordinary meeting is about to happen, and I have to thank you for making it possible. We (you, I, Coco) have had an interesting few months of communication and I will finally get to meet Coco –and definitely to give him a hug from you and me, not only because that is the South American way of greeting but also because it will be a truly heartfelt encounter.

Naturally, when I get back, I will write you reams and send you photos.

Have a wonderful time in the mountains, and you both take care.
Best wishes
N

:: :: ::

September 17, 2000
Coco – N,
We just got home a few minutes ago from our camping trip to Central Oregon. The first thing I did when I came into the house was to check my e-mail. We had 67 letters but the first one we checked out was the one you sent. The picture of my two good friends brought a lump to my throat. Thanks for the message. I could feel your happiness. It looked like language was not a problem – a bottle of wine soothes many problems.

I wish I had had your pictures with me this last weekend. I must have told a dozen people yesterday about the two of you – about my brother, the ship, the sub, the airplane landing in Buenos Aires Saturday morning and two strangers greeting each other at the airport. I am happy, too.

More later.
Luis

:: :: ::

September 18, 2000
Hello Lew
Well, the first words are from "El Ingles" – !
Hope you enjoyed the photos. I can hardly believe that I am here. It has been an action-packed two days, with Coco playing an excellent tour guide and already showing me most of the city and treating me to astonishing Argentinean hospitality. Before anything, and I'm sure Coco will reiterate this, it is you that I have to thank for making this special occasion possible. It means a great deal to both of us, and, I'm sure to you too.

I am impressed by what I have seen of here. Buenos Aires is larger and more European than I had expected, but, after the backwaters of the Caribbean, this is actually rather a pleasant surprise. And it's not too cold either!

Well, my plan is to stay with Coco and Martha until Saturday and then to head west to Mendoza (wine country), then north to Salta, Puerto Iguazu and finally back down to BA before heading back home on the 6th.

I'll definitely write again soon and when I get home you will receive a volume.

As far as language is concerned... well, I am trying hard with my bad Spanish, and Coco is trying hard with his GOOD English (don't believe him when he says he can't speak English). And we are managing just fine. But even if we didn't know a few words, I think we would still be able to communicate fine.

Well, I will sign off here because Coco tells me he has another bottle of wine to taste soon.

Take care Lew!

N

Everything N says is true. I'm surprised the good Spanish of N, and he replies me in a good accent. I'll tell you later all the news. It's a pleasure to have here a GOOD friend.

Bye Bye

COCO

Coco and N

∷ ∷ ∷

September 19, 2000
Friends,
Words cannot express my joy for having the privilege of talking to both of you tonight on the phone. I never imagined that I would have an opportunity to talk to both of you at the same time – especially from Argentina. My joy is made larger because I know that you two are together as "brothers of war."

I sit here with tears of happiness in my eyes. Thank you both for bringing such unique pleasure to me. I will tell the story a thousand times.

Your friend in Oregon
Lew/Luis

∷ ∷ ∷

These letters that you have just read pretty much tell the story of Coco and N. Many letters followed but they basically dealt with travels and family so I have chosen not to include them.

Coco and N

:: :: ::

October 12, 2000

Argentina

Dear Lew

This is a very short note as I am drowning under 3 weeks of paperwork after my return at the weekend.

What a wonderful time I had in Argentina. Coco's hospitality was overwhelming almost to the point of embarrassment. He is a lovely man with a huge heart, and his family is also wonderful. I was treated royally in every respect.

Quite apart from meeting Coco and his family, and spending a total of 8 days with them, I was also able to meet Captain Bonzo, an interesting and heartening experience.

I traveled around 3,000 miles within Argentina and also got to see a fair whack of this enormous country, and left with the promise to myself that I would return again in a couple of years.

I need to thank you for making the whole thing possible, for having introduced me to Coco and for enabling me to put my dreams into practice.

I'm currently putting together a fairly lengthy trip report and will send it through as soon as it's done. But I just wanted to get this off to you, to say a very big "thank you".

By the way, it was very nice to talk to you on the phone, though I'm sorry that I caught you at an awkward moment, thinking that I was selling you insurance. Coco and I were in a somewhat festive mood, as I'm sure you gathered.

Thanks again Lew.

Warmest wishes

N

:: :: ::

October 18, 2000

Hello Lew

Well, this is finally what the Guardian published today. It was heavily edited but they told me that the response was good and I got the shock of my life when a Buenos Aires radio station called this afternoon and said that they had Coco on the other line and would I agree to do an interview? So, yes, I chatted with Coco, on the radio, and then we spoke a little. I was a little embarrassed and wrote to Coco to say that I was sorry and hope he had not been bothered.

I hope you like the final article.

Best wishes

N

(This is as N wrote to me, rather than the Guardian article which was heavily edited.)

MEETING OLD ENEMIES, FINDING NEW FRIENDS

On the evening of Tuesday 19th September 2000, I sat with two men, drinking coffee in a café in central Buenos Aires. One was around 70 years old, had a white moustache and was casually dressed in a short-sleeved pullover and an open-necked check shirt. The other, in his low 60's and more formally attired, was bald, with bushy, white eyebrows and a look of sadness about him. More than 18 years earlier, I had helped to kill 323 of their companions.

In early 1982, I was a junior officer on board the nuclear submarine HMS Conqueror when it torpedoed and sank the Argentinean cruiser the General Belgrano during the Falklands War. Hit by two torpedoes on the afternoon of 2nd May, the ship sank within an hour, leaving approximately 290 crew members dead and a further 30 dying of burns and exposure as they took to their life rafts in the icy waters of the South Atlantic.

In early January 2000, I stumbled across a message on an internet web site, in which an American gentleman, Lew Holt, asked if anyone knew of people who had served in the HMS Conqueror. I responded that I had been in the submarine, and asked what I could do for him.

Lew explained that his older brother, Bill, had served in World War 2 on the light cruiser USS Phoenix – later sold to Argentina and renamed the General Belgrano. The Phoenix had survived the Japanese attack on Pearl Harbour, but Bill had died of tuberculosis shortly before the end of the War. Half a century later, Lew decided to compile a book about his brother and to research the history of the ship on which he had served and which was eventually sent to its watery grave that fateful afternoon in May 1982.

As our correspondence developed, Lew mentioned that he was in touch with a former Belgrano crew member, Captain Nestor Cenci, known universally as "Coco". I asked Lew if he would contact Coco and ask permission for me to write to him. Coco responded that he would be pleased to hear from me and so on 19th January this year, I wrote to him:

Dear "Coco"

I have been given your name by Lew Holt. What a hard letter this is for me to write. I am going to try to keep this first one short and simple, to introduce myself – and to thank you for letting me write to you.

In 1982 I served on board HMS Conqueror during the Malvinas conflict and I was a Control Room Watch Officer on board the submarine when the ARA General Belgrano was torpedoed and sunk.

Nearly 18 years later, I have not forgotten one moment of the events of the afternoon of 2nd May 1982 and whenever I think of that time, it is with profound sorrow and regret for what you and your crew experienced, and for those that died and for their families. I have been haunted by it ever since. To say that I am "sorry" would seem inadequate, but I cannot change the past, I can only help to improve the future.

For all these years, I have wanted to contact someone who was on board the Belgrano and now I have your name and address and I am writing to you with my hand stretched out in friendship, and asking you and your family and the people of Argentina to forgive us for what we did. Although what we did was our "duty", in the same way that you performed your duty, nevertheless it was a needless act and one which should never have taken place.

I hope that we will be able to write to each other, and I hope also that one day I will be able to fulfil my wish of visiting Argentina and standing at the Belgrano Memorial to stand humbly in silence and remember those who did not return home.

Yours Sincerely,

N

Just one day later, I received a reply:

Dear Narendra Sethia

Your letter made me tremble.

I am very pleased to meet you. I have to thank to Mr. Lewis Holt, a very good friend, to make it possible you and I can be in touch.

You will see, I speak a little English, and for this reason, my vocabulary is poor, and in occasions like this, I am sorry for can not to express all I feel. But the first thing I want to express to you, is I am joyful to have your letter, and to know you want to write to me. Believe me, I'm very glad for this.

It is not easy for me remember the sinking. I prefer to talk about this unhurried in the future. I was Commander at that time, and the third officer from the Captain, and 44 years. Now I'm 61, and retired since 1988, after 30 years on duty.

I live in Martinez, a city near Buenos Aires, the capital of Argentina. My wife is Martha, also 61, and I have 4 children. One girl and three boys: Beatriz (39), married and 3 children, Willie, 36, married with Laura (they live in Oakton, Virginia, USA), Fernando, 33, almost ready to get married, and Martin, 24, single.

I knew your Country in 1968, during the sixth trip from the Frigate Liberty. I was Lieutenant at that time, and we were in Portsmouth, and we visited London also.

I congratulate you for your letter, and I am glad you to think like me about Malvinas conflict. I wish you will be able to come to Argentina some day, and is for sure I will be your humble host.

I liked "my hand stretched out in friendship". I accepted it!

Nestor Cenci (Captain retired)

I was overjoyed to receive Coco's letter and, for the following few months, we exchanged correspondence. We did not talk about the Falklands or the Belgrano, but about family, and where we lived and other mundane matters.

As time passed, our cyberspace friendship grew and, finally, on 15th September, I flew to Buenos Aires at Coco's invitation. After a long journey, via Trinidad and Caracas, Venezuela, my plane touched down at Buenos Aires' Ezeiza airport at 5:30 on the chilly morning of 17th September.

Coco was waiting for me as I exited the baggage hall. Sixty one years old, and the former Supply Officer and third most senior officer on board the Belgrano, he looked older than his years and stooped slightly. I dropped my bag, saluted him and then walked towards him. We immediately embraced, like old friends.

He drove me to his home in a suburb of Buenos Aires and introduced me to his wife, Martha. An enormous breakfast waited on the table and, between us, in my halting Spanish and his slightly better English, we were able to communicate.

On the 18th September, Coco excitedly told me that he had "had a call from Bonzo". He referred, of course, to Captain Hector Bonzo, Commanding Officer of the Belgrano at the time of the sinking by HMS Conqueror. Coco told me that he had tried to arrange for me to meet Bonzo, but that Bonzo had said, "Why on earth would I want to meet a man who tried to kill me?" A fair enough response, I thought. But I also suspected that he may have second thoughts and that, like me, he would be extremely keen to meet "the enemy". Sure enough, when he called on the 18th, it was to tell Coco that he would agree to meet me in a café in downtown Buenos Aires the following evening.

The following day I could think of little else other than the meeting that evening. I donned a jacket and tie, and had my hair cut in the afternoon. I felt as if I was off for an interview, and I was somewhat nervous. Coco and I arrived at the café at 6.30 p.m. and ordered a coffee. As the minutes ticked by, Coco nervously tapped his fingers on the table, and constantly checked his watch. I looked through an adjacent window overlooking the street, and saw a man with a moustache passing by. Having seen an older photograph of Captain Bonzo, I thought that this may be him, and moments letter Coco sat up straight and said "He is here".

Captain Bonzo walked up to our table and I stood up and held out my hand. He took it and looked me squarely in the eye. "It's an honour, Sir", I said in my poor Spanish, "to finally meet you". He nodded and sat down next to me.

Coco then took charge and explained to Captain Bonzo that he had been corresponding with me for several months and that I was staying with him. "Sethia is a 'tipo phenomino'" he announced, and I tried to restrain a smile.

I noticed that, although they had not met for many years, and although both had been retired from the Armed Forces for many years and were of the same rank, Coco always addressed Bonzo as "Senor" – Sir. From time to time, Bonzo nodded and glanced at me, not in an unfriendly manner, but neither with obvious warmth. The two chatted, and occasionally I heard Bonzo mention my surname and from what I understood, he was telling Coco that he had, many years before, read the extracts from my Falklands diary which had been published in the UK Press in 1984 and 1985. When addressing Coco, he called him by his surname, Cenci, which I thought somewhat formal.

The atmosphere was tense, and whilst I understood snippets of their exchange, much of it eluded me. Bonzo then turned to me and, kindly, spoke slowly in Spanish. He told me that, in his view, the sinking of the Belgrano had been "politically criminal". I nodded and told him that I agreed with him and I felt that he hesitated at that, as if to take another, closer look at me.

Bonzo's hands were unhealthily white and devoid of flesh, his knuckles tensed. Whilst age had been kinder to him than Coco, he nevertheless did not look a well man, and Coco told me that for this meeting, he had made his first unescorted excursion from his apartment in a long time.

Coco explained that he had not been a well man, and Bonzo nodded. Three years previously, Bonzo had been involved in an unspecified accident in the city of Cordoba, some 300 miles from Buenos Aires, and had suffered two heart attacks whilst in the intensive care unit. He had also lost a great deal of blood and the hospital had no stocks. Some 40 former members of the Belgrano's crew had chartered a bus, driven to Cordoba, and all donated blood for their former Captain. I raised my eyebrows in awe, and Bonzo nodded again, as if to say "You see how my crew loved me?"

My ears pricked up when I heard Bonzo speak the name "Wreford-Brown", referring to Captain (then Commander) Christopher Wreford-Brown, Commanding Officer of HMS Conqueror at the time of the Belgrano's sinking. Coco and Bonzo both started laughing. I asked Coco to translate and he said "Captain Bonzo says that years ago, around 1983, a British journalist came to Buenos Aires and asked him if he would ever agree to meet with Wreford-Brown. Bonzo replied 'No...' and the journalist looked shocked. But Captain Bonzo then said 'No ... no problem'". I smiled.

Suddenly, Bonzo looked at me and said, in English, "So you were born in Scotland? My wife and I were there, many years ago. It is a lovely place", and he smiled at me. The ice had been broken and his smile was genuine.

He asked me where I lived and what I did for a living, and for another hour or so, we exchanged pleasantries. Neither Conqueror nor the Belgrano nor the Falkland Islands came into the conversation again. There seemed to be no need to include them. The fact that Bonzo and myself were sitting at this table really said it all. A retired Argentinean Naval Captain, "El Comandante" as I heard him referred to, and a retired junior Lieutenant were chatting and drinking coffee in a café in Buenos Aires. One had had his ship torpedoed with the loss of 323 members of his crew. The other had been Ship Control Officer of the Watch of the submarine which fired the weapons. But at this moment, it was as if the singularity of the human spirit had transcended the gulf between victor and vanquished, and there was warmth.

Earlier in the day, I had bought a book written by Bonzo, "Los 1,093 Tripulantes" ("The 1,093 Crew"), a detailed account of the operations of the Belgrano during the Falklands War, and of the sinking and its aftermath. I asked him if he would sign the book for me. He took it and looked pensive and then started writing and then he handed it back to me and I saw that he had written, in Spanish, "By coming to Argentina, you have demonstrated to me all of the qualities of a true gentleman". I blushed.

Bonzo then put his hand in his pocket, turned to me, and spoke slowly. "This", he said, taking something from his pocket, "is for you. And I want to make it clear that it is only for you, for no-one else, do you understand?" He then handed me a small ceramic brooch and told me that it was one of a series that had been specially struck for the survivors of the Belgrano. I was touched.

Coco then turned to Bonzo and said to him "Sethia would like to have a photograph, Sir". Bonzo did not look happy and shook his head as if to say "No". I turned to him and said "Sir ... Please!" And he then nodded and said "Alright". He then turned to me and put one arm around my shoulder and clasped my hand and beamed, and I turned to him and took his hand but, regrettably, the apprehension of the moment was reflected in the photograph in which I appear to be regarding him somewhat arrogantly, as if to say "We won", whilst his demeanour is infinitely more relaxed.

The meeting was over. We stood up and shook hands and Coco and I turned around and walked out of the café without looking back.

For a week I stayed with Coco and his family and, on occasions, usually over lunch, when the wine bottle was more empty than full, he would speak of the Belgrano. At the moment that the first torpedo hit the cruiser, at 4.00 p.m. on 2nd May 1982, he was in his bunk. The lights suddenly went out, he heard a muffled explosion and smelled an acrid odour. He immediately rushed up to his watch keeping position on the bridge and, whilst on his way there, the second torpedo hit the ship and blew its bows off. I felt myself blushing as he spoke, but there was no animosity in his voice. Within 20 minutes the ship was heeling some 30 degrees and the order was given to abandon ship. "On my life raft, there were 33 men'" he said. "The life rafts were designed to hold 12 people". He smiled. "They were very good life rafts, yes, very, very good".

"What was it like in the life rafts?" I asked.

He looked pained. "Cold," he said, shaking his head, "very cold. It was 36 hours before we were rescued. The sea was very rough, with 30-foot waves. Fortunately, the body heat from 33 men enabled us to survive. Some life rafts had only 4 or 5 people in them, and they died from exposure". I blushed again.

When they were rescued by the destroyers Hippolito Bouchard and Piedrabuena, the survivors were taken to the Argentine Naval base at Puerto Belgrano. "The Press were not allowed there," Coco explained. "When you went home with HMS Conqueror, you had the Press to meet you and your families to welcome you back. When we went home, there was no one. They wouldn't allow anyone to welcome us. It was as if no one wanted to see us, as if we were to feel ashamed." He paused and looked sad. "It was a terrible time," he said, "a really terrible time. But the worst moment of all came when we assembled in an aircraft hangar to work out who was alive and who wasn't. We called out the names of the crew. Sometimes there would be a response and you knew that the person was alive. But often there was no response, and you knew, with great sadness, that the person was dead. I lost 65% of the men in my department. When the first torpedo hit, it slammed through the accommodation spaces where the men in my department were sleeping or working. Sixty five percent of my department wiped out."

Coco retired from the Navy in 1988, 6 years after the sinking of the Belgrano, and with the rank of Captain. His pension, after 30 years of service, is $US 1,200 (about 750 Pounds) per month. Although he didn't say it, I sensed that he felt poorly treated by the Navy, forgotten and put out to grass. I asked him about Bonzo and he told me that Bonzo had been sent into retirement and now spent his time trying to help the relatives of those who had perished on the Belgrano. Eighteen years on, I felt that Bonzo was a tormented man who was inextricably trapped in one moment of time, four o'clock on the afternoon of 2nd May 1982, a moment imprinted on his memory and soul as it must have been on the other 770 survivors.

One afternoon, Coco took me to the Centro Navale in Buenos Aires, a yacht club with tennis courts and a cafeteria. We sat down with a coffee and a plump, middle-aged, fair-haired man with a moustache walked into the cafeteria. He looked unremarkable and wore shorts and carried a tennis racket. Coco glanced at him furtively and then turned to me. "Remind me to tell you about that man when we leave here," he said. I asked him to tell me there and then, but he shook his head and said "No, only when we go outside".

The unremarkable man turned out to be Captain Alfredo Astiz, the gentleman who had signed the surrender of South Georgia in the early stages of the Falklands conflict, and who was well known for having hurled French nuns out of aircraft flying over the South Atlantic. "Astiz," said Coco, "is known as the Blonde Angel of Death". A sort of modern day Dr Mengele, he was generally regarded as a state-sponsored terrorist whose hobbies included torture and murder of anyone remotely suspected of anti-Government sentiments during the years of Argentina's military dictatorships.

"Astiz cannot go anywhere except to this Club," Coco told me. "If he was to go to a restaurant, the Press would be called within minutes, and members of the public would attack him. He lives alone, under guard, and can only come here." He shuddered and I asked him why

Astiz seemed to enjoy the protection of the Navy. Coco shrugged. He did not know.

When we drove home later that evening, he pointed out an attractive building with manicured lawns and cypress trees at the front entrance, and proudly said "And this is the Naval Mechanics' School". A shudder went down my spine, recalling that the Naval Mechanics' School had been the infamous torture centre for "The Disappeared", those who were summarily executed during the military dictatorships. "Nice building Coco," I said.

For 2 weeks I set off to explore something of Argentina on my own. I went first to Mendoza where I was met at the bus station by a uniformed Colonel and a camouflaged guard, something of an embarrassment as I staggered off the bus after a 14-hour journey, looking disheveled and haggard. One of Coco's friends, a retired Army Colonel, had written to the Commandant of Mendoza's Mountain Infantry Brigade, to alert him of the arrival of a "British War Veteran". My reception committee drove me to the Casino Officiales – not a gambling house, but a comfortable Officers' Hotel in the centre of the city.

Treated with overwhelming hospitality by the Argentine Army in Mendoza, I was sent to meet the Commanding Officer of the 8th Infantry Regiment and made a hopeless fool of myself when I attempted to tell him that I was embarrassed by the hospitality being extended to me. Unfortunately, the Spanish word "embarrazada" means pregnant but I did not know this until everyone collapsed in laughter.

From Mendoza, I went to the Chilean border, close to Mount Aconcagua, then to the colonial city of Salta, to the spectacular waterfalls at Puerto Iguazu on the border of Paraguay and Brazil, and then back to Buenos Aires for my last few days in Argentina. When I arrived in Buenos Aires, Coco greeted me excitedly. "Barcena wants to meet you," he said. I asked him who Barcena was. "Barcena? The captain of the destroyer, the Hippolito Bouchard".

The Bouchard had been one of the destroyers escorting the Belgrano at the time of her sinking and it was reported after the war that one of HMS Conqueror's torpedoes had actually hit the Bouchard but had failed to detonate. After this incident, the Bouchard had apparently sent a message to the Argentine fleet headquarters to say that she was "returning home to carry out repairs after storm damage". Later it was found that she had four 5-inch cracks in her hull and it was stated that the torpedo had in fact exploded, but close to the destroyer rather than on contact with her.

Captain Washington Barcena and his wife arrived at Coco's house around 8:30 p.m. one evening. He looked somewhat younger than his 61 years, wore a jacket and tie and had an air of formality about him. We shook hands and then sat down with a glass of wine. He spoke little English, and so Coco acted as interpreter. "He wants to ask you a question, " said Coco.

"Fire away," I said.

"Sethia," said Barcena, "when did you first detect our ships?"

"Well," I said, "on the afternoon of 1st May 1982, I was on the periscope and saw your ships, 2 destroyers, the cruiser Belgrano, and an oil tanker, all steaming abreast of one another, carrying out a fuel replenishment." Without thinking, I then added "And I thought to myself 'What a great target that would make'".

He nodded. I then told him that I had a couple of questions for him.

"After we sank the Belgrano, Sir, we felt explosions close to the submarine and thought that we were being depth-charged. Did you or your sister ship, the Piedrabuena, drop any weapons on us".

"No," he replied, "we never fired any weapons. What you felt must have been the exploding ammunition and boilers on the Belgrano".

"Didn't you ever fire any weapons?' I asked. "Surely after our attack on the Belgrano, you must have tried to drop a few depth charges, in the hope of hitting the attacking submarine."

He looked pensive. "No," he said. "You see, we didn't have many weapons on board. And we wanted to keep them … maybe for a later engagement."

I nodded, uncomprehending. "Oh, I see. You mean that you didn't want to waste your ammunition on an uncertain target?'

He beamed. "Yes, that's exactly it!"

"Why didn't you ever transmit on your sonar?" I asked. "Surely you would have had a better chance of detecting the submarine? Wasn't your sonar working??"

He replied that this sonar was indeed working but that "it was a very old sonar, with only a short range. I didn't think it would be much use." Didn't think it would be much use? I nodded, uncomprehending.

"So how long after the Belgrano was hit did you realize that there was a problem?" I asked, knowing that the Hippolito Bouchard had been only a short distance away, less than half a mile from the Belgrano at the time of the attack.

"Oh, not for about 15 minutes," replied Barcena. Not for about 15 minutes? Hadn't he seen the smoke and flames coming from the Belgrano? No, he hadn't. Hadn't his passive sonar detected the explosions coming from the Belgrano? Apparently not. I nodded, uncomprehending.

"So what did you do once you realized that the Belgrano had been sunk?" I asked.

"We moved away from the area," said Barcena. "You see, we were worried that the submarine might come back and try to attack us. So we moved away".

They moved away. And the 770 survivors from the Belgrano spent 36 hours in their life rafts before rescue came.

Barcena excused himself and went to Coco's study and shortly afterwards returned with an envelope which he handed to me. Inside was a photograph of the Hippolito Bouchard, and Barcena had written in Spanish "Dear Lieutenant (Retired) Narendra Sethia, 18 years have passed since we were mutual enemies. Today I have had the opportunity of meeting you personally and appreciating your human values and moral virtue. They confirm to me, once again, the importance of meeting and communicating with other human beings and also of the tragic and cruel realities of a war in which you conducted yourselves with true Naval professionalism. Your nobility motivates me to present you with this photograph of my ship, the destroyer ARA (Argentine Armed Forces) Bouchard. My best wishes to you for a full and fruitful life. May God be with you. Capitan de Navio (Captain) (Retired) Washington Barcena".

DESTROYER ARA HIPPOLITO BOUCHARD

Buenos Aires, 3 de octubre de 2000.
Estimado Teniente (R) NARENDRA SETHIA:

Pasaron 18 años en que nosotros queríamos destruirnos mutuamente. Hoy tuve oportunidad de conocerlo personalmente y apreciar sus valores humanos y virtudes morales. Ello me confirma una vez más la importancia del conocimiento y la comunicación entre los seres humanos, como así también de la dolorosa y cruel realidad de la guerra, la que se debe tratar de evitar por medio de una excelente formación naval profesional.

Su noble proceder me motiva a hacerle entrega de una fotografía de mi buque, el Destructor ARA "BOUCHARD".

Mis mejores deseos de una vida plena y fructífera Que Dios lo bendiga

WASHINGTON BARCENA
CAPITAN DE FRAGATA
Comandante del Destructor
ARA BOUCHARD

Cap. de Navío (RE) WASHINGTON BÁRCENA.

I was touched and thanked him, and, in Argentine fashion, we embraced. When he left, I asked Coco if Barcena was a close friend of his. Coco replied that he had not seen him for many years and did not know him that well, and I asked if he would mind if I spoke candidly. He said that that would be fine.

"I cannot understand," I said, "why he never apparently made any effort to find the attacking submarine, why he left the area, why he didn't go to your assistance any sooner".

Coco bowed his head. "I have often wondered," he said, "why it took 36 hours for us to be rescued. I have often wondered."

On 6th October, I finally said goodbye to Coco and flew back to my home in St Vincent and the Grenadines. I had been in Argentina for nearly 3 weeks and had managed to put some of my ghosts to rests. I remembered clearly the words of an officer on board HMS Conqueror on the evening after we sank the Belgrano – "We are the instruments of the politicians' incompetence" – and realized that Bonzo, Coco, Barcena and all of the others were no different to me. Men, who had been doing a job, some well, some not so well. But men with the same emotions, the same humanity, the same pride, the same fears, the same frailties.

As I wrote to Coco when I first contacted him, and as I said to Captain Hector Bonzo when I first met him, "Sir, I cannot change what has happened in the past, but I hope that I can help to improve what happens in the future". For myself, and for some of the people that I met in Argentina, I believe that my visit has, in some small way, done some good. Eighteen years ago, I should never have believed that one day I would count amongst my friends a man whom I had helped to send into the frigid waters of the South Atlantic and whose comrades I had helped to send to their deaths. But today it is the truth.

© Narendra Sethia
October 2000

:: :: ::

October 13, 2000
Your letter

N,

I sat down to be comfortable and carefully read your 13-page account of your visit to Argentina. It was so clear and descriptive that I felt that at times I was there with you. Your writing touched me very much, bringing tears to my eyes.

"I dropped my bag, saluted him and then walked towards him. We immediately embraced, like old friends." Such powerful words, N, my heart pounded along with yours.

The brooch that Bonzo gave you must have come from his heart. The simple things can often become the most valuable. Coco sent me a Belgrano cap and a Belgrano paperweight that Bonzo had given him. Coco had given up the paperweight that must have meant very much to him. I will always cherish it.

It was amazing how the pieces of the jig saw puzzle came together – first you and Coco meeting, then Bonzo agreeing to meet with you and finally to meet Barcena. Men of history and you met them all. And you were one of them.

When Bonzo said in English, "So you were born in Scotland..." It sounds like something out of a movie – the element of suspense and surprise. Why hadn't he spoken earlier in English?

And there were other sentences that caused me to flush emotionally – real "grabbers." I look forward to reading about your visit to the Falkland Island War Memorial, too. If only other people from the trouble spots in the world could do as you have done.

I now look forward to more words from you – whether it is your story of your trip or of "life in the Caribbean." Welcome home. Thanks again.

Lew

:: :: ::

Chapter Seventeen

PHOENIX REUNION

August 21, 2000

N,

Is the hurricane I have been seeing on TV close to you? I take a special interest in watching the progress of a hurricane, wondering if it is in your area.

I have been following the Russian sub reports. It has been even more sensitive for me after reading your article. I have shared your article with several friends – the local paper didn't pick up on it. They wanted "local" people who might have been sub people.

Tomorrow I go Washington State to the reunion of the USS Phoenix/ General Belgrano. A friend is picking me up in his Porsche and will do all the driving – I won't mind. It will be 150 miles for him up to here and then another 100 miles to Kelso – and the return trip that evening. He is 15 years younger than I am – and enjoys driving his Porsche.

Lew

:: :: ::

This is a letter I wrote to a friend after returning from the reunion of the Phoenix.

August 22, 2000

I have anticipated this day for "a long time." Last spring Andy Wilson, president of the Phoenix Association sent out a notice that the reunion of the Phoenix veterans would be held in Kelso, WA. Knowing that Kelso was only 100 miles away, I planned to attend. We had lived near Kelso 65 years ago, before I started to school – a long time ago. (1934)

As I have written before, my brother, Bill, served aboard the USS Phoenix from August 1941 to January, 1943 when he was diagnosed as having tuberculosis and was transferred to an Army hospital in Australia. Later he was in hospitals in the U. S. and died in the veteran's hospital in Walla Walla, Washington in February of 1945.

It has been an interesting day. Dave Cloud, an associate and friend of mine for almost 40 years, drove 150 miles from Roseburg, Oregon early this morning to attend the reunion with me. We left Salem at ten o'clock, crossed over the Columbia River and arrived in Kelso shortly after 11:30. His little black Porsche cruises right a long.

We could see the Red Lion from the freeway. Dave took exit 39 in Kelso to the Red Lion. We parked, went inside and asked for directions to the Phoenix reunion hospitality room. We were sent down the hall to the Oak Room. I had no idea what would transpire at the reunion, whether I would be "in the way" or how I would be received. I soon found out.

When I walked into the room, I recognized Joyce Wilson and she recognized me. She blew her whistle to get everybody's attention and introduced me. She pointed out my book on a table that I had compiled about my brother who served aboard the Phoenix. Instantly I was a part of the reunion and made to feel welcome.

A lady who was reading the book commented that she could relate so well to the early part of the book – my hard working mother with sons in the service. In a few minutes I asked for everybody's attention – which is rather difficult to get when over half of the people were wearing hearing aids (my figures). But they listened intently as I told them a bit about my brother and Nester Cenci, "Coco," in Argentina, telling them I write to him often on e-mail. I called their attention to his pictures. Coco was on the Belgrano/Phoenix when it was sunk by a British submarine in 1982 during the Falkland Island War. I also told them about "N" who was served aboard the HMS Conqueror, the submarine that sank the Belgrano/Phoenix and that I had received many interesting letters from him. They listened intently nodding their heads in approval. Later the book went about the room as men looked at the pictures.

Several Phoenix veterans came to me to visit. I heard many stories about the Phoenix, the men, and some "girl stories." David took pictures of some of the men and of me visiting with others. Several of us visited in great length.

Later I met Ed Lettari from Argentina. I had a brief but important visit with him. I showed him Coco's pictures. He showed me a picture of the Falkland Island War Memorial. I was glad that I had come to the reunion.

About 3:30 David and I followed a van to the American Legion Building in Longview where the activities were to continue. When we walked in, most of the veterans were already there and sitting at banquet tables. I went to Joyce to asked what the schedule was. She told me that they were having a banquet, hospitality time and at 6:30 Ed Lettari would make a presentation about the sinking of the Belgrano. This would have extended Dave's and my schedule to the limit so we slipped away and had a pleasant 100 mile drive back to Salem and Dave soon continued his 150 drive home.

Lew Holt and Ed Lettari

I still have several things to follow up on. The reporter for Longview newspaper is to e-mail me the story that she will write about the reunion. Russ Telecky is to send me a two hour audio tape where he tells about his experiences aboard the Phoenix. Another man is to e-mail me reminding me to send him Coco's account of being on the General Belgrano when it sank and N's account of the HMS Conqueror sinking the Belgrano.

I would imagine that the youngest Phoenix veteran attending the reunion was 75 years old and others were older. I felt fortunate to be able to attend this reunion of men who had given some much during the war. Many had T-shirts noting they were survivors of the attack on Pearl Harbor.

There was a large poster with names of "departed veterans" from the Phoenix. Time is taking its toll.

Lew

:: :: ::

Phoenix Reunion Scenes
(names as reported to me)

Harry Rogucki   *Lew Holt & Ed Pelikan*

Ben Christiansen

Frank Costagliola & Lew Holt

Russ Telecky

Mel Fragassi

Jean and Ray Pevehouse

Lew Holt & Ed Lettari

Chapter Eighteen

Locating Japanese Aviators

I had my brother's account of the attack on Pearl Harbor. I had letters from men and women who knew him. I had Coco's account of the sinking of the Phoenix/Belgrano and I had the account of the sinking from the submarine from N. After having such luck meeting Coco and N and getting their stories, I felt that I had reached the end of my story and was willing to call it quits.

In the summer of 2001, knowing that the 60th anniversary of the attack on Pearl Harbor was approaching that fall, and with the luck I had been having, the idea came to me to try locating a Japanese aviator who had participated in the attack on Pearl Harbor. I had thought maybe the 60th anniversary would be a good time to be able to contact Japanese aviators. I was sure that several Japanese aviators would participate in the 60th anniversary recognition at Pearl Harbor.

A couple of months prior to December 7th, 2001, I wrote email letters to the Pearl Harbor Anniversary address asking for help locating a Japanese aviator who had participated in the attack. I explained why I wanted to have such a contact. I received an answer back that they were too busy and for me to check back "after the first of the year." I was disappointed but I didn't give up.

Just before the film "Pearl Harbor" came out, there was a story in our local paper about an 88 year old veteran of Doolittle's raid on Tokyo in 1942. The article in the Statesman Journal about Mr. DeShazer told of him being a prisoner of war for 3.5 years in Japan. The article told of him returning to Japan after the war for 25 years as a missionary. During that time he befriended a Japanese aviator who had participated in the attack on Pearl Harbor.

Since I had been thinking about trying to contact a Japanese aviator who had participated in the attack, I thought maybe Mr. DeShazer might be able to help me. I called Mr. DeShazer to ask if I might bring my two grandsons to visit with him for a few minutes. He said that if we came over right now, that he had time. He lives less than two miles from my place. We drove up Market Street, under the freeway and after a quarter of a mile beyond Lancaster Ave. we turned into a nice retirement village.

We were greeted at the door and invited in. Mr. Jacob DeShazer introduced himself as "Jake" and made us welcome. He introduced Taylor, Chase and me to his wife, Florence. I was hesitant. Would I be imposing on him? Would he talk about his experiences? I need not to have feared any reluctance on his part. His mementos of the raid were evident. Large pictures of B-25s were on the wall, pictures of reunions, his military ribbons were framed and displayed and other items. His wife said that they often had visitors about Jake's participation in the raid so that they were used to having company.

Chase, Taylor and Mr. DeShazer

After a short visit, he invited us into his study where there were more pictures and mementos. He gave both Chase and Taylor little "keep sake" items. He gave all three of us pamphlets that briefly outlined his military and missionary work. Then he gave me a paperback book that had been written about him. He showed me a book *Thirty Seconds Over Tokyo* which was dedicated to ten men. Inside it read, "They didn't get back. God help them." Jacob DeShazer was one of the ten. But he was proud to tell us that he did make it back.

When I asked him if he could help me locate an aviator in Japan, he told me that he wasn't able to help me. The aviator he had befriended had died ten years earlier.

We visited a while longer, I took pictures, thanked him, shook hands and left. That afternoon I went downtown to a used bookstore and luckily was able to find a first edition of *Thirty Seconds Over Tokyo*. Another time I visited with Mr. DeShazer to have him autograph the page that was dedicated to him and to "the others who didn't come back." I feel very fortunate to have met Mr. DeShazer.

Mr. DeShazer

:: :: ::

After other letters to various locations and no results, I had given up and was ready to write "that it just wasn't to be for me to locate an airman in Japan who had participated in the attack on Pearl Harbor." I knew that there were only a few living airmen from Japan who had participated in the Dec. 7, 1941 attack so the odds were against me locating any of them. The difference in language was a big obstacle. I couldn't just send out random letters and really believe that I would get an answer.

Late at night on January 4, 2002, just a month after the 60th anniversary of the Japanese attack on Pearl Harbor, by chance, a simple letter gave new meaning and purpose to my search for a Japanese aviator. The following series of letters will tell the story. Some will be shortened – editing out the irrelevant parts.

:: :: ::

On January 4, 2002 a letter appeared on the Fiddle List on my computer. It is a LIST for people who share a common interest in fiddles and fiddle music. I am a member. When I first read the following letter, I didn't think much about it.

Somebody on the Fiddle List wrote:

Is there a Japanese literate on the list that would share a translation of this CD? I'd like the sparse liner notes translated, but mostly I would like to know what Heja is singing about on track 3. Is this an ode to a long lost love, or perhaps just a remembrance of breakfast? I did learn the last verse, but I would like to know what she is singing about on the others.

:: :: ::

With in a few minutes the following response appeared on the Fiddle list:

Date: Fri, 4 Jan 2002
From: Christopher Girsch
Subject: I'm a Japanese to English translator
I am literate in Japanese – I would be glad to translate something

into English for you – that is my profession.

Bye for now,

Christopher Girsch

:: :: ::

Christopher's letter caught my attention and intrigued me. I saw Chris's response as an opportunity for me to have a letter from me in English translated to Japanese. My original intent was to have a letter translated and mailed before December 7th when I was sure that veterans would be attending the Pearl Harbor Anniversary ceremonies. I feel now that I was fortunate that I was not able to get a letter in Japanese prior to the anniversary. Had I had a letter translated locally, I would have mailed it to various addresses that I might have found on the Internet and possibly would not have received any answers. Repeating myself – I would have shrugged my shoulders and said, "I tried, I guess it wasn't meant to be." Had that been the case, the following exciting story would not have been told.

That same evening I read Chris's letter volunteering to translate the CD, I wrote the following letter to him:

:: :: ::

January 4, 2002   Friday 10:29 P. M.

Translation

Christopher Girsch,

I am going to try take an advantage of your offer on the fiddle list – only mine has nothing to do with fiddles or CD.

I had a brother who was on the USS Phoenix on Dec. 7, 1941. Later in the war he contacted tuberculosis and died in 1945. In 1951 the Phoenix was sold to Argentina and the British sank it in 1982 during the Falkland Island War.

I have an account of the battle on Dec. 7 that my brother wrote before he died. I have an account of the sinking from a veteran in Argentina who was on the ship when it sank. And I have an account of the sinking from a British veteran who was on the submarine that sank the Phoenix/Belgrano. I introduced the two men via e-mail and a year ago last September; the British veteran went to Argentina and spent 8 days in the home of the Argentine veteran whose ship he helped sink.

Now I am trying to locate a Japanese veteran of the attack on Pearl Harbor on Dec. 7, 1941. I would prefer an aviator but would even be pleased to even contact someone who might have been a sailor on a ship. My purpose is to have accounts from men from all four nations who were directly or indirectly involved with the attack and with my brother's ship. I have written a book for the family – including my brother's letters home, letters to him, the history of the ship, letters from men who remembered my brother and from his girl friend in Australia after 54 years. (She died Dec. 2, 2001.)

I feel that my story won't be complete until I contact a Japanese veteran. This is what I am asking of you – hope it sounds logical. I would like to have the following text translated into Japanese so I could send it to others who in turn might be able to get it to a Japanese veteran.

:: :: ::

In Japanese:

I am trying to contact a Japanese veteran who participated in the battle at Pearl Harbor. I am soliciting a Japanese veteran for the following reasons:

1.   I had a brother on the USS Phoenix
2.   He died later in the war from tuberculosis
3.   Ten years ago I wrote a family book with his letters, letters from Pearl Harbor veterans, history of his ship, etc.
4.   The Phoenix was sold to Argentina in 1951.
5.   The British sank it in 1982 during the Falkland Island war.
6.   I have become a good friend of an Argentinean sailor who was on the Phoenix/Belgrano when it was sunk.
7.   I have become a good friend of a British sailor who was on the sub that sank the Belgrano.

320

8. I introduced the two men – the British sailor has visited and stayed in the home of the Argentinean sailor.

9. Now I would like to have a letter from a Japanese veteran so I would have a personal contact with men from the four nations that are a part of the history of the ship.

Thank you very much.
Lew Holt

:: :: ::

Does this look/sound logical to you if it were translated into Japanese? Maybe it would give a Japanese veteran a better understanding of what I am wanting.

Thanks, Christopher.
Lew Holt
Salem, Oregon

:: :: ::

January 4, 2002   Friday 11:07 P.M.
Re: Translation
Lew,

It will be my highest honor to translate this letter into Japanese for you.

To add value, if you need assistance in communicating with folks beyond the letter writing portion of your project, please do no hesitate to call on me as your liaison in Japan.

If I can help you locate someone here, let me know what I can do for you.

Since Japanese characters can only be viewed on a Japanese language system, why don't you supply me with your fax and a mailing address to which I can send the original.

I will get to it right away – shouldn't take more than an hour or so.

My best regards to you...
Bye for now,
Christopher Girsch

:: :: ::

January 4, 2002   Friday 11:08
Wow, Chris. I am glad that I stayed up – sure didn't expect an answer from you so soon – if at all. I left the computer on line just in case any mail came in – while I was enjoying a dish of ice-cream before I went to bed.

Lew

:: :: ::

January 6, 2002   Sunday 5:40 P.M.
Lew,
I am doing some digging around for you right now on the Japanese Internet. If I can locate some folks here, I'll just call them and explain the details of your project. If you would like, I can email that letter right now to Mr. Yoshida to get the ball rolling for you. I contacted him the other day.

My translation of your letter covers the story that you described – without the numbered points. I think it covers and explains your interest well and I have written in very polite language for the recipient to feel somewhat honored by your approach.

Let's see what happens.

:: :: ::

January 6, 2002   Sunday 6:48 P. M.
Nr. Two
In a message dated 1/6/02 5:40:50 PM, Chris writes:
>I am doing some digging around for you right now on the Japanese internet. If I can locate some folks here, I'll just call them and explain the details of your project.

I think that would be excellent Christopher. I have "yelled into the dark" many times – it takes a lot of leads to finally connect. So, whatever you might do sounds fine to me.

>If you would like, I can email that letter right now to Mr. Yoshida to get the ball rolling for you...

Yes, I think that will be fine. He might better understand and appreciate what I am after (interrupted by a phone call from Chris in Japan at this point – but will continue) with you knowing and better understanding the culture.

(My comment in the above paragraph is that Chris gave me a call on the telephone from Japan. We had a nice visit.)

>My translation of your letter covers the story that you described – without the numbered points.
As I just said on the phone, today as we drove into Portland I thought, "why didn't I tell Chris to change the letter to fit the culture?" And you did, Thanks!

>Let's see what happens.
I don't get too excited about Christmas, 4th of July, my birthday, a new car and such events but after receiving your letter the other evening, I have been on a "high." Finally, I have a chance – may not make it – but at least I have a very good chance. But I am being optimistic – "my glass is half full" thanks to you.
You sure took me by surprise. I get quite a few calls from fiddle friends and people, so when you said, "Chris," I didn't catch on until you said, "Japan." I was picturing Chris in Woodburn – maybe somebody else – so it was a very pleasant surprise.
When "N" (the British veteran) arrived at "Coco's" in Argentina, they called me that evening and we had a nice visit. They also sent me a photo of the two of them holding up a sign that said, "Thanks Lew" (for introducing the two of them). Life is fun.
Lew

:: :: ::

January 6, 2002   Sunday 5:52 P.M.
Let me know if you want anything changed, Lew. I will email the letter when you say it is ok. That way Mr. Yoshida can read the letter and he and I can communicate for you.

By the way, I think I mentioned to you before that my oldest brother is an endodontist in Salem, right where you live and I have visited your town many, many times. I have another brother and a sister who live in Portland. Another brother was a veterinarian at the Dove Lewis Emergency Animal clinic years ago, but died of breast cancer two years ago at the age of 48. Too young to go. I was there to be at his side the last few hours, there in Portland, two years ago.

Anyway, let me know what you think.

Bye for now,

Christopher Girsch

:: :: ::

January 7, 2002   Monday 3:12 P.M.

Re: No subject

Lew,

I have yet to hear from Yoshida San, but then it has only been a day. I asked my wife to ask her father where we might poke around with a better rate of hits, so to speak. Her father was in high school during the war and was enlisted at the very end. His oldest sister married a man who was captured by the Russians early on and spent most of the war in hell in a miserable camp in Siberia. I have met him many times, since we are family, and have shared drinks with him on many occasion at which he rambled on and on about the experience. Must have been very hard for him.

Anyway, I'll keep my ears to the rail for you – and you will be the first person I contact when I have any information.

Take care – out on a business call to my customer for the day.

:: :: ::

January 7, 2002   Monday 11:04 P. M.

Re: No subject

In a message dated 1/7/02 10:54:23 PM, Chris writes:

> I will wait a little while before trying another route for you.

Great, Chris. You are a winner! Since you are a fiddler, too, we'll have to talk about fiddling someday.

I hope to get a positive answer from my response to the chairman of the Pearl Harbor Ceremonies. As soon as I hear from him – good or bad – I'll let you know.

Again, I am very appreciative of what you are doing. The whole process will add drama to my story and, I feel, make it unique. An idea just came to me – could you print out some of the letters that you are sending out – so I can add them to my files? I have printed 15 copies of the book – not bound like a real book – but just with a spiral binding. I included every letter that I wrote, a journal of letters, answers – everything to show the process. A copy or two of some of your letters would add to the story – and in Japanese would make them that more interesting, I feel.

My original book does not include Coco in Argentina or N in the Caribbean or Chris in Japan ... but the material will be added. I am in the process of shortening the manuscript – leaving out sample letters, unanswered letters, etc., to make it more readable – but Coco's story of the sinking, N's story of the sinking – and then what might be in the future, yet, will add to it.

I feel that you have expressed "our" desires for a contact in such away that would show that I am not looking for sympathy or humbling the defeated or glorifying the victor. I feel that the men who actually went to Pearl Harbor to visit during the 60th celebration have put the war behind them and might very well be willing to share a bit.

Another story – I have a friend who was on Corregidor who has given me his story. Another friend who graduated from high school with my brother was a POW in Germany. I have his story. I recently met Mr. DeShazer who was on Doolittle's raid on Tokyo...

I have a friend in his 80s who was with Chennault in China. I asked him if he had ever written his story – he hadn't – but he started writing to me. Now I have a lengthy story of his military experience. And the best part is, now his grown children have their Dad's story.

So you can see that I kind of have a "hang-up" for this kind of thing.

OK, another story – I have two Helland Hardanger fiddles. It is a long story but to make it short. Marvin and I have become very good friends. His father died when Marvin was two years old. His mother remarried 5 years later and moved to Oregon so Marvin grew up not knowing his Helland heritage. I came along and he brought up a box of family memorabilia from the basement. From this box, a story is coming. I have many pages of newspaper clippings, birth certificates, marriage certificates, ships records, etc., most of it I have gotten by writing many letters and help from other people – such as you have done for me. My goal is to write a book about Marvin and his family. Its title is "A Box From the Basement." In October Marvin fell into Mill Creek that flows passed his place – 8 feet down onto pieces of concrete in the water. He was lucky to have survived.

I have irons in several fires – all of them very interesting to me. It is no wonder I don't learn many new tunes.

But midnight will be striking by the time I get to bed – so I better head that way.

Lew

:: :: ::

January 7, 2002 Monday 11:39

Lew,

I asked my 70-year-old mother in law if she knew where we could go, and she called a neighbor who was on a bomber flying to some country in the south Pacific on the 7th of December. He seemed to know of some people...

So, I pressed her to ask that man if he knew anyone – and – She just called me as I am writing this to you with the following information:

Chiharu Naito 1-10-18 Asake, Kofu City Yamanashi Prefecture

She has said that Mr. Naito is in good health, but I will talk with you before calling him personally tomorrow.

Congratulations.

Bye for now,

Christopher Girsch

:: :: ::

January 7, 2002   Monday 11:48 P.M.

In a message dated 1/7/02 11:41:01 PM, chrisg@d1.dion.ne.jp writes:

> ONE LAST THING Kofu City is a 20 minute drive from my house – it is where my wife is from. I live up, outside of town in a farming village, so I can go see the man for you, if he is agreeable.

You bet, Chris, it is agreeable. I don't want to appear greedy but if you had a digital camera – or a regular camera, pictures would add so much more to the significance of the letters – pictures would make the people real. Yes, I am getting greedy ... but I am higher than a kite, right now.   Lew

:: :: ::

January 7, 2002   Monday 11:53 A.M.

Re: No subject

At 02:49 02/01/08 -0500, you wrote:

>In a message dated 1/7/02 11:41:01 PM, Chris writes:

>You bet, Chris, it is agreeable. I don't want to appear greedy but if you had a digital camera – or a regular camera, pictures would add so much more to the significance of the letters – pictures would make the people real.

Actually, that was going to be my surprise to you...I bought a digital camera last May when my brother from Salem (Dr. William J. Girsch) was here for a visit. I was going to get to this guy, take some photos and send them on.

However, I want to talk with you a little more to clarify things in order to approach Mr. Naito in the appropriate manner.

I'll talk with you tomorrow.

Bye for now,

Christopher Girsch

:: :: ::

January 8, 2002
Re: No subject
> but his oldest sister married a man who was captured by the Russians early on and spent

Chris,
Rereading your letters – I find that experience very fascinating. It won't be long until those men will all be gone and their stories with them. I read one time and believe it almost "religiously" that "if it isn't written down, it never happened." Guess that is my driving force that pushes me on to record the things that I have. There are millions of stories out there – many gone now – but once in a while, one will come to the surface. Perhaps, too, it fascinates me to meet people and to wonder how they stood those ordeals, walk away, and for the most part, lead normal lives.
Lew

:: :: ::

January 8, 2002
Re: Follow up
At 23:30 02/01/08 -0500, you wrote:
>Chris,
>After I talked to you on the phone, I called my friend on ham radio and had another chat with him. He sat up and took notice since he was in Japan for three years – probably in the 50s. He was stationed at Misawi Air Base (think that is correct) on Northern Honshu for three years.
>He asked me where you lived and I couldn't answer that. I told him that I would ask you.

Lew,
I live in Yamanashi Prefecture. It borders Tokyo – but I live on the western edge near the neighboring prefecture of Nagano. The capital of Yamanashi is Kofu City – which was completely wiped out by the war – and I live in Akeno Mura – a farming village.

Bye for now,
Christopher Girsch

:: :: ::

January 8, 2002
Re: Follow up
Lew,

As you requested, I spoke with Chiharu Naito. He was scheduled to bomb Pearl Harbor, but fell ill and was waylaid. Incidentally, he said 'the guy that went in my stead was killed.'

He later went to Saipan and other southeast Asian countries. He responded favorably to my request and introduced me to a principal of a kindergarten who was a pilot that participated in the attack on Pearl Harbor. The man said that I could use his name in an introduction and that he will be very agreeable to speak with me. [Turned out to be Mr. Harada.]

I will ask to meet him – it is only an hour or so from me – and record him to get a tailored description for your book.

Then, when he approves the original Japanese, I'll render it in English for you.

How's that for a few days of poking around?

Bye for now,
Christopher Girsch

:: :: ::

Chapter Nineteen

Mr. Harada in Japan

January 8, 2002   Tuesday 9:00 P.M.
Re: Follow up
Lew,
Just for your files:
The man's name and address are:
Kaname Harada
Nishijo 472
Nagano City, Nagano Prefecture
Tel: 026-296-1151
Bye for now,
Christopher Girsch

:: :: ::

January 8, 2002   Tuesday 9:02 P.M.
Re: Follow up
In a message dated 1/8/02 8:55:17 PM, chrisg@d1.dion.ne.jp
writes:

>How's that for a few days of poking around?
Chris,
I think that is just "fabulous!" Beyond my greatest imagination. And
all because of our love of fiddling, I might say...
Lew

:: :: ::

January 9, 2002   Wednesday 12:53 A.M.
Lew,
I have just hung up the telephone with Harada San and he is more
than agreeable to meet me and to discuss the entire event – including
introducing me to the other members of his flight crew who dropped

331

torpedoes on several famous ships in the harbor (though, in the excitement, I forgot the names). Those other gentlemen are a little far away – more than a day's drive, so I actually told him that we wanted HIS story. He was tickled, I could tell.

Due to my strict schedule this month – 5 patents and a 150 page text on a semiconductor testing machine, all due at the end of January – I tentatively set a date to meet him and interview him on the morning of the 18th, though he invited me to come any day of the week. Sorry to put the meeting off a week, but I am actually now feeling menaced by my deadlines.

I will take my digital camera to take some photos for you and will tape the entire meeting – and try to produce a document that illustrates the terror he experienced, as well as the glory of his bravery, despite losing the war. The Japanese fought admirably.

I will take him some extra special visiting gifts bearing your name and offering.

Bye for now,
Christopher Girsch

:: :: ::

January 9, 2002
Good morning Chris,

Everything is looking great – you best get back to your work – a week is but a "second" in this whole drama that has spread over years. I feel so fortunate that you have given so much of your time to this point. It should all be frosting from here on out.

You can call it "greed" or "creativity" but I might request – if the interview lends itself for such information – to make Mr. Harada San's story more meaningful, if at possible, I would enjoy having a picture of him – say – in his uniform – by an airplane – as a child – a marriage picture... I think you understand what I am asking for. But you will need to be the judge as to whether you ask him or not. I would, also, appreciate a biographical sketch of his life – birth place, family, school, military, marriage, – again "what ever."

In 1985 Alice and I took an extended trip around the U.S. – with our primary focus being Vermont during the peak of the fall color. As we rounded a corner and saw a new splash of color, we always exclaimed something to express our enthusiasm. We repeated it hundreds of times. I feel the same every time I talk to you or read another letter from you. I always think, "Wow," and other descriptive words...that express the same meaning. I just walked a mile to get a hair cut and back home. It gave me a chance to walk and to think about this whole experience... and to think, it isn't over yet.

Enough.

Lew

:: :: ::

January 9, 2002   Wednesday 4:14 P.M.

Lew

WOW, is the same expression I have been using for the last 24 hours.

Yesterday, after having spoken to this man, I sensed that I was beginning to slip into a profoundly lonely state of a pride of having found this incredibly unique individual after only three telephone calls, of having spoken to him over the telephone, of having developed in a matter of minutes his trust, of having been invited right into his home, in knowing that not only was he there and that he participated in one of the defining moments of modern history – he survived the war. I know that through this he and I will probably remain close friends for the rest of his life partly because of his enormous generosity and humanity and because of my eagerness to honor him, and of a new curiosity directed at myself where elation and a sense of a loss of myself mingle. What events in my life would have led me from an upper-class midwestern American family 22,222 miles to the east not only to appreciate but to make an essential part of my adult life a culture in which old truths hold untrue, where white is black and day is night.

Bye for now,

Christopher Girsch

:: :: ::

January 9, 2002   Wednesday 4:46

Lew,

I don't think that I mentioned to you that after calling Harada, I called I called Mr. Naito who introduced us, ourselves having never met, to thank him. He said 'Harada was the top of the top...you will never, ever find anyone like him. In those days he was top of his class and the cream of the crop. He was a top flight officer and very powerful and fought valiantly in the war. Now he represents ALL Zero pilots as the head of the Zero fighter pilot's association. He was at the Arizona Memorial last year and there was a photo in the newspaper of him shaking hands with one of the living American Generals.'

Harada is 85 years old, but when I spoke with him on the phone yesterday, he was sharp as a tack.

Bye for now,

Christopher Girsch

:: :: ::

January 9, 2002

Lew

From web sites I read that Mr. Kaname Harada is one of the few Japanese pilots who participated in the attack on Pearl Harbor who survived the WW II. He flew cover over the aircraft carrier Soryn while others from the carrier attacked Pearl Harbor. Early on after the war Mr. Harada struggled with mediocre jobs but later years he has devoted much of his life to the education of kindergarten children to whom he has become an outspoken advocate of international understanding.

Christopher Girsch

:: :: ::

January 10, 2002

Lew,

I am going to go out this weekend and pick out a nice bottle of wine or Japanese sake with gold leaf plus maybe a special local delicacy as a treat for Mr. Harada.

Bye for now,

Christopher Girsch

:: :: ::

January 10, 2002

Chris, you are one of a kind. I feel so fortunate to have met you and to have you do so much for me. Your generosity and understanding of what I want combine for the best. And there is more "down the road" yet to come. I have friends who are sweating out this story with me.

Only two more days and counting – stay in there, Chris.

Lew

:: :: ::

January 12, 2002

Lew,

You might find it interesting that I have been telling this story to folks here to find that everyone is greatly interested. I went to the wine shop last night to pick out a nice bottle of wine for Mr. Harada, and asked the keeper to help me pick out something special and proceeded to tell him the story...His response was 'most of those guys won't talk to anyone about that time. You are really lucky.

I am going to take a tape recorder with me and record our talk, but my plan of approach is to first sit and talk with him to get acquainted and to let him warm up to me a little. I will decide then whether it is within protocol to ask him to produce a piece of writing covering his birth, young life, the general atmosphere of the country just before the war, when he found out the plans (remember, he was a officer – my father in law says that you don't get any higher in the Japanese military at that time) to attack Pearl Harbor, and what he did subsequent to the end of the war.

If it seems like that would be asking too much of him, then I will ask him questions along that line and ask him if I can produce the piece for him. In that case, I will take it back to him for approval.

I have learned that this man spent a great deal of time making speeches opposing violent conflict and war and that he spent most of his time working with children. I also know that to have risen to be an officer before the war in Japan at that time, he must have been from a very well-to-do family because he was given a top flight education,

335

so to speak. People did not get such opportunities in Japan at that time. His family was probably descendent from local power holders – even samurai.

Bye for now,
Christopher Girsch

:: :: ::

January 15, 2002
Lew,

I saw one photo, last night. Very impressive fiddle back...almost makes you want to play the thing upside down to let everyone appreciate the little seen side...

On a more serious note, so to speak, you might want to sit for 24 hours and muse over some questions you would like me to ask Mr. Harada on Friday. I imagine that he and I will be in contact regularly, during and after this project, but rather than call him all the time and pester him, I would prefer to visit him personally periodically, if ever I need more information. I have questions of my own, but this is your project. I am only the mule, so any specifics from you would be highly welcome.

I have not set a time, but it is two and one half hour drive there to Mr. Harada's home, plus time searching for his place the first time. So, I imagine that I will leave here quite early Friday morning. That means you can only contact me tomorrow, or email my portable phone, if you have any bright ideas while I am at Mr. Harada's house on Friday (Thursday night, your time.)

Bye for now,
Christopher Girsch

:: :: ::

January 15, 2002
Lew,

I have just returned from the photo shop. We were able to print one of each of the three photos. They came out well and without much of a hitch, save for my scraping one meter of the front end of my new BMW on the cement planter (cement planter...why cement...) on the way out of my parking space. Next month, I have to take my car in for its one year checkup and will have them replace the front bumper then.

So, I have a bottle of fine wine, my wife's parents are going out to get the delicacy I ordered tomorrow, and now I have the photos... Looks like things are going well.

Bye for now,
Christopher Girsch

:: :: ::

January 15, 2002
In a message dated 1/15/02 9:57:17 PM, Chris writes:
>save for my scraping one meter of the front end of my new BMW on the cement planter

Chris,
I feel badly about that – it will leave a blemish on this positive and exciting episode.

>So, I have a bottle of fine wine. . . . Looks like things are going well.
I don't think a professional public relations team could have come up with a better approach.
Lew

:: :: ::

January 15, 2002
Re: Phoenix
> it will leave a blemish on this positive and exciting episode.
Carelessness on my part...should have looked and should have been more careful...but I wanted to get the happy news to you and to get back to my patent...due today...
>>I don't think a professional public relations team could have come up with a better approach.

This is just normal protocol in Japan. I believe my living here for 17 years has caused me to behave in a manner beloved to Japanese people.

Bye for now,
Christopher Girsch

:: :: ::

January 16, 2002
Re: Another signature
I just got off the telephone with Mr. Harada and he is planning to meet me at the train station at 10:00 AM. That means I leave here at 7:00 AM...

Now, to get your letter composed...
Bye for now,
Christopher Girsch

:: :: ::

1625 19th St. NE
Salem, Oregon 97303
January 18, 2002 (Written by Chris.)
Dear Mr. Harada,
My name is Lew Holt, and I am a retired teacher and school principal living in Salem, Oregon in the United States. Indeed, it is a great honor and a unique privilege to be writing this short note to extend my hand in friendship and brotherhood to you and your family. Undoubtedly, by the time you have had a chance to read this letter, hand delivered to you by my friend Chris, you will have heard the amazing story of the USS Phoenix, about which I have done much research to write a book.

In preparing my story, I felt a strong need to complete this very personal story by making a meaningful contact with a Japanese veteran of the war. Chris was instrumental in locating you. Thus, the years of my research and correspondence with people involved with my brother's ship, around the world, will be complete with my reaching out to you, another honored veteran.

I would be forever grateful if you and I could periodically correspond and share our experiences of the past and present and of our hopes for the future via letter. In closing, I look forward to hearing from you and to learning about your life and the many things that we actually have in common, namely our lives as teachers. Take care and all the best to you.

Lew Holt

:: :: ::

January 16, 2002   11:55 p.m.

Watch your email tomorrow night, maybe, if the timing is right, I can email you a short message from my phone while I am in the company of Mr. Harada. JUST MAYBE...

Bye for now.

Christopher Girsch

:: :: ::

January 17, 2002   12:29 a.m.

Re: Another signature

1. Wine and delicacy are readied and waiting at the door.

2. Letters completed and in a plastic file with photos and a 'Greetings from Harada Kaname to Lew Holt' sign for a photo.

3. Contact made and location to meet set.

4. Finished an assignment due tomorrow and delivered it to my client today.

5. Roads look clear, no rain or snow.

6. Camera with new batteries and film floppy.

7. Addresses and phone numbers safely registered in my cellular.

That's it. Your dream is coming true.

Bye for now,

Christopher Girsch

:: :: ::

Chris had told me that he had his cell phone and that it could copy short email letters. I guessed as to the time he might be at Mr. Harada's house and sent the following letter hoping that Chris might receive the letter while he was talking to Mr. Harada.

January 17, 2002

Good morning Chris and our friend, Mr. Harada. My greetings to both of you this morning as you are visiting. My warmest good wishes to you. Thanks to you both for your friendship.

Lew Holt

Salem, Oregon USA

:: :: ::

January 17, 2002   6:18 p.m. PST

I am sitting here in Mr. H's house! He is signing a book he wrote! For you!

:: :: ::

January 17, 2002   9:52 p.m.

I am on my way home, so check your mail in 2 hours.

:: :: ::

January 17, 2002   10:40

Chris,

I'll be up...

Lew

:: :: ::

January 18, 2002   12:09 A.M.

Lew,

The photos are on the way, but they are not very clear...have no fear, I have a feeling that I will be seeing Mr. Harada again, so I can get clear photos later...wait until you see the photos he is sending you...they are REALLY REALLY great. You will really get a kick out of them.

Bye for now,

Christopher Girsch

:: :: ::

January 18, 2002
Chris,

I finally have the pictures downloaded. My computer was indexing as it does after midnight and it was too much and froze on me – so I had to restart and start over. Got all the pictures. There is one nice sharp one which I will be able to send to friends tomorrow to show them the results of your visit.

Yes, they look like very nice people – I can see their charm in the pictures. I wish I could have been there with you. I shall be forever grateful to you and hope that in someway, someday, I will be able to repay you…

Now I look forward to the book and other memorabilia when that time comes. It has gone beyond the "maybe" or "I hope" to reality. I no longer have to wonder "if" or "when" but now I know that "one of these days" I'll have the information.

Yes, I would be pleased if you could contact one of the seven survivors of the actual attack. And I know that realistically that you must put everything in its place – your job, your family, your father. I will "take a number" and take my turn.

More later. I am overwhelmed at this moment.

Lew

:: :: ::

January 18, 2002   12:43 A.M.
Lew

I am sure that by now you are well beyond counting sheep and are actual nestled in among their wool. Just to keep you up to date, I just got off the telephone with Mr. Harada to thank him for a lovely day at his home and to ask if he would mind introducing me to Mr. Maruyama.

He said he intended to call him tonight, and that he will call me later this evening to give me the outcome of his introduction – from there it is up to me…but, you know me…, sort of… I get things done.

Unfortunately, I have just received word that my father is on his death bed and may need to get back to Iowa in the next few days if he does not recover, so hang on. I will get you more details tomorrow.

Bye for now.

Christopher Girsch

:: :: ::

January 18, 2002   4:48 p.m.

Lew,

I called Mr. Maruyama again about 7:00 last night. He is a little ornery, but he said to call back at the beginning of the week to give him time to check his schedule. He said 'We have a schedule around here, you know, and we just can't drop everything at any time...you know.'

So, I am going to try to set a date in early February.

Bye for now,

Christopher Girsch

:: :: ::

January 18, 2002   5:12 p.m. Lew

Yesterday, I held the originals in these very hands. He is making special copies for you...I also held that hat in my hands yesterday... He offered to introduce me to Mr. Abe, who is also alive and well... but Mr. Maruyama is the star of the show, if you ask me. He sank the Oklahoma. He also seemed to remember a slower ship getting away – maybe your brothers...

Bye for now,

Christopher Girsch

:: :: ::

January 18, 2002   5:25 p.m.

Re: Another signature

WOW...By the way, feel free to write directly to Mr. Harada. I told him that you will probably be sending him things from time to time and that he can call on me to translate for him – and vice versa...That produced a huge smile on his face and his lovely wife said 'It really is nice to have language ability.'

So, the door is open to Mr. Harada for you and Mr. Maruyama is not far behind.

Bye for now,
Christopher Girsch

:: :: ::

January 18, 2002
Another "Wow." I'll have to come up with some pictures, maybe a short letter.

I am showing my grandsons the picture of Mr. Harada. I want them to remember this experience 50 years from now. I took them to meet Mr. DeShazer – the man on the B-25 during Doolittle's raid. Mr. DeShazer bailed out over China and was a prisoner until the end of the war. I want the boys to read what I wrote and to look at the picture 50 years from now. And to point to a picture of Mr. Harada and say, "My grandpa knew him."

Lew

:: :: ::

January 19, 2002   4:23 P.M.
Lew,

I was thinking that you can see the photo of Mr. Harada holding the sign, but the others have special import and I wanted to make sure that you knew what they were...The interesting thing is that you emailed us right as he was signing the book and as I was taking that picture in tribute to the two of you. Also, I wanted make sure that you knew that he was reading the letter that I had drafted in both languages for you...You see the happy expression on his face and thought you should know that those are the things of which those pictures are composed.

From the outset, I understood your dire need to seek making your dream come true and I happened to fit the role. So, rather than just translate your letter and shotgun email it to every Japanese site, I offered my help to you out of goodwill and honor because I knew that I could get what you wanted or at least tell you whether or not such things were still available. From the outset it was never my motive to seek anything in return, nor would I divulge to you my costs because that would spoil the joy of knowing that I did something good.

That philosophy was reaffirmed for me by Mr. Harada, himself. I walked away from his table enlightened, in a way. Accompanied by his wife at his side, he said to me, and I quote 'Chris, I missed my waylay point which meant that I would not be able to meet the escort back to my carrier...so I had no choices...Getting captured was disgraceful... they would take away my citizenship and running away was punishable by the firing squad, so right then and there I decided to ram my plane into the row of planes on the tarmac and kill as many British soldiers as possible, and myself...I was prepared for that eventuality when I joined the service, so it made no difference to me. I was going to be a hero, rather than a disgraceful coward. That is one of the main reasons why we lost the war...morale was down. We were dead either way...the Americans tried to stay alive...

'I turned my plane around and began heading back to the British camp and was picking out the best site where I could do the most damage. As I began my decent into the camp, other Zeros appeared at my side – manned by three of my comrades...They were holding up three fingers which meant that they had destroyed three targets and they were quite jubilant; they didn't seem to know that they were late for the way point and that we would be left behind for dead...and that I was heading back to do the deed...Just then, I began thinking... thinking that I was already 25 and had lived that long, while those other three men were only 19 or 20. If I went back, they were going to follow and I would be responsible for their losing their short lives. I made a decision right there...I could do something bad and hurt a lot of people, or try to do something good and help even more people, so I turned my plane back and started heading for the carrier, even though I knew our chances were slim...I have lived my life in that philosophy ever since. That's why I became a preschool teacher...start early and do something good because when you do good, good things happen...very simple, isn't it.'

I said to him...'yes, Mr. Harada, I can agree, because in truth, I don't know Mr. Holt at all…never met him, don't know him or anything about him…I am here out of goodwill and that's all. When you two get together, I will know that I did the right thing for you and for him. My coming here to get you two together is all…there is nothing in this for me…its simply a good thing.'

He smiled warmly at me and offered me more tea. After a sigh, we both chatted about and bemoaned the poor quality of Japanese young people today, again another point whereat we both agreed.

Anyway, I have work to do and while my father seemed to recover two days ago, I just got word that his condition is deteriorating rapidly…I must stay close to the phone for the coming week.

More later.

Bye for now,

Christopher Girsch

:: :: ::

January 19, 2002   4:42

Lew

I don't know if you knew this or not, But I asked Mr. Harada what 'Zero' meant. He told me that the true word was 'Rei Rei' which is Zero Zero in English. It comes from their belief that the Yamato clan, or the Japanese people were celebrating their 2600 year history – and the final two numbers – 00 were the symbol they used for the name.

So you know…

Bye for now,

Christopher Girsch

:: :: ::

January 19, 2002   12:05 a.m.

Just chatting

Chris,

>But I asked Mr. Harada what 'Zero' meant.

No, I didn't know what it meant. Very interesting. Thanks.

Next letter:

Your letter was absolutely "fabulous!!" I enjoyed your retelling of your visit. Mr. Harada's story was most interesting. As I wrote in the other letter – which I will resend to you – people are following this saga – literally all over the world. I just received a letter from a lady in Wisconsin – she wrote –

HI Lew,

Thanks for all the interesting letters and photos. I have been enjoying reading about your projects and activities. Now that is how retirement should be! Packed with enjoyable jaunts and participating in all the fun times that you can pack into a week. I am green with envy. (I'm still working) She titled her letter "Keep them coming."

I typically send out a Sunday night letter to maybe 25 people – and many have written back in anticipation of the next chapter.

Chris, I can sense what you are doing, is what you have chosen to do. The choices are all yours and I feel your anticipation and enjoyment – probably as much or more than mine because you are there "living the reality" of the people and the environment. If I were able to share something with you from this end, I would only do it because I want to and not because I am trying to buy your loyalty. If I am able to get fiddle and if I don't tell you how much it cost, it will come from my heart – because I want to show my gratitude. But let's cross that bridge when we come to it.

I could not have set out to buy what I have gotten from you. I can't imagine that there is anybody – anything – that could have duplicated what you have done. OK, the original translation – I would have sent it out – just "yelling in the dark." It would probably have fallen on "deaf ears." The only satisfaction that I would have gotten is "that I tried." I would have shrugged my shoulders and said that it wasn't to be and gone on with my business but with that one void at the end of my story. Now my story will be complete and if the reality/actuality someday of you meeting Mr. Maruyama comes about, then I will have attained the ultimate. This would be frosting on the cake.

Last October my 84-year-old friend, Marvin Helland, fell 8 feet into Mill Creek hurting himself badly. His yard was covered with leaves. His 86 years old wife, Chris, was raking them. I couldn't see her doing that so this 72-year-old man went over 3 times carrying many loads of leaves to their garden. They kept talking about paying me. I tried to explain that I wasn't there for any reward. Marvin has 4 of his father's and uncle's violins – two beautiful ones built in 1913 – still new instruments. Now he says that he wants me to have one to be in my possession until I die – and I am to will it to a museum. Yes, that is exciting but I had to say to them that I wasn't hauling leaves for any reward. In our Christmas card from them was $40 – to go out to dinner.

I can sense this is what you are saying about me. And I understand.

And my carriage just turned into a pumpkin. Good night from Salem.

Please keep me informed about your father.

Lew

:: :: ::

Feb. 23, 2002

Lew,

I got your letter yesterday. I will translate the letter from Mr. Harada here.

Greetings,

Thank you very much for coming all the way to Nagano, on roads you may not know well. It was too bad that we had to part company without being able to take our time together more slowly. The nice weather of spring will soon be here so we are looking forward to seeing you next time you come and hoping that we can spend more time together then. (Lew: literally, he is saying we can take it slow, which is a way to say we won't be rushed and can enjoy our time together.)

I am planning to write, as promised, about my feelings regarding my experiences of the past, but in the meantime, I am sending you the photos.

It is still cold these days, so I hope that you and your family take care of your health and not catch cold.

Harada.
To: Mr. Girsch

Lew,
Some things just don't translate well into English, though they sound perfectly natural in Japanese.

I will call him today to thank him and to explain why I have not responded sooner.

Take care.
Bye for now,
Christopher Girsch

:: :: ::

February 23, 2002
I just got off the phone with Mr. Harada. He has received your letter and was very pleased. I passed along your thanks and appreciation.

You can rest assured that he got your message.

Now, I have to get a hold of Mr. Maruyama
Bye for now,
Christopher Girsch

:: :: ::

Now I'll jump forward to June 2004. I received the following letter from Mr. Harada:

Translated as follows:

June 2004
To my dear friend Lew,
I was relieved to see in the letter the other day that you are well.

As usual, I am spending many happy days. I am thankful for the environment that allows me to mix with the children of the kindergarten and I pray to God that I can continue for a long time to come.

From the 15th of last month to the 22nd, I spent a week in Los Angeles to participate in the Japan/America veteran's events. While I was busy every day, it brought back a lot of memories.

親愛なる友人 ルーホルトさん
お元気な お便り 昨日 拝愛して
安心しました。
お蔭様で 私共も相変らず
楽しい毎日を過しています。
幼稚園の子ども達と交流して
いる環境に感謝し永く続く
ことを神に祈っています。
先月15日から22日までの一週間
ロスアンゼルスで 日米 ベテラン
親善行事に参加しました。
忙しい毎日でしたけれど 想い出の
多い旅になりました。
特に 沢山の報導陣に囲まれた
ことや 日本で捕虜生活を体験
した idop idallaron 氏のスピーチ
には 感動しました。
彼が今「オニの故郷は 日本だ」と
発言したことが印象的でした。
又 山本五十六大将を撃墜した
P38 搭乗員に 会ったことや
航空母艦 ミッドウェー 甲板で 日米
両国歌の演奏裡に 両国ベテラン

349

の握手交歓会と想い出に残る
一コマでした。
Chino
41航空博物館で催された
航空ショーは盛会でした。
零戦に面会し驚く感じました
13年前に会った零戦が今と若々
しく爆音を響かせて飛ぶ姿は
流石零戦!! だと思いましたし
アメリカの古い物を大切にする優しい
心に尊敬の念を懐きました。
ではお元気で又会う日まで
長生きしましょう。
　　　　　　原田　要より
　　　　　　　稿

　　Particularly, I was moved by being surrounded by the many people from the press and the speech given by Hap Halloran. His saying that his 'second home is in Japan' left a deep impression on me.

　　Also, I enjoyed meeting the men on the P38 that shot down Admiral Isoroku Yamamoto, the sign from the carrier Midway and singing both of our national anthems with the veterans from both countries.

　　That one shot brings back memories of the time we shook hands.

　　The air show held at the Chino 41 airplane museum was a great success. I was able to get a view of the zero planes which brought back many memories. It made me think of the solid form they had when I saw them 13 years ago. I thought that they still have the roar of the wonderful zeros! I was also impressed and filled with admiration for the kindness of the American people in their dedication to taking care of antiques. I hope you will be healthy and live long until we can meet again.

Yours,
Kaname Harada

Persimmons near Chris's house.

Chapter Twenty

CHRIS IN U.S.

Chris was originally from Iowa where his parents live. His father was seriously ill and not expected to live. Chris flew to Iowa to be near his father and with his mother until his father died. The following letters tell of him stopping on the way home in Salem, Oregon to visit with his brother who lives in Salem. This, also, gave Chris an opportunity to stop at my place to visit.

:: :: ::

January 30, 2002   6:16 p.m.
Lew,
Just to keep in touch, I will be flying in on the morning of the 13th and should be in Salem by the afternoon. How about getting together at your house then? My brother Bill will be with me. On the 14th, Bill and I intend to travel to Stayton to visit Cartwright's music store and buy some CD's and accessories there – I'm sure you have a wealth of information to relay to me about what to listen to, so have your idea book open to the old time music page.

Then on the 14th, I will visit my brother's office and then the family intends on going out to dinner, and I am leaving on the next morning for Japan. Will we be able to meet for a few hours on the afternoon of the 13th?
Regards,
Christopher Girsch

:: :: ::

January 28, 2002
When you have time
Chris,
I wasn't going to bother you until I heard from you but thought I would impose on you to ask for a suggestion. I went to "Made in

Oregon" today to buy a gift for Mr. Harada. Would he like – say – some jars of jelly/jam? And/or chocolate covered hazel nuts? Or do you have any other suggestions. I want to get on the ball and send him something.

I have been thinking about you and your family – hope things are leveling off. I know how busy you must have been and the feelings that go with the loss of a father.

Lew

:: :: ::

February 9, 2002
Re: Only if you want to...
>... if you chose to open my letter from Mr. Harada, it would be fine with me.

:: :: ::

Lew,

Nope...I am just not going to do it...It is addressed to me, but my wife sent it unopened by federal express to me to hand deliver to you. It is your letter. The letter is probably only a page, not anything more, but there are photos, and I want to watch YOU open it and experience it for yourself...I imagine that I can render what he has to say in minutes...if it is legible.

This is YOUR dream and YOUR life and YOUR pleasure and...I am only a mule. I am glad that I made YOUR dream come true.

Merry Christmas and yes, I AM the Easter bunny, as you said before...and you can still believe.

I was online today with Jay Ungar, asking about a violin shop in Portland that he recommended earlier to me when I was looking for a dark sounding fiddle and I told him to keep his eyes on the list for a post from Lew Holt about an amazing and true adventure that we two have experienced. His response this morning to me was:

>I'll keep my eye on Fiddle-L for future developments...my curiosity is piqued.
>Jay

So, when you get through yelling and wowing, you would be well advised to put this wonderful experience to paper...Looking forward to meeting you and Alice next week.

Regards,
Christopher Girsch

:: :: ::

February 9, 2002
Re: Only if you want to...
> This is YOUR dream and YOUR life and YOUR pleasure and...I am only a mule.

Chris,
Thanks for your generous and unselfish attitude. I guess I picked up the right bottle and when I rubbed it, out came the genie in the form of "Chris." It is truly a "dream" which I am and will cherish – always hoping that it might come true but never expecting it to really happen. Now it is so close.

Lew

:: :: ::

February 9, 2002
Re: Only if you want to...
Lew
Oh, and don't let me forget to complete the story of my day with Mr. Harada...there are some details, personal to me, that are uncanny.... and make this seem as though the years in school and all of my days in Japan were...meant...to do this....

Regards,
Christopher Girsch

:: :: ::

February 9, 2002
Re: Only if you want to...
In a message dated 2/9/02 8:54:03 PM, Chris writes:

>and make this seem as though the years in school and all of my days in Japan were...meant...to do this...

Chris,
To read those words brings a warmth and almost a tear. I look forward to "the rest of the story."
Lew

:: :: ::

February 9, 2002
Lew,
There is more to come...I am going to be seeing THE man... Mr. Maruyama and you will have a personal introduction to him... Remember, he is famed (depending on your viewpoint) for having dropped a torpedo that struck the Oklahoma...Remember that it is the one of the ships behind your brother's vessel as it escaped out of the harbor, in your photograph. You are going to get to know this gentleman...

I am only the shadow that made it happen. And I have had doubts about visiting...actually.

I figured that being anonymous made this whole thing so poetically beautiful...

We'll see you next week.
Regards,
Christopher Girsch

:: :: ::

Chris stopped by our house on February 13, 2002. We visited as fast as we could for several hours.

Mr. Harada had mailed a packet of books, pictures and a letter for me to Chris in Japan. Because he was in Iowa for his father's funeral,

Hiromi sent the packet to Chris in Iowa. Chris delivered the packet to me in person. What a thrill it was to open the packet to see what Mr. Harada had sent to me.

Just before Chris left, I asked him to go upstairs with me to see some of my fiddles. I had three on the daveno. He played the three of them. He especially liked the DeSalo – which was one of my favorites. I asked, "Do you like that fiddle?" He told me that he did. I looked at him and said, "It is yours, take it home with you." Chris was very pleased. It was one small way that I could show my appreciation for all that he had done for me. But not realizing that he would do even more in the future.

:: :: ::

February 16, 2002

Welcome Home

Welcome home, Chris. Maybe things have settled down a bit – you were glad to see your family and they were equally glad to see you. Just a minute. There is only one of you but three of them so you had more reasons to get home.

I asked Yuiko to translate the stickies on the back of the pictures. You had mentioned what they said – but it wasn't in my memory.

1934   *When I practiced how to use a fighting plane style of 90.*
1936   *When I served in a war in China.*
1941   *I was nervous about of leaving for Pearl Harbor.*

I'll scan them and send them to you one of these days when things settle down at your place and see if you can't refine the translation a little better.

I made copies of the three photographs on one sheet so I won't have to handle the originals so often.

Oh, another thing, I would like to send you a copy of Mr. Harada's letter and have you translate it, please. Please send me your address.

Alice is at Patty's place. She just called to invite me up for dessert – so think I will take them up on it.

Lew

Chapter Twenty One

Mr. Maruyama in Japan

February 27, 2002
Re: A new friend

Just a quick note from my phone to let you know that I contacted Maruyama and he agreed to meet on 3-13. He was very agreeable. More later.

:: :: ::

February 27, 2002
Lew,

Well, I'm sure you got my mail of yesterday, from my cellular phone. I will fill in the gaps here. I finally got the nerve and had my schedule fairly finalized to make the call to grumpy Mr. Maruyama.

He immediately asked about my father and was very friendly. We soon agreed to meet on March 13, and I offered to take him out to lunch.

I will relay the same message to him as I relayed to Mr. Harada – and will take better photos this time. However, I intend to use a different camera, so don't expect them over the Internet right away.

He lives about 3.5 hours away, so it will be a long day – one well worth the trip, I'm sure.

Hang on, just a little longer.

Bye for now,

Christopher Girsch

:: :: ::

March 7, 2002   3:52 p.m.
Lew,

Just a quick update...Mr. Maruyama just called me (8:45 AM) and said that although we had made arrangements to meet on the 13th, his hips are aching very badly and he can hardly get around his own house.

He asked if I would mind letting him recuperate. He said that he would call me in April when it got warmer and he was feeling better.

Obviously, I agreed. He is well over 80 and I didn't want to put him out. So, we'll just have to wait a little while longer.

Bye for now,

Christopher Girsch

:: :: ::

Chris was not able to schedule another meeting during the spring and summer. I was disappointed but didn't give up.

:: :: ::

August 29, 2002

Photos

Lew,

I am walking out the door in about thirty minutes to have prints made of the three photos you have sent. I'll put them in the envelope and send the letter off to Maruyama this afternoon – meaning tomorrow, really, and then you can wait to hear from him...However, he is not really into this and seems a bit ornery, so don't expect the wonderful embracing tone of Harada...he is just a different man from a different time and probably is not happy about reliving painful memories.

Just wanted to let you know that the gears of progress are still energized.

By the way, I was teaching myself some Scottish fiddle – Cape Breton, nice stuff...

Do you play that style too?

Chris

:: :: ::

September 2, 2002
Lew,
I had larger photos printed, and the letter ready to go, but something was bothering me about this, and I hesitated to send it until I could put my finger on what was bothering me.

Last night, as I was taking my usual evening walk in the pool, it occurred to me what was wrong about this whole thing with Mr. Maruyama...I realized that the whole form of protocol had been lost, so I am going out today to get him a bottle of the finest Japanese sake I can find, and maybe some treat as a gesture of good will to him. Maybe he will get the urge to write after warming up to some fine tasting booze.

Chris

:: :: ::

October 1, 2002
Thanks
Lew,
I wasn't home today, but my wife said that Harada San called and was thrilled with the gift that you sent.

My wife said that he said: 'I didn't do anything to deserve this wonderful gift, but please relay my deep thanks to Lew. I will enjoy this very much.'

So, now the bond is solidified. You have access now. Feel free to write or call or do anything now with Harada san. He trusts us.

Chris

:: :: ::

In the spring of 2002 I sent a gift to Mr. Maruyama and an invitation inviting him to correspond with me. I wrote him again in the fall.

I eventually received a nice package from Mr. Maruyama with pictures of him as a 19 year old – just before leaving for Pearl Harbor, a picture of him holding a model box of the Kate airplane that he flew in, and very important – a ten page document that he had written about his participation in the war – starting with the attack on Pearl Harbor.

:: :: ::

19 year old Mr. Maruyama

A year later I received the following post card from Mr. Maruyama.

When I visited the Pearl Harbor Memorial, I had the opportunity to meet Daniel Martinez, Historian. He told me about two videos of an interview with Mr. Maruyama. I later received the two videos.

:: :: ::

Translation of a letter sent to me by Mr. Maruyama from Japan.

:: :: ::

Pearl Harbor on Dec., 8th 1941

I attended this operation as Thunder Shooting Party No. 40 of the first attacking parties which had 183 planes in total. I belonged to the battleship "Hiryu (Flying Dragon) and my boss was Captain Hirata. We attacked Battleship Oklahoma.

It was at 6:00 am Hawaii Time when we turned into Oahu Island since we had left Hiryu and completed formation flights. The altimeter indicated 3000m and the weather was clear. We confirmed the shape of island between white waves, which was the north part of Cape Kafuku. While we were in the path of the west side, we received the order for final attack from the general. We flew down slowly to the south and aimed at Pearl Harbour. The first sign of the attack of the battleships alongside of Ford Island was confirmed. Our target was "West Virginia" and "Oklahoma". We flew low right next to a battle cruiser staying near the bay and watched a couple sailors looking up and trying to figure out what was going on.

A mass of battleships in Ford Island was coming up. At an attitude of 20m, we fired on the Oklahoma at the order of captain Hachiro Sugimoto and then tried to take shelter from return fire. Torpedo hits were confirmed by columns.

Port Darwin Attack

On Feb. 19th 1942, the mobile unit of the imperial Navy attacked Port Darwin in Australia with the 1st and 2nd parties. The Target was harbor facilities. I belonged to an attacking party of the battleship Hiryu, in a level and formation flight I bombed 800 kgs. The return fire exploded near our formation and the airplane shook up and down. But our plan was succeeded and we all returned safely.

Battle of Midway on June 5th, 1942

We departed Hiryu and bombed an antiaircraft position in Midway Sand Island with 800 kgs bombs in a level formation flight. The 1st and 2nd parties were attacked by the air defense at the base using Grumman F4F and so on. They rushed through our offense and two airplanes were shot down. But we fought back and shot down most of the Grumman. Since we made way for the attack, their aim was very accurate and intense. A Missile was exploded near us and all of us endured the blast. A platoon was dispersed and a captain made an emergency landing on the sea.

On the way back from Midway, we received a wireless to confirm finding enemies. We landed on Hiryu through the B17 attacks and started missile preparation immediately. Only a few of Kobayashi parties with 24 airplanes came back. Soon we received a notice that our three battleships "Akagi" "Kaga" and "Soryu" were sunk. When I climbed up the deck and I doubted what I saw there.

Then we were given a special instruction from General Yamaguchi and Captain Kami. What you see now is the reality. You must take revenge for all of them. We were all encouraged to shoot down a new battleship following the bravery of the party and departed with a most resolution. Our commander was Lieutenant Tomonaga. In an hour another battleship was found and we separated into two parties. Soon after that we were attacked by Grummans, which were really fast, shooting from behind and turning and shooting again from above. We tried to escape but our movement was slow as we were carrying 800 kgs bombs. Finally my airplane was shot from behind and a correspondent was shot in his leg. The level and horizontal tails were filled with holes like beehive and gas started leaking from the left tank. But I managed to deploy the torpedo.

All I could think about was that I couldn't die in this situation, so I decided to rush into the middle of fighting. The Grummans weren't able to make to shoot us down and left. Their battleship was near at hand and continued to shoot. Even though two torpedoes had hit us, the gas leaking had stopped and we succeeded to land. Yorktown was seriously damaged with 168 (error?) torpedo strikes and later sunk.

Hiryu was sunk after that and the Japanese Navy suffered a crushing defeat. This was the turning point of WW2.

Kobayashi party 13 airplanes returned out of 18
Naoire party   3 airplanes returned out of 6

Guadalcanal (Santa Cruise Battle)

On Oct., 17th 1942, 9 airplanes each from Hisho (flying eagle) and Hayabusa (eagle) as the 2nd air fleet attacked and bombed horizontally an American transport ship. However, they were attacked back by Grumman and almost annihilated. Hisho couldn't sail at high speed as the engine was broken, therefore we decided to go back to Truck islands and fit the engine. We, Hiryo supported "Hayabusa" in the Santa Cruise Battle.

On Oct., 26th 1942, we departed the battleship Hayabusa and attacked Hornet. Our squadron consisted of 15 airplanes. The battleship "Hornet" had already been damaged by our attack and was leaning. It was being escorted by their battle cruiser and navigating at 10 knot. No enemy planes were in the sky.

Before we started attacking, the battle cruiser released a rope tied to the battleship. Three torpedoes hit Hornet and it was sunk. We lost five on our side, which were captain Irai-in and his one subordinate, Captain Shirane and his two subordinates.

:: :: ::

(Permission given to use this article.)
Island Military Honolulu Star-Bulletin Sunday, December 9, 2001

"Yesterday's enemy is today's friend."
–Taitsuke Maruyama, Japanese airman who torpedoed the USS Oklahoma on Dec. 7, 1941

Pearl harbor attack, as seen from above

A Japanese pilot makes a visit to the Dec. 7 memorial and brings with him a unique perspective on the events.

By Leila Fujimori

On Dec. 7, 1941, 19-year-old Taitsuke Maruyama donned his leather flight helmet, then tied on his hachimaki, a white cloth headband emblazoned with the red rising sun.

Underneath his uniform, the 19-year-old navigator wore a new undershirt and new underpants, knowing he was embarking on a grave mission, he said through an interpreter at the Ala Moana Hotel.

Maruyama climbed into the middle seat of the Kate torpedo bomber, which took off from the carrier Hiryu and launched a 1,600-pound torpedo that struck the USS Oklahoma in Pearl Harbor, he said.

Maruyama is one of the three Japanese airmen who returned last week for the 60th anniversary of the bombing of Pearl Harbor.

Only 30 Japanese airmen of the 777 who flew in the attack remain; 56 were killed at Pearl Harbor.

His mission last week was to shake the hands of American Pearl Harbor survivors, some of whom he has met on his two previous trips to Hawaii.

"Yesterday's enemy is today's friend," he said.

Maruyama said both sides accomplished their missions, so there is no resentment against one other.

On Dec. 7, 1941, when Maruyama's plane flew into Pearl Harbor, he could see the faces of Navy personnel on the deck of a cruiser docked at Ford Island.

"They looked up, wondering what was happening," he said.

The aircraft moved across Ford Island to its designated target, the USS Oklahoma, dropped low, and Maruyama released the single torpedo strapped to the plane's belly into the harbor waters 50 feet below.

When "a pillar of water appeared," the ensign knew he made a direct hit.

The battleship USS Oklahoma was hit by up to nine torpedoes, overturned and sank 20 minutes after the first hit.

Of the more than 400 on board the Oklahoma, only 32 sailors survived.

The crew, having accomplished its mission, flew back to the Hiryu.

Maruyama, who joined the Japanese imperial Navy at 16, said he was fighting "for both emperor and country" and didn't know if he would survive.

"A soldier's duty is to accomplish his mission, so I was ready to die," said Maruyama, now 79.

He returned to a hero's welcome in Japan. But at the war's end, Maruyama said, "My head was empty." After flying so many operations in the pacific, he simply said, "It's finally finished."

Maruyama survived after missions in Australia, Ceylon, Santa Cruz islands, where he torpedoed the carrier the USS Hornet, Guadalcanal and Midway, where he hit the carrier the USS Yorktown, which sank on June 6, 1942.

...The pilot and gunner/radioman who flew with Maruyama survived the Pearl Harbor attack but didn't survive the war. Maruyama said 80 percent of the pilots who flew in the attack were killed during the war.

Taitsuke Maruyama, a Japanese airman who took part I the Pearl Harbor attack, was demonstrating Wednesday how he came in for the attack on Dec. 7, 1941. Maruyama showed a photograph of the airplane he flew for most of the war, in Nakajime, B5N2, known by Americans as Kate.

:: :: ::

on 9/20/02 7:56 PM, Lew Holt wrote:

> Dear Leila,

> On September 16 I received a package from Mr. Taitsuke Maruyama in Japan. In the package was a copy of The Honolulu Star-Bulletin where you had interviewed him on Dec. 9, 2001. I am requesting permission to quote your article as I write and share my story about Mr. Maruyama. I would like to quote your interview if I have your permission. Thank you.

> Lew Holt Salem, Oregon

Mr. Holt:

I would have no reservations about allowing you to quote the interview if you credit both the Honolulu Star-Bulletin and myself.

Thanks for your interest.

Leila

Chapter Twenty Two

ALICE AND LEW GO TO HAWAII

February 24 to March 3, 2003

Alice and I had several reasons for going to Hawaii at this time. On February 14th we celebrated our 50th wedding anniversary. A trip to Hawaii would be, we thought, an excellent way to celebrate our anniversary. It was, also, our 50th state to visit. Earlier in our marriage we had driven to the other 49 states. And as you might have expected, a trip to Hawaii also gave me an opportunity to go to Pearl Harbor and to the Arizona Memorial.

We had been advised to get to the park at Pearl Harbor early before the lines got long. We caught a "discount ride" to the park, entered the park and spent some time looking at the displays and the many books and mementos for sale. I asked at a desk if I might see Daniel Martinez, a historian at the park with whom I had talked to on the phone. He came out to greet us. We had a nice visit.

Bill embarked on a journey in 1941 to Pearl Harbor. He could never have imagined what the next four years would bring and that they would ultimately lead to his death. The attack on Pearl Harbor on the morning of December 7, 1941 changed his life as it did for so many others.

We got in line to see the film that set the stage for our visit out to the Arizona Memorial. After the film, we went on board the small boat that took us to the memorial. We got off with many others and walked silently into the memorial. It hinted nothing of what had happened 62 years earlier. But to look down into the water and see the outline of the Arizona below us, made it real.

I asked permission to cast some flowers into the water as a memorial to my brother, for those who were there on December 7th, for the over one thousand men who lay entombed below in the sunken Arizona, for the many others who fought in the war and for those who did not survive the war. The Park Ranger explained to me that it was against the rules to cast a lei into the water, the string might entangle wild life. He cut the string to my lei. I pulled off several blossoms, stood at the railing for a moment and then tossed the flowers over the railing into the water over the Arizona. Perhaps other visitors saw me and might have wondered what my purpose was but only my wife knew why I was making that symbolic gesture. Only I knew what I was feeling at the time. I was thinking of the many men below in the Arizona and I was thinking of a cousin of mine who had asked to me to cast some flowers into the harbor for "Billy." As Alice and I stood at the Arizona Memorial, I wrote a note, "I am here to finish the journey for Bill." I feel that I brought Bill back to Pearl Harbor 62 years later. I was thinking of my brother.

It was time to go. I walked toward the boat that was to take us back to the shore, looked back and thought of that terrible day in 1941. I was sad when I left, thinking of what had happened there but realizing that visiting Pearl Harbor was a dream come true for me.

Our hotel room near Waikiki Beach was on the 11th floor. One afternoon Alice and I sat in our room resting after a busy morning. The sliding glass doors were open to the balcony. A little bird with a blush of red on his head lit on the balcony railing, raised his head and began to sing a beautiful song. The bird sang what seemed like several minutes. I sat there enjoying it and thinking what a beautiful song it was.

Back home when I told a friend about the bird singing, she asked, "You know who the bird was, don't you?" At first I didn't know what she was asking. I looked confused. She said, "It was your brother, Bill, singing to you." I can't say that it was Bill singing to me but the more I think about it, the more beautiful the thought becomes. I had been to see the Arizona Memorial and when I threw the flowers from the lei into the water over the Arizona it was my way of sending a message to my brother. My imagination just might let me believe it was Bill coming to see me and singing a beautiful song there on the balcony. He would have done that if he could have. Maybe he did.

:: :: ::

Chapter Twenty Three

San Francisco – Coco

August 3, 2000

My dear Luis:

. . . . . But I felt a deep sentiment when I read: " maybe someday, someway, somehow, we will have real hugs." Heartily, I wish some day we can join, and enjoy this hug, our friendship, and can stay a few days together. This is one of my wishes, and I hope, with God's help, I will try to accomplish.

Coco

:: :: ::

This dream of both Coco's and mine became real on Wednesday, March 26, 2003. Coco had written to me earlier that he and Martha would be visiting their friends, Ricardo and Nelly, in the San Francisco area the last two weeks in March. Alice and I checked our calendar and saw no reason why we couldn't visit Coco and Martha at their friends' in March. I wrote to Coco asking if we might visit them at that time. He replied:

:: :: ::

February 20, 2003

My dear friend Luis:

YES! BE SURE WE WILL LIKE TO MEET YOU, LUIS AND ALICE!! It is very nice for you to try to join us. With God's help, we will be there between the 18th to 31st of March, and we will stay at our friend's house, so there will not be any inconvenience to meet and to give each other a big embrace, and to talk, to have some photos and to enjoy the visit of truly friends! My friends Ricardo and Nelly will be very pleased to have you at their house!

Your friend,

Coco

:: :: ::

Coco and I exchanged several letters, Ricardo sent me specific directions to his place. On Monday, March 24, Alice and I drove 400 miles to friends in California where we stayed the night as their guests. Tuesday we drove another 250 miles where we stopped to visit my brother, Charles, and his wife, Helen, and then drove late that evening to within 26 miles of Ricardo's. Wednesday morning we easily drove the 26 miles to Orinda, California.

:: :: ::

I wrote in my journal...

March 26, 2003

This morning in Concord we went to a nearby restaurant for breakfast. The night clerk at the motel had suggested that the traffic was very heavy from 7:00 to 9:00 so we were in no hurry getting away. We only had 26 miles to drive. We left about 9:30 and had an easy drive to Orinda but missed our turn off – drove maybe 3 miles too far, through a long tunnel, turned around, drove back and easily found Ricardo's place.

We arrived at Ricardo and Nelly's home at 10:45. I nervously walked up the steps to the front door. Alice rang the doorbell. We waited a few seconds anticipating our meeting. After a bit, the door opened and there stood Coco. When I hugged Coco, my fears were for nothing. I thoroughly enjoyed meeting him and felt very relaxed. Ricardo and Nelly made us feel right at home. Language was not a problem. Martha does not speak English so we couldn't talk directly to her. I will always cherish that day the rest of my life. It was certainly a dream come true.

I especially enjoyed the visit. I was not with "strangers" but rather, with old time friends. I felt that I had known them all forever but then, I guess our visits on the phone, our many letters and the many pictures prepared us for our visit.

Ricardo, a true Argentinean host, prepared shish kabobs, barbecued ribs and empanadas (stuffed, fried pies).

And a nice salad. We ate the shish kabobs out side and went inside for the ribs.

We were joined by Ricardo's and Nelly's daughter, Marcella, a very pretty and charming young lady.

After we had eaten, Coco left and came back with a wrapped package. He handed it to me. I opened it.

I knew it must be a book but I had no idea what it might be about. It was a beautiful book in English about Argentina. I will always cherish it.

Alice and Coco had a nice visit about his computer and genealogy.

Coco, Lew, Nelly, Martha, Ricardo (Alice took the picture.)

We knew we must take a picture and send it to N – as N and Coco sent me a picture, when N arrived to visit Coco in Argentina. "Envy" was Coco's idea.

We visited, took pictures and shared many stories before we left by 5:00. We hugged and sadly said our "good byes."

We meandered up the Oregon Coast, arriving at home two days later. The dream of someday meeting Coco had become reality. I can't imagine anybody being more gracious and willing to share, than Coco.

:: :: ::

March 28, 2003

Dear Friends Alice and Lew:

It is not necessary to tell you how wonderful we felt with your visit.

I need to thank you again for the long travel you did to make possible our encounter, and believe me, that was one of the moments more expected for me, and more moving I had.

Dear Alice, you are a wonderful woman, I felt with you very comfortable, and I felt you gave us all your friendship. Luis, you are a fortunate man.....

Luis, it was a great moment for me, for all us, having you at home, and sharing ourselves, as an old friends........It was a gift for me having you both at home....

Thank you also for the CD's you brought to me, it is a resume of our friendship, and I am proud of having them; they are a truly gift in this such special occasion. Thank you, thank you....(The CD was a copy of all of our letters and pictures since our first letter.)

Ricardo and Nelly are also delighted with your visit, and they think our friends are also friends of theirs......(you saw, Ricardo is quite funny joking with you.....he is a truly friend...)

We hope you have a good returning trip, and we will be in touch again, now with the satisfaction of being more close than before......

Coco and Martha

:: :: ::

March 28, 2003

Re: A wonderful visit

Dear Coco, Martha, Ricardo and Nelly,

We arrived home this evening about 6:15 after a week of adventure. The highlight of the week was at 10:45 on Wednesday when we finally arrived at the Ricardo's and Nelly's home. I nervously walked up the steps to the door. Alice rang the door bell. We waited a few seconds and I wondered for a moment but when I saw you, Coco, my fears were for nothing. I thoroughly enjoyed meeting you and felt very relaxed. Ricardo and Nelly made us feel "right at home." I will always cherish that day the rest of my life. It was certainly "a dream come true."

I especially enjoyed the visit. I was not with "strangers" but rather, with "old time friends." I felt that I had known you forever but then, I guess our visits on the phone, our many letters and the many pictures prepared us for our visit.

We feel very honored to have all of you as our friends. Meeting all of you was an experience that I will always cherish. Who knows, hopefully we can meet again someday.

But now to continue our friendship through our letters and pictures and occasional phone calls.

We easily followed route 4 to the freeway and had anticipated getting on to the freeway with no problem but several highways converged at the same time and the freeways were stacked on top of each other – signs to San Jose, signs to San Francisco, signs to the east, signs "everywhere" but not to where we wanted to go – especially at 70 mph in rush hour traffic so we ended up driving south towards San Jose several miles before we got turned around. We headed north where we saw a sign to San Rafael. We drove north to Santa Rosa where we stayed the night.

It was an easy drive to Fortuna, near Eureka, where we visited with my cousin, Doris, and her husband and stayed all night. The next day we had an easy drive home, stopping to see elk and the huge redwood trees.

Thanks again and the best to you all.
Luis

:: :: ::

Chapter Twenty Four

PLANNING MY TRIP TO JAPAN

Early in July, 2003, I wrote an email to Chris in Japan to ask him if he would translate letters for me to Mr. Harada and Mr. Maruyama. Chris wrote back "Why don't you come to Japan and talk to them yourself. I will meet you at the airport in Tokyo, drive you to visit the two men, translate for you, put you up in a local hotel for four nights. ..." I thought about his offer, Alice and I eventually got our passports "in case" we went and it eventually became "when we went." In the end it turned out that Alice decided that I should go by myself. She sent me with her blessings.

Here are a series of letters that lead up to my trip to Japan.

:: :: ::

August 2, 2003
Lew
That is really where I earn my keep. I would be worried about you lugging your bags around, looking for your hotel...the stress...forget it...

I will make sure things go smoothly and effortlessly...you just sit back and enjoy the ride and listen to music.

Without me being a guide...it just wouldn't be much fun...it would be a chore, not like traveling to the Midwest at all...So, consider yourselves taken care of in that department. If you want to extend it a few days, we can get you EASILY to Nara, Osaka and Kyoto a night at each place, then back to the airport in Tokyo...meeting Harada and maybe Yoshida or someone else there too.

Chris

:: :: ::

August 27, 2003

Lew,

I know you are sitting on pins and needles waiting to get the news... did it arrive...did he understand it...is he grumpy and disagreeable?

Well, to my surprise, my phone rang about fifteen minutes ago and an old man on the other end grumbled, 'Is this the residence of Chris Girsch?' Then, 'Are you Chris Girsch?'

Answering yes to both questions, the man then spoke up and said 'This is Maruyama from Nagoya.'

I graciously asked about his health and his wife and family – which is customary – and said I had been wondering about him – and that you were desperate to meet him.

He described his receiving a letter from you with chocolates and stating your plans as I had written in the letter and said: 'Lew says he is coming to Japan to meet Harada...and wants to meet me, too...Now, my hips are very bad and my wife is not real well...so you know, we can't be entertaining people around here...you know and...'

I agreed and said: I really do not want to disturb you at all...and I am very sorry if you were bothered...

He said: Now, you are going to see Harada? Isn't he near you? Why would you come all the way out here. I mean, Nagoya is half way across the country...nowhere near you.... Why would you take the train way out here?

I said that I was driving...He balked: DRIVING?? I took that as my lead and said: Well, really, Lew has been so eager to learn about you and to strike up a relation and has been asking me to get a letter or a photo from you...but I knew you were not feeling well and decided that I didn't want to bother you...Actually, it was my idea for him to write to you personally and ask to meet you...and that he should come to meet you personally...It was I that suggested this idea...and I am doing all the driving and organizing to meet Harada...and I love Kyoto and suggested that we see Kyoto (which is not true, but it was my lead to convince him that we were in the general neighborhood, so ...) I continued: And I figured that since we were near, Lew really just wants to meet you and shake your hand and share some time with you...but we really do NOT want to bother you... So I said: Write the letter and ask for yourself...and you could reject it without any pressure.

He said: Well, I live way out here, and my wife is not well...and we don't want to entertain folks here...since you'll be interpreting...why don't you get yourself to Nagoya station and I'll get there to meet you.

WOW...so, I said: That would be very generous and kind of you...I know Lew will be thrilled that you are making such a big effort for him...I said...we don't want to put any load on you...so, maybe we could just enjoy a quiet cup of coffee together, shake hands...photos... and then let you go on your way...

He said: Lunch...let's have lunch together.

So, then I said you were thinking about October 7, or so, and we would head out to Harada around the ninth or tenth...then, see him on the tenth or eleventh of October...

I asked if there was any time in particular that he would prefer and he said 'NO...you just make your plans and call me when they're settled...park under the station and we'll meet for lunch...

Other than that, I asked about a good time to call, so that I wouldn't disturb him...and wished him good health and said that I would contact you immediately. He sounded very glad to make the time.

So, there you have it – you HAVE to come now....

It looks like my theory worked well for us again. Congratulations.

Chris

:: :: ::

Oct. 7, 2003

Lew

OK, back from my long, refreshing walk.

I spoke briefly with Mr. Harada last night to confirm where to meet. We are going to meet in front of the Nagano City train station, which is where we met before. Our date is set for 12:30, so we will have no trouble getting there by that time. I invited his wife and him to join us for lunch somewhere. You will be surprised. His wife is the same age, but does not look it at all. I offered to take us all out for lunch.

Then, I called the grumpy old Mr. Maruyama. He is the one I am most worried about. We agreed to meet at 11:00 in front of the Nagoya train station by a set of stairs. I gave him my cellular phone in case we get mixed up, but I am keeping my fingers crossed that we got our signals straight. He said in front of the station where there is a fountain...I have been to that station and I don't remember seeing a fountain.

He then said that he didn't know the area very well...so I will be very relieved when we really do actually meet up with him.

I will call my friend and ask if the big sculpture in front of the station is a fountain.

Anyway, that time means that we must leave here very early to get there and to get parked and make our way to the station on time.

I will see you tomorrow. About five hours after you leave, I leave, too, to pick you up.

Talk to you tomorrow.

You can write emails from here while you are here, so you may want to print out or copy and send you pals email addresses to write them from here.

Chris

:: :: ::

October 7, 2003
Chris,
I just glanced at the clock – I have to be up in 12 hours, catch the HUT bus at 6:30 to ride to the airport in Portland – be at the airport at 8:00 to check in and catch the plane at 11:00. I have been giddish all day like a ... don't know what ... but Alice said that I would live. My daughter and family have volunteered to take me to the airport here in Salem in the morning at 6:15 to catch the HUT. Then I am on my own – until I see you.

We just got back from shopping – picking up nametags for my luggage, things like that. I am basically all packed. I may choose to carry my luggage. I'll see. I'll be carrying a book bag, a camera case and a back pack. It may get to be too much.

Lew

Chapter Twenty Five

THOUGHTS FROM MY JOURNAL

The impulse was to include my complete journal, that not being wise, I have included the highlights of each day.

:: :: ::

October 8, 2003   Wednesday

I was up early, caught the airport shuttle from Salem to Portland. It was basically easy to go through the lines, take a small plane to Seattle and there get on the large plane to Tokyo. I had a window seat so enjoyed the view, often just the ocean. It was exciting when I saw the coast line of Japan and when the plane landed.

Oct. 9, 2003   Thursday (We had crossed the International Date Line.)

It must have taken an hour and a half to go through all the check points. I walked into the lobby and heard "Lew." It was Chris. My name has never sounded so good. We had a long drive through Tokyo and to his place. His father in law, Suguru Kato, was with him.

We went to Chris's house. I met his wife, Hiromi and their sons, 14-year-old James and 9-year-old Marty. We visited for a bit, had a snack and then Chris took me to my hotel in Nirasaki.

October 10, 2003   Friday

I was up early. When I looked out of my 4th story window, I enjoyed the view. I felt that I was really in Japan. I was very pleased to see Mt. Fuji.

I ate breakfast. Chris picked me up shortly. Then to his house, where I met his family again. Chris and I took his dog for a walk. I enjoyed the terraced rice field, the houses, the people, the persimmons, the grapes and row crops. To me it was like something out of an old fairy tale book.

That evening we drove to Kofu where Chris and I ate in a restaurant – tempera – sushi. Then to a school for an English class he teaches.

October 11, 2003 9:15 Saturday Nirasaki Hotel

Chris came to get me at 8:00. We went to his house. I called Alice back home in Salem.

The drive to Nagano City in Nagano Prefecture through the mountains to meet Mr. and Mrs. Harada was very interesting. At 12:30, Chris spotted Mr. and Mrs. Harada approaching. They were an alert, sharp couple – he at 87 and she at 82.

Mr. and Mrs. Harada with Chris

Following their car to the school and their house

We followed the Haradas as they wound through the narrow streets to the school – for ages 3, 4, and 5 – where he is the principal. We were taken on a tour of the school and were shown his pictures that were taken when he met with veterans of WWII. One was of John Sykes and him, a British pilot whose plane he had shot down during the war. And a picture with Joe Foss, leading U.S. Ace, who had shot down Mr. Harada's plane. These pictures were hanging in his office.

We followed them to their interesting home. We removed our shoes, put on sandals and went into the living room. We were invited to sit down on the floor at a low table. We visited and exchanged gifts. I autographed the book I gave him. He autographed his pictures that I had of him.

Words cannot adequately tell my feelings about this visit – the opportunity to sit at the table of a Japanese WWII ace and to discuss the war. He is a "man of history." He helped create the history of the war – along with millions of others. But today he represents perhaps less than five aviators out of over 700 who participated in the attack on Pearl Harbor. For him to have survived the war was a miracle. And I felt a miracle – as I visited in his home that afternoon.

We snacked on a variety of foods. There was a dish of larger rolls that I hadn't eaten yet when they announced that we were going out for lunch.

Mr. Harada & Lew

Chris drove his car—Mr. Harada and Chris in the front seats and Mrs. Harada and I were in the back seat. We drove into the mountains to a beautiful restaurant. We were served a bowl of excellent noodles. I was the last one to finish as I fumbled with my chopsticks.

On the way back to Nagano we wound our way through the mountains – many sharp curves, steep roads, tunnels, forested hillsides starting to show that fall is coming, an occasional rice paddy and small villages tucked between the mountains. We stopped at the Harada's, bid them good-bye and headed back home – 150 kilometers.

Mr. Harada telling me about the watch that stopped
when his plane crashed into the ocean.

October 12, 2003 8:07 p.m. Sunday (I can't believe that I am writing this in Japan.)

We were on our way by 8:00 to Nagoya to meet Mr. Maruyama. At 12:05 Chris's cell phone rang. It was Mr. Maruyama asking where we were. He was a half a block away. We found him quickly, shook hands and went inside, up to the third floor, to find a restaurant quiet enough so we could talk and eat. I had sushi, a large shrimp and rice dish, raw tuna and rice, raw squid and rice, salmon eggs and rice, and a mixture of something in a bowl that I liked.

We exchanged gifts. Mr. Maruyama got out picture albums of WWII gatherings – at Pearl Harbor and at Pensacola, Florida. He had the pictures that I had sent him.

I had my notebook with pictures and stories about him. He autographed his pictures and the model airplane box that I had brought with me. I showed him the aerial picture of Pearl Harbor that was taken by a Japanese aviator during the attack. The cruiser that he had written about was not the Phoenix. I was disappointed but I can't rewrite history. Had he seen the Phoenix, my story would have even more meaningful. I would have had a story about an enemy actually seeing the Phoenix.

Lew and Mr. Maruyama

Mr. Maruyama autographing the model box that I brought to Japan.
My son, Steve, found the model for me.

We left Mr. Maruyama shortly after 2:00 – a gamble that had paid off. I/we gambled that meeting would come off – that he would be agreeable to meet with us, that Mr. Maruyama would be there, that he would visit. On the way to the car I gave Chris a hug. I thought, "I feel like King Midas, everything I touch has turned in to gold." But with out the consequences the king faced. Mine was happy gold with valuable results.

We found our way to the interstate and headed for Kyoto to be tourists. That evening Chris and I went to little restaurant. We shared a variety of dishes from deep fried chicken, to deep fried squib, a stew, and a potato dish, to a corn and cheese dish. We ate until we were stuffed. I have missed much because of the language but have gained so much from the trip and the experience.

October 13 Monday This morning as I saw the rain coming down, I wondered if it would be worth plodding through the rain all day. Chris came down at 8:00. During breakfast he suggested that maybe we should go home and not fight the rain. I agreed. We packed, got refunds, checked out and headed for home.

... We stopped at a grocery store to buy me a snack/lunch. I bought a seaweed sandwich, a large sushi and a yogurt that I could drink. And a bottle of BBW sauce that I could take home. Then back to Chris's for the evening. Hiromi prepared an excellent meal – pork cutlets, vegetables, sweet beans, etc.

October 14, 2003 Tuesday My last night – Nirasaki, Japan.

I could never have imagined that I would go to Japan by myself or to ever go at all. It could only have happened because of Chris, Hiromi and Alice. I will be forever grateful to the three of them. It is hard to imagine that I am sitting a hotel in Japan so far from home – from Salem – from my family. Tomorrow night at this time I will be on my way home. I will be richer for having had the experience.

I invited Chris and his family out to eat this evening. We went to a nice restaurant, went into a room just for us, with a low table. We sat on a thin cushion on the floor, with our legs dangling in a pit under the table. Chris, Hiromi and James sat on one side. Marty and I sat on the other side. We ate plates of chicken, gizzards, potatoes, deep fried gristle – the gristle being a strange dish for me but I enjoyed it. I am getting better with chopsticks, but far from mastering them.

October 15, 2003 – Wednesday

I went down for breakfast about 7:15, had a leisure breakfast of link sausage, eggs and things I couldn't identify. But I had vowed that I would be open-minded so I tried a bite, at least, of many things. I have found nothing on the trip that I couldn't eat easily.

Chris came about 8:30. We drove back to his place. While we were talking, Hiromi brought in a special delivery package from Mr. Harada – the two videos from the Discovery Channel about the Battle of Midway. I never opened the package – just tucked it into my larger bag. With tears in my eyes I gave Hiromi a hug and then Chris, Marty and I left for Tokyo.

We picked up Hiromi's father, Suguru Kato, then the long drive to Tokyo/Narita Airport. We went to a restaurant to eat. I had pork on rice.

I paid for our meals; they walked with me part way to where I was to board the plane. I shook hands with Marty and Suguru Kato and tearfully hugged Chris good-bye. I can't imagine anybody doing what he has done – giving up 5 days of his work and spending many dollars/yen on us. I will be forever grateful. I boarded the plane – a Boeing 777 – at 4:30. The plane took off at 5:00 for Seattle.

:: :: ::

Some notes I made to keep myself straight with the calendar and events.

Wednesday	Oct. 8	Left Salem – Portland – Seattle
Thursday	Oct. 9	Arrived in Tokyo. Went to the English class
Friday	Oct. 10	Relaxed at Chris's. Walked the dog. Played the fiddles.
Saturday	Oct. 11	Drove to Nagano to visit Mr. Harada
Sunday	Oct. 12	Drove to Nagoya to visit Mr. Maruyama. Went to Kyoto.
Monday	Oct. 13	Drove home from Kyoto.
Tuesday	Oct. 14	Went shopping, played music, and out for dinner
Wednesday	Oct. 15	Drove to Tokyo, flew to Seattle, Portland and home.

:: :: ::

Seattle – I unloaded easily, followed the crowd through the checkpoints, picked up my luggage, carried it through customs and checked it for loading to Portland.

Because we were late, I knew I had missed the HUT in Portland to Salem and dreaded the 1.5 hour wait for the next one. In one of the lines I struck up a conversation with a Japanese man. Later as we walked together down the terminal, I started to tell him that it would be nice if my daughter were here to meet me. I looked to the right and there stood Patty. I was one happy father. She was in Portland for a meeting. Patty and I walked to the parking structure, got into her car and I sat back and visited as she drove home. My trip was now a dream – something to enjoy reflecting on the rest of my life.

:: :: ::

Chris wrote this for me – it summarizes my trip to Japan so well:

The world of fiddles has drawn two people of disparate backgrounds and produced something that should have great meaning to all people in the world, and that the world of fiddles has allowed us to play a part in history in the making – I contacted Chris Girsch, a fiddle-List member in Japan, who responded to someone's earlier request about translating a Japanese CD. Chris answered the call from me to fulfill a personal dream to find someone who participated in the bombing of Pearl Harbor, not by simply finding a list of names, but by actually making calls to find one of only seven living participants on the Japanese side – and that he actually introduced me to the man who put the direct hit on the Oklahoma to put her under. Fiddles have allowed us to actually become a part of these historical events.

A simple rose expresses the beauty and joy of my trip to Japan.

A lovely red rose
Showing beauty of Japan
For this visitor

Chapter Twenty Six

Hector Ricardo Caballero

Again I had thought my story had come to an end but I was haunted by the 323 young men that died when the Belgrano was sunk. They have stories to tell, too. A month after I returned from my trip to Japan, I wrote to Coco to ask him if he would be willing to contact a family of a boy who had died because of the sinking.

November 11, 2003
Coco – I hesitate asking and I apologize if I shouldn't write about it – but one time we wrote about you locating a family of a young man who died when the Belgrano was sunk. I think it would be interesting to have a short story about him and a picture of the young man who lost his life. It would serve to show the tragedy of the sinking and his story would represent the sorrow of Argentina. It is too easy to brush off the sinking and make it not important. What I desire would be maybe just a paragraph – name – parents – family – where he lived – maybe he was an athlete or liked to ride horses ... just simple information – his birth date and death date. And a picture.
    The best to all of you.
    Luis

:: :: ::

November 11, 2003
My dear friend Luis:
About the second paragraph, to the man who died in the sinking, let me tell you I had forgotten about your asking, so, I will ask again to get the information for you.
    About the third paragraph, my answer is: At the same time, I apologize with you, because I didn't do that when you asked me... and my answer is, I'm sorry, and I will ask to make your question possible.

I'm glad we can have enough confidence to talk about these things, and I appreciate you make me remind about that.

Let me tell you I'm proud of our friendship.

Coco

:: :: ::

November 11, 2003

Re: Answer

In a message dated 11/11/03 1:25:14 PM, coco@cencis.com writes:

>I'm glad we can have enough confidence to talk about these things, ...

My friend, Coco,

I felt very happy when I read what you had written. I had confidence that our friendship would allow me to remind you. But at the same time, I hesitated because I did not want to ask you to do something that you might not want to do. I did not want to take advantage of you and our friendship.

>Let me tell you I'm proud of our friendship.

Thank you, Coco, I value our friendship very much. Getting to know you has opened a whole new chapter in my life. Your friendship has allowed me to better understand men and the experiences they have had. I don't think that I could have met anybody better than you – all because in a letter to Andy Wilson, you signed your name – "Nestor Cenci (Republica Argentina)" I took a chance and wrote to you. On May 13, 1999, you wrote back to me. You ended your letter with "I appreciate your interest, and I am glad to write to you, and I wish you to write to me again. Keep in touch."

And I think we have done a good job – don't you!! For me the highest point in our friendship was last March when I rang the doorbell at Ricardo's place and stood there wondering what it would be like when the door opened. I did not need to wonder, you opened the door, we hugged and I felt that I had known you forever. I will remember that afternoon and will always cherish it. My thanks to you for making it possible.

I look forward to your next letter.

All the best,

Luis

:: :: ::

November 12, 2003

Just a short note

Greetings Coco,

I was just thinking – if you should be able to locate a family of a sailor who died during the sinking of the Belgrano, any writing in Spanish would be fine. I would be able to find somebody here who would translate it for me. That would take the pressure off of who ever was doing the writing. And a nice picture would mean a lot.

Thanks, Coco.

Luis

:: :: ::

November 12, 2003

Re: A quick note

Dear Luis:

I already got a family telephone number, and the person I contacted, promised me to give me another telephone number of another family, who's son belonged to the department where I was the boss. Today, I am going to call the first family, which surname is Caballero. I will tell you how it was, as soon I speak with them.... Do you prefer I make some particular questions to the parents? If yes, please let me know what you want me to ask. I will be happy if I get what you want.

Big big hug for you

Coco

:: :: ::

November 12, 2003
Re: A quick note
Coco,

Thanks for your quick reply. I will suggest some questions but you may choose not to use them. Some of them are very personal and it may not be right to ask them. You be the judge.

1. Name
2. Birth date
3. Name of parents
4. Brothers and/or sisters
5. Where he lived when he joined the Navy
6. His age when he joined the navy and his age when he died
7. Was there a reason why he joined the Argentine Navy?
8. Did he come home on a leave after he joined the Navy?
9. Was he married?
10. Did he write home about the war? His last letter?
11. What were his plans for the future?
12. And maybe a story about him growing up – in school, at home, sports, hobbies or about the family.
13. Was there a telegram telling of his death? How were the parents notified? This is very personal but there might be an incident that would help explain the tragedy of his death. You be the judge whether this topic should be discussed or not.
14. And a picture

Coco,

As you visit with the family, please express my sorrow for the loss of their son and tell them of the loss of my brother who served on the same ship 40 years earlier. And that I am very grateful for them sharing their son's story with me. If my book ever becomes a reality, then I would like to have his story represent all the young men on the Belgrano who died.

Thank you very much, my friend, Coco.
Luis

:: :: ::

November 12, 2003
Dear Luis:
I arranged a visit to the house of Mr. Caballero, and Mr. Grosso, both parents of sailors died during the sinking of the Belgrano. They accepted I make an interview about their sons.... Also both told me on the phone, they have a picture of their sons..... I hurry to tell you that, you to be sure I will get (I hope), the information you are waiting. I will write you soon.

Coco

:: :: ::

November 12, 2003
Thank you very much Coco. You are the best. I hope the experience will not be too sad for you. Again – thank your very much.

My best to you.

Luis

:: :: ::

November 13, 2003
Dear Luis:
I was this morning at Caballero's house, and I had an interview with the parents. It was quite hard for me, and, of course for them, as you can imagine...

I made a small resume of the things I get of them, but I'm sure you will need more explanations, but I will hope you begin working with this initial things, and you will ask me more things....I imagine you would like to ask me more, and, please, don't hesitate asking me....

Maybe tomorrow I am going to visit the parents of another family, and I will tell you how it was as soon as I get it.

I'm sorry to write to you in Spanish, but, you are right, it is easier for me to explain you everything I get in my own language.

A big hug for you.

Coco

:: :: ::

:: :: ::

November 13, 2003

My friend, Coco,

I just looked at the attachment. The pictures and letters bring emotions of tears and a big lump in my throat. I can feel the pain of the parents. My gratitude to all of you for the information.

Thank you very much, Coco. I am very grateful for what you have done. I know it must have been difficult for all of you – I am sorry. I hope that I can do the young man justice and give him a place in history that he deserves.

Thank you very much.

Luis

:: :: ::

Berta Lidia Belgeretti & Ricardo Felipe Caballero

Hector Ricardo Caballero

Father's name: Ricardo Felipe Caballero
Mother's name: Berta Lidia Belgeretti
Only son. Single

He enlisted the Navy as a soldier on April 1981(Mandatory for all the citizens at age 18) and was sent to the Naval Base of Puerto Belgrano, and his assignment was the Cruiser General Belgrano. (Formerly the USS Phoenix.)

While he was there, he went back to his home (a distance of about 700 km) in his license periods, or days off several times, and his mother visited him also several times in Puerto Belgrano.

He went back to his parents house for the last time on March 14th of 1982, his parents became aware of his death on May 9th of 1982, by the visit of 2 officers of the Navy, who went there to give them the bad news.

Before enlisting the Navy, he attended the primary school N° 41 of Pablo Podesta (a very near district to his parents' current home) where he finished his basic education.

Afterwards he worked as an employee in a shoe store, and then in a paint company.

His father encouraged his son to sign on with the railroad, since he was an employee of Ferrocarril Urquiza, (Urquiza Railways) where he retired, but Hector expressed his desire to become a police officer, which he would do after the mandatory military service.

There is a bronze plaque with the soldiers' names in Martin's Coronado plaza and another bronze plaque in the Cemetery of Pablo Podesta. He was a very loved boy, with many friends and very educated.

I'm attaching a photograph of his parents, taken today in their house along with a copy of the note notifying them of the death of their son (May 11 of 1982).

Coco

Hector Ricardo Caballero
1964 – May 2, 1982

ARMADA ARGENTINA

BUENOS AIRES, 11 de mayo de 1982.

A la Señora
Berta Lidia BELGERETTI
Teniente Espora 9740-Pablo Podestá
(1657) PABLO PODESTA
Pcia. BUENOS AIRES

        Con motivo de las acciones bélicas libradas en el mar el día 2 del corriente y que derivaron en el hundimiento del Crucero A.R.A. "GENERAL BELGRANO", luego de realizadas las tareas de salvamento de los tripulantes, el C o n s c r i p t o Héctor Ricardo CABALLERO , no figura entre los rescatados, presumiéndose su fallecimiento.

        La ARMADA ARGENTINA, le hace llegar la seguridad de que esta muy lamentable desaparición integra la cuota de sacrificio que la Institución ofrece a la Patria, en estos duros momentos históricos que se viven.

        Hoy la Patria se yergue sobre el sacrificio de su h i j o . De aquí en más, los pliegues celestes y blancos de nuestra bandera, que señala los cielos desde el brazo de sus mástiles, llevará estampada la imagen de su h i j o proclamando ante los ojos de la historia, que su rostro resplandecerá para siempre en ella, con el gesto imborrable de los héroes que respondieron al llamado de la Patria.

        En la certeza que la fe en Dios y el legítimo orgullo de haber ofrendado el máximo sacrificio, le traerán la seguridad y paz interior que le reconforte, reciba el testimonio de un especial afecto.

RODOLFO A. REMOTTI.
VICEALMIRANTE
DIRECTOR GENERAL

Argentine Navy

Buenos Aires, May 11th, 1982

To: Mrs. Berga Lidia Belgeretti
Teniente Expora 9940 – Pablo Podesta
(1657) PABLO PODESTA
Pcia. Buenos Aires

In regards to the warlike actions on the sea that came off badly on the 2nd day of the current month after the sinking of the ship ARA "GENERAL BELGRANO", after accomplishing the mission of saving the sailors, the enlistee Hector Ricardo Caballero, is not among the rescued; his death is presumed.

The Argentine Navy assures you that his lamentable disappearance serves as proof of the high level of sacrifice that the Armed Forces offers our nation in these very difficult, history-making times.

Today the nation is uplifted by the sacrifice of your son. From here on, the celestial and white folds of our flag, that salutes the heavens from the mastheads, will be embossed with the image of your son, proclaiming before the eyes of history, that his face will shine on it forever with the indelible courage of the heroes who answered the call to service of their country.

With the certainty that faith in God and pride of having offered the ultimate sacrifice will bring the comfort and inner peace that consoles you, receive my testimony of special affection.

Seal of the Argentine Navy.

Rodolfo A. Remotti
Admiral
      Director General

MUNICIPALIDAD DE LA
CIUDAD DE BUENOS AIRES

Registro del Estado Civil
DEPARTAMENTO
INSCRIPCIONES

Tomo 2:IMA. Acta N:233. Año 1983. En Buenos Aires Capital de la República Argentina, a 8 de Febrero de 1983. Yo, Funcionario del Registro del Estado Civil, en virtud de lo solicitado en la Nota de la Armada Argentina N:39/82 Letra DIINER? de fecha 21-12-1982 que se archiva bajo el N: de esta acta procedo a inscribir la partida de Defunción que transcripta dice: N: 210. En Ushuaia, Capital del Territorio Nacional de Tierra del Fuego, Antártida e Islas del Atlántico Sud, República Argentina, a 11 de Octubre de 1982. Yo, Jefe del Registro Civil, procedo a inscribir la Defunción de: Hector Ricardo CABALLERO DNI 16.212.352, nacionalidad argentino, sexo: masculino, nacido en Basavilbaso, Entre Rios, el 21-11-1962, marino, soltero, domiciliado en Tte Espora 9740, Podesta, Pcia Bs As. Ocurrida en Mar Territorial Argentino Jurisdicción Ushuaia, a las 13 horas del 2 de Mayo de 1982, muerto en combate, según fallo N: 131/82 archivado bajo N: de la presente, otorgado por Juez Federal del Territorio. Hijo de Ricardo Felipe CABALLERO y de Berta Lia BELGCRETTI. Esta inscripción se efectuó por orden Judicial. Daniel Alfredo Vergara Vacareza, domiciliado en Base Naval Ushuaia, obra en virtud de representación del Estado Nacional, Comando en Jefe de la Armada. Leída y ratificada el acta, así la firma, por ante mi que certifico. Hay una firma ilegible y un sello Fdo: Daniel Alfredo Vergara Vacareza, domicilia. Es conforme en lo pertinente con su original doy fe... Fdo.: Ilegible. NO omi

POR LA J. P. de TORRES
JEFE DPTO NAL DEL PODER LEGAL
REG RESOLUCION Y COM FEDL
... TERMA DE HODIERNO

(Translation of the hand-written death certificate.)

Volume I: IMA (unknown abbreviation), Action 237, in the year
1983: In Buenos Aires, capital of Argentine Republic, on the 8th of
February of 1983. I, Registrar for Civil Affairs, in accordance with
petition Number 39/82 Letter DINERG (**) dated December 12,
1982, and filed by the Argentine Navy under the referenced Number,
hereby issue the death certificate, which under Number 210, reads: In
Ushuaia, capital of the national territory of Tierra del Fuego, Antarctica
and Islands of the South Atlantic, Republic of Argentina, on the 11th
of October of 1982. I, Chief Civil Affairs Registrar hereby declare the
death of Hector Ricardo Caballero, DNI (***) 16212352, of Argentine
nationality, sex male, born in Bosavilbaso entre Rios on November 21,
1962, seaman, single, residing at Tte Expora 9740, Podezla province,
Buenos Aires. In Argentine territorial waters, jurisdiction of Ushuaia,
at 1700 (5:00 P.M) on May 2, 1982, died in combat, according to
document 131/82, filed under section N. This certificate is issued per
the Federal Judge of the Territory. Son of Ricardo Felipe Caballero and
of Berta Lia (sic) Belgeretti.
This certificate is issued per the mandate of Justice Daniel Alfredo
Vergara Vacarezza, presiding in Ushuaia Naval Base, representing the
Nation and Commander-in-Chief of the Armed Forces. This document
was read, ratified, and certified by me, as was the signature. (There
is an illegible signature and a seal on which appears Daniel Alfredo
Vergara Vacarezza)
(**). It is consistent in pertinent details with its original to which
I set my seal:
Perla J.P. de Torno (**)

Translator writes:
Legends;
(**) illegible
(***) abbreviation/ probably his identification number
Tte is he abbreviation for "Teniente."

1625 19th St. N.E.
Salem, Oregon 97303
USA
November 17, 2003
Dear Mr. and Mrs. Caballero

I am honored that you would allow Coco to visit with you about your son and what your son meant to your family. I want to thank you very much for sharing the story of your son with Coco and me. I know that you must be very proud of him and still miss him. I will always be thankful for the story of your son.

I have received several interesting letters from my friend, Coco. I realize that I have brought back many painful memories of the death of your son. I apologize for making you sad again. I am attempting to write a book about my brother who served aboard the USS Phoenix/Belgrano from 1941 to January 1943 when he became ill with tuberculosis. He died in 1945. My mother and my brothers and I experienced sorrow with my brother's death when he was 21. It has been 63 years since he died but my brothers and I still feel the sorrow. His name was "Bill."

The book I am writing is about my brother, about Coco, about N from England and about two Japanese aviators who participated in the attack on Pearl Harbor. These men have all been involved one way or another with the Belgrano/Phoenix. Now I will have a short story about your son. He will represent the many young men from Argentina who died when the Belgrano was sunk. I want the readers to know that many young men from Argentina died and that their families have much sorrow.

In October I visited Japan where I had lunch with two Japanese aviators who participated in the attack on Pearl Harbor. One is 82 years old and the other is 87. There are less than five aviators still alive who participated in the attack.

Again, thank you very much for sharing the story of your son with Coco and me.

Respectfully yours,
Luis Holt

Chapter Twenty Seven

CLAUDIO GROSSO

November 14, 2003
A new interview
Dear Luis:

This morning I've been with Pedro Grosso, father of CLAUDIO NORBERTO GROSSO, for about five hours, and I had a wonderful (and very very emotional and touching) interview.

His wife doesn't want to participate, because she is still feeling much sorrow. I need some time to prepare things to send them to you.

I have a Photo of the young sailor, and a copy of a letter he sent to his parents from 04/11/82 (about 20 days before the sinking).

I think I will get some more information than I already have, in a forthcoming interview, I suggested to Mr. Grosso with his agreement.

Coco

:: :: ::

November 14, 2003
Re: A new interview

Thank you, Coco. I can understand the mother's feelings. And the feelings of everybody. I would not want you to continue but I feel that the story of the two boys will express the loss in Argentina which is so easy to skim over. The human tragedy is too often forgotten.

Our nightly news might simple say "two more Americans killed today in Iraq." It sounds so simple – but the death of the young men and women and the loss for the family will continue for years as it is with the mothers and fathers of the 323 young men on the Belgrano. Their loss doesn't go away when the television is turned off.

Thanks again.
Luis

:: :: ::

Dear Luis: This is the interview with Pedro Grosso from 11.15.03

Name of the sailor: CLAUDIO NORBERTO GROSSO (this young boy was in the "Sol" (sun) Division which was the personnel division of the Supply Department, and I was the chief of that department...you imagine Luis, how I felt...)

Birth date: October 9th. 1962

Father name: Pedro Grosso

Mother name: Teresita Grosso

No brothers or sisters.

Single

The family lived in a suburban area, about 5 miles from the Capital, called Ramos Mejía, a middle class neighborhood.

Claudio joined the Navy as a Soldier, when he was 18 years old. (It was a mandatory bond to all citizens, until 1990...and for two years remaining in the Navy, and one year for the Army) At the present, Argentina has only paid soldiers.

He worked as a waiter in the room of low officers. His drop out (casualty) will be to June 1982...

He was a student, and he liked martial arts and sports. The boy has a very white skin...and always looked very healthy. He was also a futbol player, and fan of San Lorenzo de Almagro football team.

He was very very close friend of his father. During his staying in the Navy, Claudio traveled every week from Puerto Belgrano to Buenos Aires, to join his parents. When he was on board, his father used to talk on the phone every day with him around 13:00 hours.

He had a girlfriend, Alejandra.

Father and son were very close friends. On weekends when Claudio would go out dancing and not get home until the early morning hours his father would wait up for him and fix him breakfast while they talked. When Claudio turned 18 years old, dad gave him a small Fiat 600.

The death of his only son created a lot of pain in their marriage that they could not overcome, it was the same for both of them, they have suffered tremendously, and have moved from the house where they lived with their son to get away from those memories.

Mr. Grosso is retired from Volkswagen after 43 years in service.

In 1995 he discovered there was a cemetery located in Pilar, about 50 kilometers from the capital, on Province Route 25, named after General Rodriguez. It was started in April of 1992 by Father Fernandez, a priest that was in Malvinas accompanied by the Argentine Army. It occurred to him to create an exact replica of the cemetery that actually exists in Malvinas.

It is located on Provincial Route 25 (General Rodriguez Road) at Kilometer 6 you find the Malvinas Monument, started on the 2nd of April 1992. This monument is located on 600 acres and has 649 crosses identifying with names, branch of army and grade of our heroes that died in the war in Malvinos. In the same area you will find an exact replica of the Catholic Saint "Santa Maria" from Puerto Argentino.

The building, which is located across the road is permanent homage to the ones that fought defending the sovereignty of Malvinas. It was made possible through the effort and personal dedication of Priest Dr. Jose Fernandez, president of the center for civilian veterans of the war "Operation Malvinas", chaplain of the Argentine Army.

The objective of this monument is to offer relatives and friends a place to gather where they can honor the memory of those who gave their lives for their country.

The center and chapel can be visited daily. Father Fernandez personally attends to visitors and offers details of the building that is like no other in the world. There are 649 croses, 325 are from the Crucero, and 324 are from the army and air force.

:: :: ::

Pedro Grosso met Father Fernandez and they became instant friends, a fantastic friendship. Father Fernandez enlightened Mr. Grosso and helped him bear his life without his son. Pedro Grozzo started to go, accompanied by Father Fernandez, to the cemetery. He even stayed and slept there because he found healing for his pain, little by little his spirits were raised.

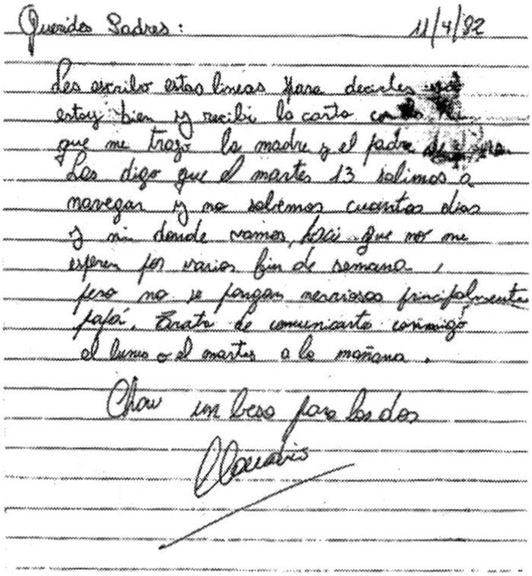

(handwritten letter in Spanish)

11 April, 1982
Dear Parents,
I am writing this letter to let you know that I'm fine and I received that _____ mom and dad brought me. I am letting you know that on Tuesday the 13th we are going out to sea, we don't know how many days nor where we are going. So don't wait for me for a few weekends. But don't get nervous especially dad. Try and contact me on Monday or Tuesday in the morning. Chow, a kiss for both of you.
Claudio

Claudio Norberto Grosso
October 12, 1962 – May 2, 1982

Chapter Twenty Eight

END

This will be the end. It has been a long and tedious, often an exciting task, which began in 1988. I did not know in 1988 that I was writing a book. I was writing an account of my research, not realizing that it would turn in to a book. The story has come to an end several times but something new presented itself and another chapter was suggested and the story continued. Maybe there is "one more page" waiting to be discovered. I have yet to meet "N" in person or...

Bill's life ended long ago and Rita's life more recently. The last twenty years have been a narrow time frame to gather the material and to write this book. Bill, Rita, and the four men from the Phoenix who remembered Bill are all dead. Time will take the rest of us but the story will be forever – only because of the people like Bill, Rita, Coco, N, Mr. Harada, Mr. Maruyama, Chris – all who have made a story possible.

Technology has changed. With Email I have been able to accomplish something in a matter of a few minutes or a few hours or a day that might have taken weeks or months or years to accomplish using regular mail. Or maybe never. The early exchange of letters between Coco and me, N and me and Chris and me demonstrate my point of email being expedient. Before the advent of email, it would take many days by mail, as my early letters to Phoenix veterans and others show.

High on my list and one of the greatest contributors was a person who wasn't even born at the time Pearl Harbor was attacked. Christopher Girsch, born in Iowa in 1960, who has lived in Japan for over 20 years, made it possible for me to contact and get to know Mr. Harada and Mr. Maruyama. Without his interest, desire, effort, creativity, money and the cooperation of his family, the trip to Japan would not have been possible. Nor would the letters and gifts from Mr. Harada and Mr. Maruyama have been possible. I will always be grateful for Chris's contributions and efforts which gave me the contacts and the interesting material from Japan. Without it one big piece of the jig-saw puzzle would be missing.

Coco's friendship and his willingness to write have been unique. To meet Martha and him in person in San Francisco, California was "frosting on the cake." I will always be grateful to the two families in Argentina and Coco for giving me the story of the two young men from Argentina who lost their lives when the Belgrano was sunk.

The well-written and sensitive letters from N made a huge contribution to the story. I will always admire what he has written. I can't imagine another man on the submarine who would have the interest, the writing skills and a diary. Those simple words one morning, "I was on the Conqueror, how may I help you?" gave me opportunities that I could never have imagined.

Mr. Harada and Mr. Maruyama in Japan accepted my invitation to meet them. Our handshakes and bows brought "brothers of war" together.

My wife, Alice, sent me to Japan to be with Chris and to meet the two Japanese aviators with her good wishes. I appreciated that and will always be grateful. Now I feel that I have been down every path and it is time to bring the story to an end.

I must recognize two ladies, Meg Graf and Peg Willis who each read draft copies, found many errors and made suggestions. Hopefully not too many errors have slipped by us.

I want to thank the readers for reading this story. It has been a pleasure sharing the letters that have told the story of the people from five continents who are truly "Brothers of War."

Lew Holt

Salem, Oregon

2008

END

:: :: ::

4th May 1982....N's diary... There is much talk of "when we get back home", but we are all very subdued. The WEO (Weapon Engineering

Officer) succinctly christened us the "instruments of the politicians' incompetence". It's interesting how now, we are effectively at war, it's no longer "exciting" or "fun" it's bloody frightening and nerve-wracking... Narendra Sethia ("N")

:: :: ::

March 9, 2000 – I'm glad that you were touched by my observations, in the same way that I have been touched by your work, You are absolutely right that a work of fiction could never have produced a story so extraordinary and so human. That, I feel, is its strength – had you written it to be a best-seller, I think it would have lost much of its human quality. It's REAL, and it's about real people, real events, real hardships, real joys, real tragedy – and it therefore appeals to the innate sensitivities of real people. What a wonderful legacy for your family, children, grandchildren and their grandchildren. Narendra Sethia ("N")

:: :: ::

Chris wrote this for me – it summarizes my trip to Japan so well:
The world of fiddles has drawn two people of disparate backgrounds and produced something that should have great meaning to all people in the world, and that the world of fiddles has allowed us to play a part in history in the making. I contacted Chris Girsch, a fiddle-List member in Japan, who responded to someone's earlier request about translating a Japanese CD. Chris answered the call from me to fulfill a personal dream to find someone who participated in the bombing of Pearl Harbor, not by simply finding a list of names, but by actually making calls to find one of only seven living participants on the Japanese side – and that he actually introduced me to the man who put the direct hit on the Oklahoma to put her under. Fiddles have allowed us to actually become a part of these historical events. (Chris Girsch)

:: :: ::

You know, Lew, in a way you have brought Bill back to life. Here I am, thousands of miles away from you and we have not even met, and yet, in spite of the differences in our age, background and life story, having corresponded with you and read your work, I feel I know something profound of you and your family, and am honoured that you have shared such an important part of your life with me. Through your efforts, Bill will not be a faceless, forgotten victim of a long-ago war in a far-flung land. He is now as real to me as he is to your family, and as I write I can even see his face and imagine who and what he was.

Narendra Sethia ("N")